Managing
the Public
Organization

Managing the Public Organization

Second Edition

Cole Blease Graham, Jr.
Steven W. Hays
University of South Carolina

CQ
PRESS

A Division of Congressional Quarterly Inc.
Washington, D.C.

Printed in the United States of America

Acknowledgment: Portions of chapter 4 are quoted from Steven W. Hays and T. Zane Reeves, *Personnel Management in the Public Sector* (Needham Heights, Mass.: Allyn & Bacon Inc., 1984). Reprinted with permission.

Library of Congress Cataloging-in-Publication Data

Graham, Cole Blease.
    Managing the public organization / Cole Blease Graham, Jr.,
  Steven W. Hays. -- 2nd ed.
      p. cm.
    Includes bibliographical references and index.
    ISBN 0-87187-745-7
    1. Public administration--United States.   I. Hays, Steven W.
  II. Title.
  JF1351.G69 1993
  353--dc20   92-27396
                                                                   CIP

To Luther Gulick
for the contributions he has made
to the theory and practice of
public management

Contents

Tables and Figures

Tables

Figures

Preface

This second edition of *Managing the Public Organization* has the same primary aim as the first: to articulate as concisely as possible the various activities that comprise public management. The book explores and integrates theories and research findings, past and current, that describe the work of the public manager and surveys the management literature relevant to the study of public administration.

The book is generally organized around one of the oldest but most misunderstood frameworks in public administration, Luther Gulick's POSDCORB. An acronym for Planning, Organizing, Staffing, Directing, Coordinating, Reporting, and Budgeting, POSDCORB appeared at a time when the public administration field was dominated by the assumption that administrative concerns could be strictly separated from politics. When the inherently political nature of public administration came to be recognized by scholars and advocated by practitioners, POSDCORB unfairly came to be associated with a naive view of public management. It is often used today as a shorthand reference to the "orthodox" public administration that some believe is no longer relevant to the "real world politics" faced by practicing public managers or knowledgeable elected officials.

Without attempting to advocate or promote POSDCORB as the only authoritative approach to the study of public organizations, we are attracted by its directness, clarity, convenience, and practicality. We find that POSDCORB embodies the long tradition of administrative research that emphasizes the management functions common to all organizational executives. These generic managerial responsibilities are roughly the same for a manager in a corporate setting as in a government setting. The public sector manager must balance responsibility and action with political orientations and public-service values just like the corporate manager must relate to company policy and the bottom line.

Like other approaches, theoretical and applied, POSDCORB basically holds that defined activities must take place in order to accomplish any goal in a complex organization. The goal must be clearly identified, and deviations from the intended path must be corrected or accommodated. In the process of pursuing goals, resources must be acquired, budgets must be balanced, employees must be hired and trained, subordinates must be motivated, and outputs must be measured and evaluated. POSDCORB and its applications today represent what public managers contribute to society while they simultaneously respond to and influence political demands.

POSDCORB's emphasis on management functions is an immensely useful technique by which contemporary administrative thought and practice can be described and explained. Through an analysis of basic managerial functions, a framework for organizing and presenting what is known about the field of contemporary public administration emerges.

Additionally, we feel that POSDCORB is particularly relevant today because of society's renewed interest in economy, efficiency, and the control of government expenditures. The more effective public managers become in performing their administrative functions, the closer their agencies will come to fulfilling their basic objectives. Thus, good management is as important to the public interest as is good political leadership. Instead of being separate concepts, the two are inextricably linked by practical necessity.

The second edition begins with a discussion of Gulick's framework and recent attempts to redefine it. Other chapters are devoted to Planning (Chapter 2), Organizing (Chapter 3), Staffing (Chapter 4), Directing and Coordinating (Chapter 5, on leadership), and Reporting and Budgeting (Chapter 6). Responding to revisions of Gulick's views and framework, we treat evaluation as an important new public management topic (Chapter 7).

The second edition considers new journal articles, recent books, and new facts and conditions of concern to practitioners and students in each of these established management domains. There are updated discussions of important and dynamic areas such as employee motivation, work force characteristics and trends, public budgeting, and public information systems. The summary (Chapter 8) has been completely reorganized and extended to incorporate Gulick's latest suggestions for contemporary themes around which one may continually relate emerging research findings and policy developments.

To communicate with readers and students in many professional categories, we have not limited our analysis to a specific position, type of organization, or approach to political leadership. It comes as no surprise that we have incorporated many theories and techniques of researchers who teach and practice outside the public-management community. Administrative techniques arising from the business community, for example, are directly transferable to public agencies, as are the theories of organizational and human behavior that emerge from psychology, sociology, and other disciplines. No single field or discipline dominates the science of management. An interdisciplinary approach to its study is imperative if one hopes to make the discussions relevant and meaningful.

Our aim is to encourage readers to derive an interpretation of managerial functions that is based on the wide body of current research in public management and that is capable of changing with new experiences and with new research knowledge. We were inspired by our discoveries. We think readers will be similarly excited by the intellectual contrasts in analytic approaches to public management issues, by the range of topics confronting students of public management, and by the dynamic changes in the field.

1

Management Functions and Public Administration

Americans idolize successful managers. We are taught from our earliest days that an entrepreneurial spirit is a virtue and that behavior that is not truly purposive is a vice. We admire growth, efficiency, and productivity, and we are uncomfortable with people (and, in some cases, cultures) that lack a comparable value structure. Managers who make it big are quickly converted into folk heroes, while we reserve our most stinging epithets for managerial failures. (No parent would be so unkind as to name a child Edsel.)

Although this orientation has occasionally suffered a momentary lapse, usually in response to some major crisis or catastrophe (the Great Depression, or the excesses of laissez-faire economics in the late nineteenth and early twentieth centuries), it has never faded from America's collective conscience. In recent times, however, the number of American management "heroes" has been limited. A country that once regarded itself as the managerial model for the world has had its confidence shaken. Declining worker productivity, huge trade imbalances, and a threatened economic restructuring have led to an apparent loss of confidence in our management infrastructure.

Although this problem affects both the public and private sectors, government managers have for some time been especially subject to criticism. Most Americans cannot even remember a period when public administration was generally perceived as efficient and competent, such as was the case during and after World War II.

The public has become increasingly disenchanted with government. This change in attitude has been variously attributed to (a) excessive increases in the size and intrusiveness of government; (b) the inability of public managers to resolve the problems entrusted to them, coupled with increased public expectations; and (c) several crises in confidence that shook the public's faith in their elected and appointed public officials. The general public's disenchantment with government is shared by business also. Many contemporary businesses are reluctant to contract with government because they perceive that government pays them too slowly and has excessive paperwork requirements along with other impediments to a happy relationship (MacManus, 1991).

Between 1949 and 1976, public expenditures as a proportion of gross national product (GNP) rose from 23 percent to 34.2 percent, and the number of public-sector employees surged from six million to fifteen million (Lynch, 1977: 6). In addition to the always unpopular increases in taxes, this growth in the size of government resulted in the encroachment of public officials into areas of activity that traditionally had been off limits to them. The public's legendary belief in freedom and individualism was assaulted by government regulations covering every topic from the content of peanut butter (the Food and Drug Administration demands that it be 90 percent peanuts) to bathroom safety (the Occupational Health and Safety Administration has a standard expressing a preference for U-shaped toilet seats). Yet despite its massive growth, government made little progress in solving the country's problems. Huge sums were spent on education, health, and welfare, yet illiteracy, illness, and poverty abounded.

Then, from the 1960s to the 1990s, a series of public-relations disasters further tarnished government's deteriorating image. Revelations concerning the illegal and immoral activities of several public agencies became almost fixtures on the evening news. It was revealed, for example, that the FBI had engaged in unlawful wire-tappings and burglaries, that the CIA had engineered assassinations and other forms of political interference in the internal affairs of foreign nations, and that the U.S. Army had secretly administered LSD to some of its own personnel in an attempt to determine the drug's effects (Woll, 1977: 5). More recently we learned that government installations have been some of our worst illegal polluters, carelessly dumping hazardous chemicals on public lands, and that many members of Congress have written bad checks. Events such as these—along with the residue of Vietnam, Watergate, the *Challenger* disaster, and other confidence-shattering crises—have led some citizens to question both the efficacy and legitimacy of government activity. According to recent opinion polls, not even the military victory in the Persian Gulf had a lasting positive influence on the public's attitude toward government.

Not surprisingly, public managers have borne their share of the antigovernment outbursts. Vitriolic attacks on public administrators at all levels are now so fashionable that they are becoming clichés. Government administrators are typically portrayed as officious, unresponsive, and inept, while the bureaucracy is depicted as a mindless beast that devours taxes and spews forth impertinent regulations. Presidential elections since 1976 have criticized bureaucratic mismanagement of national problems to the point that even elected politicians are now caught up in the public's disgust with government. The phenomenon of Ross Perot's campaign reflects the depth of public dissatisfaction with present politicians, and highlights the extent to which public management is a profession under assault.

Amid all of the rhetoric surrounding government's perceived shortcomings, a few voices have been raised in defense of public managers. Those who argue this case in the court of public opinion assert that the performance of public administrators compares quite favorably with that of their private-sector counterparts. Researchers have recently begun to provide empirical support for this contention, and a growing body of both empirical and anecdotal data tends to confirm the assertion that government is much more efficient and responsive than is generally believed (see Goodsell, 1985; Bowsher, 1992).

The effect of such findings is bolstered by the general observation that, while the basic functions of public and private managers are nearly identical, leaders of public organizations must contend with a number of limitations that are not found in business and industry. Public managers are expected, for instance, to deal with ambiguous and contradictory goals, absurdly unrealistic expectations on the part of their "owners" (the public), and inadequate control over their own administrative resources. Such differences led Allison (1983) to entitle an important article "Public and Private Management: Are They Fundamentally Alike in All *Unimportant* Respects?" (emphasis added). Public managers, the argument goes, have been tried and convicted for crimes they did not commit. Considering the context in which they toil, Allison argues that government's managers perform quite competently.

This second edition is grounded on one of the basic themes of public management's chief defenders: that government executives perform essentially the same functions as private managers, but they do so in a much more demanding institutional environment. While a major portion of the book is devoted to discussions of the similarities in managerial functions between the two sectors, care is taken to point out the unique problems and obstacles that complicate the practice of public management. The book is not intended as a polemic, however. Our goal is not to convince but to inform. By describing the functions and problems of public administrators, we hope to provide our readers with a better understanding of public administrators' role in the managerial world, so that they can be in a better position to judge for themselves whether public managers deserve to be America's heroes or its scapegoats.

THE ROLE OF PUBLIC MANAGEMENT IN GOVERNMENT

It seems that one of the most widely held beliefs of many contemporary Americans is that taxes are unnecessarily high. This perception is strengthened by presidential pronouncements and has become a favored topic of conservative talk show hosts and columnists. Many citizens believe that most people do not receive equivalent benefits for the taxes they pay. Because public opinion is so intense in this regard, and since politicians are so quick to exploit the issue, politicians are often trapped by their own rhetoric. Repeated budget deadlocks in Congress and state legislatures point to the fact that politicians are immobilized by a public perception that they have helped to create.

That this flawed view of reality is so widespread speaks eloquently of the level of misunderstanding that currently infects public administration in the United States. Implicit in this position are the beliefs that most government expenditures are devoted to social-welfare programs and that other public activity is almost irrelevant to citizens who do not receive direct public benefits from such programs. It seems necessary to counter this view by providing an accurate description, and thereby a justification, of the role of public administration in government.

THE PARAMETERS OF PUBLIC ADMINISTRATION

As of 1990, total civilian employment in state, local, and federal government stood at 17.3 million, or nearly 20 percent of the entire labor force. Local governments accounted for 58 percent (10.1 million) of these employees, state governments for 24 percent (4.1 million), and the federal government for 18 percent (3.1 million). Moreover, an additional 1 to 2 million workers were employed by industries that are almost completely reliant on government funds, such as defense and highway construction. The annual government payroll was more than $320 billion, while total public expenditures were more than $1.6 *trillion* (U.S. Department of Commerce, 1990: 300, 310, 324).

One way of making some sense out of these statistics is to determine what all of those people are doing with their time and how they are spending our money. Table 1-1 provides a breakdown of the numbers of public employees by the types of activities in which they are engaged. More than 7 million of the 17 million public employees are engaged in educational activities, either as teachers or support personnel. Another

Table 1-1 Public Employment by Level of Government and Function, 1988

Function	Number of Employees (Thousands)			
	Federal	State	Local	Total
National defense[a]	1,099	—	—	1,099
Postal service	807	—	—	807
Space research and technology	23	—	—	23
Education	15	1,804	5,584	7,403
(Teachers)	—	(553)	(3,600)	(4,153)
Highways	4	251	302	557
Health and hospitals	265	691	708	1,664
Public welfare	14	194	239	447
Police protection	73	82	636	791
Fire protection	—	—	335	335
Sanitation and sewerage	—	1	225	226
Parks and recreation	24	37	237	298
Natural resources	243	158	38	439
Financial administration	134	133	200	467
Other government administration	28	46	314	388
Judicial and legal	36	99	174	309
All others	326	619	1,082	2,027
Total	3,091	4,115	10,074	17,280

[a] Excluding members of the armed forces.

Source: U.S. Department of Commerce, Bureau of the Census, *Statistical Abstract of the United States: 1990* (Washington, D.C.: Government Printing Office, 1990), 300.

large group of workers, about 1.7 million, staff public hospitals or are otherwise involved in delivering health-related services to the public. Civilian employees of the Department of Defense constitute the third largest group of workers, 1 million, leaving about 7.3 million civil servants to deliver all the other assorted services that government provides.

Patterns in the expenditure of public revenues confirm that education and defense are two of the principal activities of government (Tables 1-2 and 1-3). Education is the largest expenditure item for state and local governments, absorbing almost 30 percent of their revenues, while defense consumes nearly 26 percent of the federal budget. With the break-up of the Soviet Union, this level of defense expenditure will certainly decline. This so-called "peace dividend" was earlier touted as a relief from increased taxes, but now seems destined to be eaten away by existing obligations and debts. A large proportion of the public dollar is also devoted to various forms of public assistance, including Social Security (28 percent of federal funds) and social services (more than 3

Table 1-2 Budget Expenditures of State and Local
Government by Function, 1988

Function	Percent of Expenditures
Education	29.3
(Elementary and secondary)	(20.3)
(Higher)	(7.8)
Highways	6.8
Public welfare	10.4
Health	2.2
Hospitals	5.2
Police protection	3.2
Fire protection	1.4
Natural resources	1.3
Sanitation and sewerage	2.8
Housing and urban renewal	1.5
Parks and recreation	1.4
Financial administration	1.7
General control	2.2
Interest on debt	5.4
Utilities (water, power, transit)	8.9
Insurance	6.6
(Unemployment compensation)	(2.0)
(Retirement programs)	(3.8)
Other	9.7
Total[a]	100.0

[a] Total expenditures = $773 billion.

Source: U.S. Department of Commerce, Bureau of the Census, *Statistical Abstract of the United States: 1990* (Washington, D.C.: Government Printing Office, 1990), 278.

percent of the federal and more than 10 percent of state and local budgets). One of the fastest growing expenditure categories in both state and federal government is interest on the public debt.

Lest we jump to the conclusion that government is little more than a collection of well-defended yet heavily indebted schools and retirement homes, let's consider for a moment the important government services that are not as conspicuous as education, defense, and welfare. Anyone who has ever visited a foreign country in which the public sector is poorly developed and maintained should be especially cognizant of the impressive array of services that our government quietly administers. Among the conditions that predominate in many underdeveloped nations are unreliable or nonexistent utilities (resulting in lights that flicker or go off suddenly, water that is undrinkable, and transit facilities

Table 1-3   Budget Expenditures of Federal Government
by Function, 1989

Function	Percent of Expenditures
National defense	25.4
Social Security and Medicare	27.1
Income security[a]	11.7
Health	4.2
Veterans' benefits and services	2.5
Education, training, and employment assistance	3.1
Housing	1.7
Transportation	2.4
Natural resources and environment	1.4
Energy	.3
Community and regional development	.5
Agriculture	1.8
Interest on debt	14.1
International affairs	.9
Science, space, and technology	1.1
Government administration	1.0
Administration of justice	.8
Total	100.0

[a] Includes unemployment compensation, workers' compensation, and retirement and pension programs.

Note: Total expenditures = $1,137 billion.

Source: U.S. Department of Commerce, Bureau of the Census, *Statistical Abstract of the United States: 1990* (Washington, D.C.: Government Printing Office, 1990), 310-311.

that make Amtrak appear to be the epitome of efficiency); unlicensed and unregulated practitioners of every imaginable profession (ranging from the taxicab driver who picks you up at the airport to the physician who treats the injuries you may receive in a traffic accident); acute levels of pollution (due to untreated sewage, unregulated industrial discharges, and inadequate waste-removal systems); unsafe or unsanitary living and working conditions (as exemplified by the absence of building codes, zoning standards, and inspection programs for drugs, foodstuffs, restaurants, businesses, and other public conveniences); and untrustworthy systems of social and economic control (inadequate police and fire protection, the absence of government insurance programs to protect savings and income, and unsatisfactory methods of maintaining monetary stability). Americans, in contrast, have grown accustomed to having their government protect them from these and many other such occurrences. In fact, a substantial part of the United

States's vaunted quality of life is as much attributable to the protective umbrella of government regulations and services as it is to the largess of the economic system. And because most of these services are delivered efficiently and unobtrusively, many Americans are not even conscious of the role that public administration plays in their everyday lives.

PUBLIC ADMINISTRATION AND PUBLIC MANAGEMENT

Up until now, we have used the terms "public administration" and "public management" interchangeably. However, there is an important distinction between them. Specifically, public management is an *aspect* of public administration.

In ordinary usage, public administration is a generic expression for the entire bundle of activities that are involved in the establishment and implementation of public policies. It is perceived by most academics, if not by most practitioners, as the part of politics that focuses on the bureaucracy and its relations to the executive, legislative, and judicial branches of government. It is concerned with such broad questions as equity, representation, justice, the effectiveness of government, and the control of administrative discretion. Students of public administration study the various institutions of government in an attempt to determine how these and other issues are dealt with in our society. The role that public administrators play in setting, implementing, and altering public policies and programs is therefore a primary concern.

Public management, in contrast, focuses more succinctly on the administrative activities that occur *within* government agencies. Instead of emphasizing the political considerations that permeate the policy process and pervade the external relations of government organizations, public management is primarily concerned with the policy implementation. While public managers do deal continually with political problems and relationships, public policies are taken more or less as given, and attention is fixed on the *methods* by which civil servants carry out their assigned tasks. Thus, students of public management are concerned with efficiency, accountability, goal achievement, and dozens of other managerial and technical questions.

This approach to the study of public administration has both advantages and disadvantages. The primary advantage, we believe, is that an analysis of the managerial (how-to) side of public administration can be helpful in identifying ways in which the delivery of public services can be accomplished more efficiently. Given the extreme pressures for economy and efficiency that presently confront civil servants, an emphasis on these practical aspects of public administration is both necessary and inevitable. A potential side benefit, moreover, may accrue to public managers from a comparison of administrative practices in the public and private sectors. If the activities of managers in the two sectors are shown to be substantially the same (and we contend that they are), then public managers may come to share in the respect accorded to business executives.

A potential disadvantage of this approach is that important philosophical questions may be obscured or neglected when public administration is examined from a strictly applied perspective. While we do not wish to downplay the significance of this possibility, we believe that the benefits that could be gained from a more efficient delivery of public services are worth that risk. Among the major themes of Frederick C. Mosher's work is that the public service is pivotal in the success of the nation and that public management has to *work* as well as be accountable (Stephenson and Plant, 1991). It is taken here as a matter of faith that, if public management is performed in an effective and efficient manner, greater progress will be made in the pursuit of the underlying goals to which major public policies and programs aspire.

But the big picture ought not be ignored in a discussion of the techniques of public management. Public management practices cannot be properly understood and appreciated without being placed in a political and economic context. For this reason, an examination of environmental factors that influence internal management activities is a central component of our discussion. It is therefore our contention that a careful analysis of management practices inside public agencies can teach us a great deal about *both* public management *and* public administration.

THE COMPETENCY/ACCOUNTABILITY DILEMMA

Prior to the emergence of formal merit systems, the lives of public managers were (at least theoretically) much simpler than they are today. Because public employment was so dependent on politics, everybody who was connected with public management played by the politicians' rules. When elected, politicians cleaned house by tossing most of their predecessors' appointees out of office and replacing them with their own supporters. Through this "patronage" or "spoils" system, elected officials built and maintained the party machinery, fostered party loyalty, rewarded faithful service, bought off political opposition, and kept the government running.

Although the patronage system represented an important (perhaps crucial) step in the maturation of America's political institutions— playing an instrumental role, for example, in the development of political parties during the nineteenth century—it carried with it certain drawbacks that virtually ensured its ultimate demise. Most politicians were not terribly concerned about the ability of the individuals they appointed to office, and many did not even appear to pay much attention to their appointees' honesty. This situation became especially troublesome as society became more complex and as industry grew. Corrupt and inept bureaucrats were an inconvenience before industrialization, but they became a serious problem when they inhibited the growth of business. Unreliable postal services, inefficient regulatory programs (most notably those affecting the stability of the currency), and the necessity to pay bribes in order to get any government business accomplished led to a widespread call for reform. Business interests, lawyers, the wealthy, and the urban middle class advocated the creation of a professional civil service selected on the basis of merit rather than on political connections. When this became a reality in the late 1880s, it was heralded as a major step in the modernization of America. Today, when private-sector attacks on the bureaucracy are so common, it is interesting to note that business and industrial interests were largely responsible for the initial adoption of merit systems by government.

As is implicit in the name, merit systems are premised on the belief that public employees should be selected on the basis of competence rather than on their political service. From this fundamental belief grew the idea that government's business should be conducted by a corps of specialized, professional, and neutral civil servants whose relationship to politicians would be that of servants to masters. In other words, a new conception of public management arose in which public employees were viewed as passive and neutral tools with which politicians would build their visions of America. Known as the "politics-administration dichotomy," this was the popular perception of public management for the first few decades after the introduction of merit systems in 1883 (Wilson, 1887).

As the understanding of public management advanced during the early- and middle-twentieth century, political scientists came to realize that tension frequently exists between political values and professional expertise (Riggs, 1991). Whereas politicians may want a given agency to pursue a certain policy, the training and experience of neutral experts may well point in a different direction. Moreover, politicians come and go, but the bureaucracy remains. In one sense, the real power is in the hands of the permanent bureaucracy (Heclo, 1977). If civil servants disagree with the politicians' policy goals, they can use their expertise to convince the politicians to change the policy; they can ignore the politicians' commands and simply not implement the policy, perhaps in the hope that changes will be made when new elections are held; or they can subvert the policy by interpreting it according to their own preferences. Each of these courses of action raises questions about the responsiveness of appointed officials to elected representatives. Whereas the patronage system provided accountability without a corresponding measure of competence, the merit system has reversed the situation, providing competence but not accountability. To many observers, the "arrogance of expertise," coupled with the extensive job protections that are provided to most public managers (see Rosenbloom, 1984), has created a governmental style in which public policy is forged in the crucible of bureaucracy and heated by the contending forces of accountability and competence. Although some traditional scholars have argued that the degree of opposition between these values has been exaggerated (Willoughby, 1936: 219), an appreciation for the underlying strain between them is a prerequisite to understanding the unique environment of public management.

As is implicit in the foregoing discussion, the job of public managers is not as clear-cut as it might seem to be. In addition to having to thread their way through the treacherous minefield of public opinion, public executives are pushed and pulled by the competing pressures of politics, professionalism, and expertise. But there are still other forces with which civil servants must contend, including the following:

> Their agency's enabling legislation and any relevant statutes concerning the agency's mission
>
> Court cases that interpret the agency's range of authority and responsibility
>
> The influence of other agencies with missions that are either complementary or antagonistic to their own
>
> The individual manager's own sense of agency loyalty, which may very well come into conflict with a professional or political outlook
>
> The position of the various interest groups that support the agency but also make demands on it
>
> The structural and procedural impediments that are placed before public managers in the continuing struggle to make them accountable to the popular will—including, for example, externally imposed budget levels, personnel ceilings, staffing practices, organizational structures, and standards by which their performance is judged

FUNCTIONS AND TYPES OF PUBLIC MANAGERS

Despite current tendencies to think of bureaucrats in the public sector as a separate class of citizens, the roles they play are not very different from those played by their counterparts in the private sector. Almost any job title or occupational category that exists in private enterprise has a public-sector equivalent. Governments employ accountants, attorneys, chemists, physicians, janitors, secretaries, engineers, teachers, truck drivers, and thousands of other technical, professional, and service employees. It is also true, however, that governments provide the primary (in some cases, the only) occupational outlets for people in many job categories, such as air traffic controllers, penologists, police officers, social workers, military careerists, and highway engineers.

The individuals who supervise the activities of public employees are generically referred to as public managers. Of these, some are elected and others are appointed. Elected public managers include members of the executive branch of government: the president, governors, and mayors. Legislators are also often considered to be public managers, especially if their jurisdiction does not have strongly defined powers for a separate executive, as in urban governments using either the commission or weak-mayor forms of administration. Under the commission form, each commission member serves in a dual role. Each member individually serves as head of one of the jurisdiction's administrative departments. The commission collectively is the policy-making body. In a weak-mayor plan, elected council members exercise both legislative and executive powers. The mayor is weak because of a lack of administrative powers. These powers are exercised by the elected commissioners and their appointees.

Appointed public managers are mostly civil servants, such as bureau chiefs, agency directors, city managers and their department heads, and supervisors at all levels. While many public managers obtain their positions through patronage appointments (that is, through the sponsorship of elected politicians, which may or may not be followed by legislative approval), a majority of public managers come to office through competitive civil-service procedures. In general, the highest-level public managers (for example, secretaries of major federal departments and heads of state agencies) are political appointees, while most of their subordinate managerial personnel are civil-service appointees. It is a matter of continuing confusion to the public that both political appointees and those who are selected through "neutral" civil-service procedures are included under the "appointed" designation. (See Chapter 4.)

Our focus in this book is on all appointed public managers, regardless of how they achieved their positions. We have, however, made a conscious decision to exclude elected officials from our discussion. As we have pointed out, elected officials do sometimes manage;

indeed, their managerial decisions are frequently dramatic and widely publicized. But elected officials become embroiled in the internal management of public organizations at their peril. The point can be illustrated by President Jimmy Carter's decision to intervene in the Occupational Safety and Health Administration's (OSHA) decision process concerning the cotton-dust standard. Instead of allowing OSHA to decide the issue and therefore take the resulting heat, Carter himself became the direct target for all of the eventual criticism (Eads and Fix, 1984: 58-59). This phenomenon is partially explained by the observation of Neustadt that elected chief executives exercise authority primarily through persuasion (1964: 42-63). Their positions are more suited to general political leadership, forging the way, than to specifying the details of regulatory programs. It is generally the appointed managers who deal with the day-to-day problems, who make all the little decisions that add up to the business of government (Chase and Reveal, 1983: 13-16), and it is they who will be our primary concern.

Figure 1-1 portrays the hierarchy of employees in most public jurisdictions. In the federal government, the central authority consists of the president and, because of its critical policy-making and budgetary role, Congress. The next level, political executives, is made up of the appointed officials who occupy such positions as secretaries and assistant secretaries of cabinet departments and major bureau chiefs. These positions are labeled "political" because the officeholders serve only for the term of the elected official or "at the pleasure of the chief executive" (meaning that they can be terminated by the executive at will). Modern-day presidents generally make about 2,000 political appointments, of which 500 or so have important policy roles (Hilsman, 1985: 138-149).

Executive managers occupy the level immediately beneath the political appointees. They are drawn primarily from the ranks of government-service careerists. Under the old civil-service system, the positions at this level were known collectively as "supergrades," referring to the fact that they were located at the top three grades of the federal personnel system classifications GS 16 to GS 18. Now, due to a major restructuring of the upper reaches of the civil service that occurred in 1979, they are called senior executives. There are approximately 5,000 of these posts in the federal government. Most senior executives are appointed through the merit system, although the 1979 changes allow the president to fill 10 percent of these posts with political appointees.

Middle managers and supervisors, the next two levels in the pyramid, are composed entirely of employees selected through competitive or merit procedures. This large group of people, which accounts for hundreds of thousands, is responsible for the great bulk of the routine

Figure 1-1 A Generalized Organizational Pyramid of Government

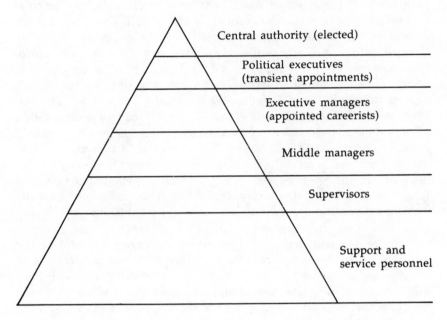

Central authority (elected)

Political executives
(transient appointments)

Executive managers
(appointed careerists)

Middle managers

Supervisors

Support and
service personnel

work of government. These people perform every conceivable type of administrative function, from supervising janitorial crews to assisting political appointees in the formulation of policy initiatives for presentation to Congress.

It has been more difficult for state and local governments to lodge political power in a single executive. This situation has led to the de facto creation of a "plural executive," in which there are several formal centers of governing power and no single office seems to be in charge. State and local legislatures—general assemblies, city councils, county councils or commissions, and the like—have not been as pliant toward their governors, mayors, and executives as Congress has been toward the president. Rather, many of these nonfederal legislative bodies have been exceedingly reluctant to provide the executive officers of their jurisdictions with the range of power and authority that we have come to take for granted in the presidency. Thus, political power in state and local government is often more diffuse than it is at the federal level. The plural executive is one result of this diffusion (Kaufman, 1969). As is shown in Figure 1-2, the plural executive is typically not organized in hierarchical fashion.

Whereas the U.S. Constitution and accompanying statutes provide the federal government with a hierarchical structure, there is often no

Figure 1-2 The Plural Executive

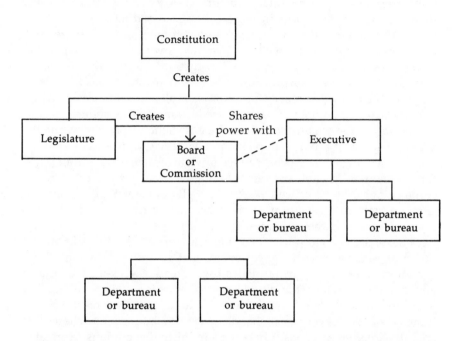

comparable requirement for state and local governments. In the absence of any such legal compulsion, and given the fact that local traditions and conditions vary so greatly among states and regions, enormous variations exist in their governmental forms. Some states have granted their governors powers that are more extensive than those given to the president (line-item vetoes, for example), while others handcuff their executives with dozens of procedural and statutory limitations. Governors' offices therefore vary greatly in their formal and informal powers and in their modes of operations (Beyle, 1983). The degree of autonomy within the bureaucracy also varies. Some states allow their agencies to exercise considerable discretion, with only intermittent oversight and legislative involvement, while in others the legislatures keep a firm hand on the throttle of government. In the former situation, agency directors may be career civil servants with no direct ties to elected officials; alternatively, the governor may have the authority to appoint some or all agency heads (usually with the advice and consent of the legislature). But where strong and active legislatures are present, policy-making authority may be exercised through a board or commission that is controlled exclusively or predominantly by legislative committees (see Figure 1-2). If there are many such boards and commissions, the result is a significant diffusion of power and authority. Executive officers in such nonhierarchical governmental structures are generally much weaker than are their counterparts in more centralized settings.

The structures at the local level are even more diverse. In general, managerial responsibility in city and county government is delegated to a chief executive officer by the jurisdiction's legislative assembly. Beyond that, different jurisdictions use one of several forms of government. In the council-manager form, for example, the chief executive is a city manager appointed by the elected council. The council retains responsibility for establishing all of the jurisdiction's policies, while the manager acts as the policy implementer, supervising the city's employees and seeking to have the council's wishes carried out in an expeditious manner. In another form of local government, the elected mayor is the chief executive officer, exercising both policy-making and administrative authority, usually with the assistance of deputies who help to discharge the managerial duties. In this arrangement, the mayor ordinarily exercises a veto power over the acts of council. This is known as the strong-mayor form of government, and it is found in most large American cities. Many smaller cities use instead a weak-mayor form of government, in which the elected council exercises policy-making and oversight authority, while the mayor presides over council meetings and, if the jurisdiction is very small, handles the few administrative chores that arise. In larger jurisdictions, where the administrative burdens are greater, many weak-mayor cities have employed city administrators to carry out the orders of their councils. Occasionally, city administrators develop sufficient informal authority to be able to exercise a measure of independent judgment in limited areas of decision making.

Figure 1-3 provides a simplified picture of these three major forms of local government. Both Figures 1-2 and 1-3 are highly generalized; many cities have developed unique forms of their own. The important characteristic to keep in mind is the nature of the formal powers that are granted to the respective offices. City managers have the authority to hire and fire department heads and to oversee the daily operations of the city without council interference, whereas city administrators generally do not enjoy these powers. Not surprisingly, then, city administrators tend to be placed in their positions through political appointment, whereas city managers are usually hired through a more competitive, merit-based procedure. Additionally, city administrators are subject to dismissal at the whim of the council, whereas city managers usually can be removed only by more formal (though not necessarily any less arbitrary) methods. Thanks to their independent and more extensive basis of authority, which is almost always codified in the jurisdiction's charter or code of laws, city managers have been able to achieve a

Figure 1-3 General Forms of Local Government

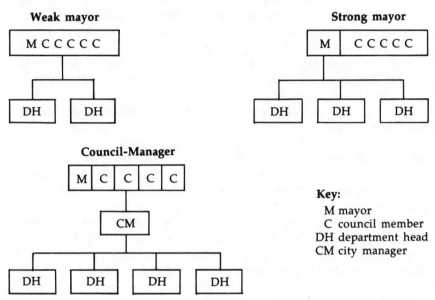

reputation for professionalism and expertise that has not yet become universally applicable to city administrators (see National Municipal League, 1964: 22-25).

Although the titles are different, county governments also contain officials who are comparable to mayors, city managers, and city administrators. County supervisors, for example, sometimes have functions similar to those of mayors, and many counties employ professional executives who have such titles as county manager or county administrator. Other political subdivisions, most notably school and public-service districts, also employ managers, whose powers and degrees of administrative autonomy are highly variable. As is observed in the next section, a proper understanding of the problems and responsibilities of public managers depends in part on an appreciation for the extreme variability that characterizes the power relationships between appointed public officials and their elected bosses.

CHANGING VIEWS OF PUBLIC MANAGEMENT

The duties normally associated with public administration include enforcement of laws, ordinances, rules, and regulations; preparation and supervision of budget and planning documents; analysis of and recommendations concerning programs and policies; selection and supervision of employees; agency operation and maintenance ("housekeeping functions"); and the maintenance of contacts with relevant groups and individuals outside the agency. In performing these many tasks, the manager is assumed to have a degree of discretion in carrying out the official policies of the agency. The options may range from the police officer's decision about whether to ticket a jaywalker to a senior executive's decision about whether the full punitive force of government should be brought to bear on a chemical company that is polluting a river.

Given the diversity we find in public management, one may well ask whether there are any "eternal verities" or commonalities in the way that managers behave. Leonard White, the author of an early textbook on public administration, was one of the first to respond in the affirmative, declaring that "administration is a single process, substantially uniform in its essential characteristics wherever observed" (White, 1939: *ix*). Shortly thereafter, Luther Gulick offered what has been perhaps the most enduring description of the common elements of public administration, discussed in the next section.

THE ORIGINAL VIEW

For a field noted for its acronyms Gulick aptly summed up the functions of public management in an acronym, POSDCORB, which stands for Planning, Organizing, Staffing, Directing, Coordinating, Reporting, and Budgeting. He described these basic managerial operations in the following way:

> Planning . . . is working out in broad outline the things that need to be done and the method for doing them to accomplish the purpose set for the enterprise;
> Organizing . . . is the establishment of the formal structure of authority through which work subdivisions are arranged, defined, and coordinated for the defined objective;
> Staffing . . . is the whole personnel function of bringing in and training staff and maintaining favorable work conditions;
> Directing . . . is the continuous task of making decisions and embodying them in specific and general orders and instructions and serving as the leader of the enterprise;
> Coordinating . . . is the all-important duty of interrelating the various parts of the work;
> Reporting . . . is keeping those to whom the executive is responsible informed as to what is going on, which thus

includes keeping himself and his subordinates informed
through records, research, and inspection;
Budgeting ... consists of fiscal planning, accounting, and
control. (Gulick and Urwick, 1937: 13)

Despite the convenience and value of the POSDCORB description,
it fell out of favor not long after it was introduced. Its decline in
popularity is attributable to the fact that it does not tell us what is *public*
about public management. In other words, it seems to assume the
validity of Wilson's dichotomy between politics and administration,
which was discussed earlier. But this dichotomy has been discredited in
a succession of insightful works (Appleby, 1949; Simon, 1946; Lindblom,
1965). Thus, the management-functions approach to public administration does not provide theory that is descriptive of, nor entirely applicable to, the world of politics and government.

Critics seized on the theoretical prominence that Gulick and others
had given to the work of Henri Fayol in "directing minds to the need
for studying administration scientifically" (Gulick and Urwick, 1937:
117). Fayol's "scientific management" emphasized detachment, almost a
revulsion to politics, and an objective, apolitical approach to problem
solving. Herbert Simon called the resulting managerial principles mere
proverbs and proceeded to lay bare their fallacies (Simon, 1946).
Additionally, Gulick's work was attacked by many other authors because
it ran counter to the "human relations" movement that had begun to
spread across the management field during the 1940s. POSDCORB, and
other classical approaches to management, were viewed as attempts to
exploit, control, and manipulate workers. In place of the virtues of
authority, structure, and control, management theorists were emphasizing the innate value of the individual worker. Accordingly, management functions were de-emphasized while theorists searched for ways to
make workers feel more comfortable and worthwhile in their organizational settings.

Gradually, the preference for what seemed to be industrial or
engineering solutions to public problems gave way to a model of public
administration that accommodated political and policy concerns. The
superficiality of any approach to public administration that is not
cognizant of political reality is now recognized by academics and
practitioners alike.

POSDCORB TRANSFORMED

Nevertheless, even though now relegated to a subsidiary role in most
treatments, the functions of management have continued to be a concern

of theorists in the field and have certainly been a topic of interest among practitioners. Successive restatements of POSDCORB have attempted to introduce a greater appreciation for the social and political context in which public management operates. Garson and Overman (1983), for example, suggested a new acronym, PAFHRIER—Policy Analysis, Financial management, Human Resources management, Information management, and External Relations. This brings in the terms that have emerged in the more recent theoretical and practical approaches to the field. Policy analysis, for example, deals with public administration's interest in the impact of public policies on the environment and in variations in the ways that policies are implemented. Human resources management connotes a broader conception of the staffing function than was envisioned in POSDCORB; in addition to the traditional operations of recruitment, selection, and classification, the human-resources approach encompasses such relatively modern concerns as employee growth and development, motivation, and equitable treatment—in short, it views employees as resources that must be nurtured and treated fairly. Taken as a whole, this transformation reflects the following differences from Gulick's treatment of public management:

> expansion of the planning concept to the broader policy-analysis concept;
> expansion of the staffing concept to the broader human-resources concept;
> expansion of the neglected reporting concept to the broader information-management concept;
> addition of external relations as a major category;
> dispersion of the POSDCORB categories, especially organizing, directing, and coordinating, for use as aspects of the new categories. (Garson and Overman, 1983: 64-65)

In their analysis of recent research on public management, Garson and Overman identify a number of utilizations of PAFHRIER concepts in public agency operations. A detailed discussion of their categorization scheme is presented in an appendix to their 1983 book (pp. 175-181) and serves as a compendium of the tasks that public managers perform today.

Another way to transform POSDCORB is to relate its concepts to a theory of managerial roles rather than treating it as simply an inventory or laundry list of managerial functions. Thus, Henry Mintzberg (1973) has proposed a management theory consisting of three major categories of activity, which are in turn divided into more specific types. The three major activity categories, or roles, are the *interpersonal, informational,* and *decisional.* The interpersonal roles are those of "figurehead," "liaison," and "leader." Informational roles have the manager acting as "monitor," "disseminator," and "spokesperson." The decisional roles encompass the activities of "entrepreneur" (making basic decisions that will influence the very survival of the organization), "resource allocator" (a more routine set of decisions), "disturbance handler," and "negotiator."

Table 1-4 presents a comparison of the major areas of emphasis in POSDCORB and the Interpersonal-Informational-Decisional approach. One way in which Mintzberg is an improvement over Gulick is that his formulation acknowledges, and tries to deal systematically with, the network of informal relations that managers have both inside and outside of their organizations. Additionally, Mintzberg contends that the old approach to management generated hypotheses (or rested on assumptions) about managerial behavior that were more folklore than fact—for example, the ideas that managers give high priority to planning, whereas they are really oriented to acting in the present rather than in the future; that they have no regular duties, whereas they actually perform a great many routine tasks; and that they operate through written communications, whereas they actually do most of their work through spoken communications (Mintzberg, 1974).

While other authors have offered further reformulations of Gulick's approach, none has been able (or, for that matter, even attempted) to refute the underlying concept that a functional approach to the study of administration is inherently valuable. Consequently, these later versions of POSDCORB constitute improvements and refinements, not replacements. The continuing interest in functional and role-based approaches to public management demonstrates that they are still relevant to an understanding of administrative phenomena.

THE APPROACH OF THIS BOOK

Interest in the applied aspects of public administration has been increasing notably in recent years. Probably the most significant factor accounting for this renewed attention is the fiscal uncertainty that characterized American society in the mid-1980s. Widely publicized taxpayer revolts, coupled with large deficits in government budgets, focused professional attention on the need to manage government more efficiently (see Hartle, 1985). This movement was reinforced by calls for greater privatization of government services (Savas, 1982), as well as by harsh criticisms of alleged waste in government. Foremost among such criticism was the Grace Commission Report (President's Private Sector Survey on Cost Control, 1984), which put forth a vigorous argument for the idea that government would run much more efficiently if it were managed according to business principles (see Goodsell, 1984: 200).

Table 1-4 Managerial Functions in Mintzberg, Gulick, and Garson and Overman

Type of Function	Mintzberg[a]	Gulick (POSDCORB)[b]	Garson and Overman (PAFHRIER)[c]
Interpersonal	Figurehead: performs ceremonial duties Leader: uses formal powers Liaison: makes contacts outside chain of command	No specific counterpart Organizing, staffing No specific counterpart	No specific counterpart Dispersion of POSDCORB functions No specific counterpart
Informational	Monitor: scans for information Disseminator: passes along information Spokesperson: passes information outside organization	Planning, reporting Directing, coordinating No specific counterpart	Policy analysis Information management External relations
Decisional	Entrepreneur: seeks to develop and improve organization Disturbance handler: responds to pressures Resource allocator: decides who gets what Negotiator: argues organizational position	No specific counterpart No specific counterpart Budgeting No specific counterpart	Human resources management No specific counterpart Financial management No specific counterpart

[a] Henry Mintzberg, *The Nature of Managerial Work* (New York: Harper and Row, 1973).

[b] Luther Gulick, "The Dynamics of Public Administration Today as Guidelines for the Future," *Public Administration Review* 43 (May/June 1983): 193-198.

[c] G. David Garson and E. S. Overman, *Public Management Research in the United States* (New York: Praeger, 1983).

Wherever one looks in the field today, the need to manage wisely and effectively is being broadly emphasized.

Yet few theorists, and even fewer practitioners, are contending that POSDCORB is no longer relevant. As is indicated by the reformulations of POSDCORB, understanding of the content and significance of the functions of management has grown. A dramatic illustration of this point is offered by Gulick himself, who, in 1983, wrote that government productivity can be improved only through "decentralization, delegation, and the participation of workers and clients in management" (Gulick, 1983: 197). Nevertheless, there is no doubt that POSDCORB still captures most of the major management activities that are performed daily in our public organizations. POSDCORB remains valuable as a basic model, though it needs to be updated in accordance with advances in management thought.

For the most part, the approach to management functions taken in this book follows Gulick's original formulation. Planning, organizing, staffing, reporting, and budgeting are all discussed. However, whereas Gulick spoke of directing and coordinating, we use the more contemporary term of "leadership."

Furthermore, our discussions of the various functions emphasize many issues that were either ignored by Gulick or had not yet been well understood when POSDCORB was first proposed. The interconnectedness of the functions is highlighted, as are the influences of extraorganizational and interpersonal factors. We also look at evaluation, for this is an emerging managerial function that is at the forefront of many of the most important issues in modern public administration. Through these revisions, and others that will be described later, we have attempted to place POSDCORB in a contemporary context that is relevant to students and practitioners of today's brand of public management.

Our intention is not to downplay the political aspects of public administration, but to draw attention to what we feel much of the literature in the field either takes for granted or underemphasizes. Although the discussion will focus on what public managers do inside of their organizations, an examination of the external environment of public organizations is unavoidable. The boundaries of government organizations are porous—that is, easily penetrated by outside influences. The effects that these influences have on administrative operations will be made visible in our assessments of the various managerial functions. A useful guide in this regard is the suggestion by Appleby (1949) that public management consists more of *cooperative roles* than of discrete functions. In other words, the public's business is conducted in an environment within which managers, politicians, employees, interest groups, and numerous other actors are involved in give-and-take relationships. Policy decisions are thus worked out within a system of relationships to which many parties make significant contributions. In this view, public management is a partnership of diverse groups working toward a more or less common goal. Once this is understood, it is impossible to overlook the essentially political nature of public management.

Our approach is also based on the premise that management is, and always will be, more an art than a science. Although the study of management principles and practices can provide many valuable lessons to public administrators, no textbook can hope to teach the entire array of skills, abilities, and attitudes that together constitute effective management.

In summary, POSDCORB is a convenient starting point from which to develop a contemporary discussion of public management. At root, today's public manager is the administrative generalist of Gulick's day, but one who is confronted by a new set of challenges and opportunities. Practitioners of the art of public management must have diverse skills in such functional areas as budgeting, personnel management, and organizational design. Today's public managers must also be experts in communication, able to handle citizen complaints as easily as they present a report to their governing body. Likewise, they must be "change agents," who are able to adjust their policy advice and operating skills to a changing technology and to the changing expectations of workers and citizens. In a sense, then, our approach to the topic is merely a reflection of what has occurred in the field of public management over the past few decades.

REFERENCES

Abney, Glenn, and T. P. Lauth. 1983. "The Governor as Chief Administrator." *Public Administration Review* 43 (January/February): 40-49.

Allison, Graham T., Jr. 1983. "Public and Private Management: Are They Fundamentally Alike in All Unimportant Respects?" In *Public Administration: Concepts and Cases*, ed. Richard Stillman, 453-467. Boston: Houghton Mifflin.

Appleby, Paul H. 1949. *Policy and Administration*. Tuscaloosa: University of Alabama Press.

Banfield, Edward, and James Q. Wilson. 1963. *City Politics*. New York: Vintage.

Beyle, Thad. 1983. "Governors." In *Politics in the American States*, ed. Virginia Gray, Herbert Jacob, and Kenneth Vines, 180-221. Boston: Little, Brown.

Bowsher, Charles A. 1992. "Meeting the New American Management Challenge in a Federal Agency." *Public Administration Review* 52 (January/February): 3-7.

Chase, Gordon, and Elizabeth C. Reveal. 1983. *How to Manage in the Public Sector.* Reading, Mass.: Addison-Wesley.

Chubb, J. E., and P. E. Peterson, ed. 1989. *Can the Government Govern?* Washington, D.C.: Brookings Institution.

Congressional Budget Office and General Accounting Office. 1984. *Analysis of the Grace Commission's Major Proposals for Cost Control.* Washington, D.C.: GAO.

Council of State Governments. 1985. *The Book of the States: 1984-1985.* Lexington, Ky.: Council of State Governments.

Downs, Anthony. 1967. *Inside Bureaucracy.* Boston: Little, Brown.

Drucker, Peter. 1974. *Management: Tasks, Responsibilities, Practices.* New York: Harper and Row.

_____. 1980. "The Deadly Sins in Public Administration." *Public Administration Review* 40 (March/April): 103-106.

Eads, G. C., and Michael Fix. 1984. *Relief or Reform: Reagan's Regulatory Dilemma.* Washington, D.C.: The Urban Institute.

Garson, G. David, and E. S. Overman. 1983. *Public Management Research in the United States.* New York: Praeger.

Goodnow, F. J. 1900. *Politics and Administration.* New York: Macmillan.

Goodsell, Charles T. 1984. "The Grace Commission: Seeking Efficiency for the Whole People?" *Public Administration Review* 44 (May/June): 196-204.

_____. 1985. *The Case for Bureaucracy.* Chatham, N.J.: Chatham House.

Grosenick, Leigh. 1984. "Research in Domestic Governance." *Public Administration Quarterly* 8 (Fall): 266-287.

Gulick, Luther. 1965. "The Twenty-Fifth Anniversary of the American Society for Public Administration." *Public Administration Review* 25 (March): 1-4.

_____. 1983. "The Dynamics of Public Administration Today as Guidelines for the Future." *Public Administration Review* 43 (May/June): 193-198.

Gulick, Luther, and L. Urwick, ed. 1937. *Papers on the Science of Administration.* New York: Institute of Public Administration.

Hartle, Terry W. 1985. "Sisyphus Revisited: Running the Government Like a Business." *Public Administration Review* 45 (March/April): 341-351.

Heclo, Hugh. 1977. *A Government of Strangers.* Washington, D.C.: Brookings Institution.

Hilsman, Roger. 1985. *The Politics of Governing America.* Englewood Cliffs, N.J.: Prentice-Hall.

Kaufman, Herbert. 1969. "Administrative Decentralization and Political Power." *Public Administration Review* 29 (January/February): 3-15.

Lau, A. W., Arthur R. Newman, and Laurie A. Brodling. 1980. "The Nature of Managerial Work in the Public Sector." *Public Administration Review* 40 (September/October): 513-520.

Levine, Charles, and George Wolohojian. 1984. "Retrenchment and Human Resources Management: Combatting the Discount Effects of Uncertainty." In *Public Personnel Administration: Problems and Prospects,* ed. Steven Hays and Richard Kearney, 175-188. Englewood Cliffs, N.J.: Prentice-Hall.

Lindblom, Charles. 1965. *The Intelligence of Democracy: Decision Making through Mutual Adjustment:* New York: Free Press.

Lynch, Thomas. 1977. "A Context for Zero-Base Budgeting." *The Bureaucrat* (Spring): 3-11.

MacManus, S. A. 1991. "Why Businesses Are Reluctant to Sell to Governments." *Public Administration Review* 51 (July/August): 328-344.

Marini, Frank, ed. 1971. *Toward a New Public Administration: The Minnowbrook Perspective.* Scranton, Pa.: Chandler.

Mintzberg, Henry. 1973. *The Nature of Managerial Work.* New York: Harper and Row.

———. 1974. "The Manager's Job: Folklore and Fact." *Harvard Business Review* 53 (July/August): 49-61.

Morgan, David, and Robert England. 1988. "The Two Faces of Privatization." *Public Administration Review* 48 (November/December): 979-987.

Mosher, Frederick. 1982. *Democracy and the Public Service.* New York: Oxford.

National Municipal League. 1964. *Model City Charter.* New York: National Municipal League.

Neustadt, Richard E. 1964. *Presidential Power.* New York: The New American Library.

O'Connell, Brian. 1989. "What Voluntary Activity Can and Cannot Do for America." *Public Administration Review* 49 (September/October): 486-491.

President's Private Sector Survey on Cost Control. 1984. *A Report to the President.* 47 vols. Washington, D.C.: Government Printing Office.

Quade, E. S. 1982. *Analysis for Public Decisions.* New York: North Holland.

Rainey, Hal G. 1984. "*Public Organization Theory: Current Contributions and Research Directions.*" Paper delivered at the annual meeting of the American Political Science Association, Washington, D.C.

Riggs, F. W. 1991. "Public Administration: A Comparativist Framework." *Public Administration Review* 51 (November/December): 473-475.

Rosenbloom, David. 1984. "What Every Personnel Manager Should Know about the Constitution." In *Public Personnel Administration,* 27-42. *See* Levine and Wolohojian.

Savas, E. S. 1982. *Privatizing the Public Sector.* Chatham, N.J.: Chatham House.

———. 1987. *Privatization: The Key to Better Government.* Chatham, N.J.: Chatham House.

Simon, Herbert. 1946. "The Proverbs of Administration." *Public Administration Review* 6 (Winter): 53-67.

Steiner, Peter. 1983. "The Public Sector and the Public Interest." In *Public Expenditure and Policy Analysis,* ed. R. H. Haveman and J. Margolis. Chicago: Rand McNally, 3-41.

Steiss, A. W., and G. A. Daneke. 1980. *Performance Administration.* Lexington, Mass.: Lexington.

Stephenson, M. O., Jr., and J. F. Plant. 1991. "The Legacy of Frederick C. Mosher." *Public Administration Review* 51 (March/April): 97-113.

U.S. Department of Commerce. Bureau of the Census. 1990. *Statistical Abstract of the United States: 1990.* Washington, D.C.: Government Printing Office.

Waldo, Dwight. 1965. "The Administrative State Revisited." *Public Administration Review* 25 (March): 5-30.

_____. 1980. *The Enterprise of Public Administration.* Novato, Calif.: Chandler and Sharp.

Weber, Max. 1947. *The Theory of Economic and Social Organization,* ed. and trans. A. M. Henderson and Talcott Parsons. New York: Macmillan.

White, Leonard. 1939. *The Study of Public Administration.* New York: Macmillan.

Wholey, Joseph S. 1983. *Evaluation and Effective Public Management.* Boston: Little, Brown.

Willoughby, W. F. 1936. *Government of Modern States.* New York: Appleton-Century.

Wilson, Woodrow. 1887. "The Study of Administration." *Classics of Public Administration,* ed. J. M. Shafritz and A. C. Hyde, 3-17. Oak Park, Ill.: Moore. (First published in *Political Science Quarterly,* vol. 2.)

Woll, Peter. 1977. *American Bureaucracy.* New York: Norton.

Young, Oran R. 1968. *Systems of Political Science.* Englewood Cliffs, N.J.: Prentice-Hall.

2

Planning

People in the field of public management know a lot of horror stories. For example, there is the one about the highway department that built a bridge that connected to nothing on the other side of the river. A related story has it that a sturdy, fixed bridge was built that connected properly to a road on the other side of the river, but that surprised the ship captain who found that his vessel was too tall to go under the bridge. No one had asked about the port and marina that were located upstream.

Planning is the first of the managerial processes in POSDCORB, but the successful development and use of plans are a constant source of perplexity for the practicing manager. On the one hand, planning seems like an activity that common sense requires; there are sound, obvious reasons to determine in advance where to build bridges and, in general, where an organization is and where it is going. And yet, as Mintzberg (1973: 38) tells us, managers seldom do plan. They spend most of their time talking, especially on the telephone, and dealing with the crises that occur every day. There is little or no time to get away from day-to-day operations in order to plan.

Planning is hard to do in practice, and even if plans are made, they may have only limited meaning because of specialization; each of the different experts who participate in the planning process has a narrow view of the situation. Mertins maintains that planning has lost "its usefulness as an integrating, encompassing concept" (1971: 254). Thus, even with plans in hand, the manager may still be at a loss as to the direction to take in future decisions. Nevertheless, whether preoccupied with daily operations or perplexed by the work of specialists, managers are influenced by plans. The impact is often indirect; performance or production standards based on plans are part of the manager's view of decisions that have to be made, and expectations of performance and production are a basis on which the manager's achievements will be evaluated by higher-level executives or political bodies. This chapter treats planning as the managerial function that is a prelude to organizing, staffing, and the other components of POSDCORB. A broad outline of the public manager's planning function and descriptions of planning activities are set forth. Planning is discussed here as an activity that helps managers anticipate specific problems in program implementation and operations. The chapter will identify and explain some basic planning concepts and the context within which planning serves an organization.

Several managerial techniques related to the planning function are also discussed in this chapter: management by objectives, forecasting, and operations research and risk analysis. The effectiveness of planning as a tool for public managers is explored in the chapter's summary in terms of the limits on planning and the role of creativity in the public-sector organization.

DEVELOPMENT OF THE PLANNING FUNCTION

Planning became especially important to public managers during the expansion of cities in the late 1800s and early 1900s. Growing cities required plans for infrastructure (roads, water, sewerage, and the like) and for housing and land use. New Deal policies stimulated further changes, and it was also at that time that economic and social planning made an appearance (Vieg, 1942). World War II emphasized the importance and necessity of planning to carry out large-scale operations. Whatever concerns there might have been about a government that was "too big" or "destructive of free enterprise," national mobilization during the early 1940s illustrated that planning could work if the acceptable stimuli were present (demands for large-scale operations and the presence of hostile nation-states) along with domestic political support for taking appropriate action.

After the war, the problem was how to restore an allocation system that worked through the market. The war effort had required extensive governmental plans and organization to supervise the allocation of economic goods for military production. Further planning was required to prepare for peace: for example, how were 2.5 million discharged soldiers to get jobs? The conversion of production capacity from wartime to peacetime uses was another major planning concern after World War II, and doing all of this in a way that would avoid the economic depression which so often follows a war. The Full Employment Act of

1946 expressed the national economic policy of the time and implied a major role for public planning.

Planning by public managers has continued to this day. It may not be the comprehensive, national planning required by war, which in peacetime would be regarded as too heavy-handed (or "socialistic"), but it is planning nonetheless. The Eisenhower administration planned for the purpose of maintaining preparedness during the cold war of the 1950s (Leuchtenburg, 1983: 5). During the 1960s, federal programs for making grants to state and local governments encouraged, then required, planning as a prerequisite for receiving this aid. At the same time, planning once more expanded its scope from the physical infrastructure of roads, buildings, and public utilities to the social needs of the community. In this respect, the Great Society programs of the 1960s reflected and extended the planning for social as well as physical development and change which originated in the programs of the New Deal.

National, state, and local units of government have strengthened their planning capacity in keeping with the rapid growth of federal aid. Planning staffs have been added where none existed before, often with the encouragement and financing of the federal programs. The multiplication of federal, state, and local planning agencies has led to many levels and varieties of plans, and coordination of these many plans has become a task in itself.

Lack of coordination is often blamed for governmental "waste and inefficiency." For example, suppose that a number of small, adjoining neighborhood water systems are to be connected into a more efficient, community-wide distribution network. One system may have 4-inch water pipes while another has 12-inch pipes, complicating the job of hooking them together. The promise of planning is that the need for pipes of equal size will have been anticipated. In a well-planned sewerage system, gravity flow would be used to the maximum, so that fewer pumping stations would have to be built. Social programs have similar planning demands. Coordinated human-services planning would allow more people to be served at lower unit costs and would reduce disease and hunger. Planning would go far to reduce governmental inefficiencies and make tax dollars more effective.

One approach to coordination of multiple planning activities has been through the use of *planning councils*. Examples have included state interagency coordination councils, usually located in the governor's office, and regional councils of local governments, which go under various names, such as council of governments (COG) or area planning and development commission (APDC). Also, many local and state *advisory groups* exist to help coordinate plans. Both planning councils and advisory groups use elected officials and citizens to ensure community input to managers' plans.

Recent revenue cutbacks and changes in federal policy have generally reduced the emphasis on planning at the national level. The Reagan administration emphasized planning by state, local, and private-sector organizations for social programs as well as for physical development. During the Reagan and Bush administrations, state and local governments have been forced to use their own revenues for planning support. These developments do not mean that planning is dead, but it does face a new set of political influences and challenges.

INFLUENCES ON PLANNING

In simple terms, planning means that the organization selects objectives and determines the means to reach them. Plans are aimed at achieving the best use of organizational resources in a future environment, and they are also the basis for managerial control and direction of the organization in its current environment. Though public managers tend to emphasize the control aspects of plans, it is unavoidable that they view planning in the larger context of the organization's interdependent relations. Organizations depend on participation by many parties and stakeholders. Planners must work to include many views if plans are to be effective (Benveniste, 1989).

It is important to point out that the concepts and techniques of planning comprise a specialized area of managerial functioning and expertise. It is from a solid base in the theoretical context of planning and in an understanding of the purposes and uses of plans that a manager will be able to devise plans that will relate successfully to the decision environment of the organization (Bolan, 1975).

The *decision environment* refers to the conditions that have a bearing on what a manager is actually able to implement. They include both external and internal conditions, so that managers have a two-front job as they develop the issues for their organization's planning agenda (Michael, 1982). Moreover, these conditions are constantly changing. Among important external developments are economic growth or recession, changes in the demographic or social characteristics of the jurisdiction, and variations in political opinions. Internal changes include changes in the composition of the public work force, the skills of the employees, and employee attitudes toward work.

It is often difficult for a manager to identify environmental changes and to sort them into categories that relate specifically to the agency's plans. Even if the outside and inside environments are analyzed and general conclusions are drawn about their effects on plans, their application to the planning effort may not be realistic. Many students of planning and organizations have wrestled with these planning dilemmas.

Two Views of the Planning Problem

Herbert Simon and Henry Mintzberg are among the scholars who have sought to discover how planners and decision makers deal with changes in their environments. Both Simon and Mintzberg acknowledge that planning is a difficult though vital part of the managerial function. Simon approaches the planning problem from the internal perspective of the manager attempting to plan with the help of an organization but within the limits of inherent human fallibilities (Simon, 1976; Simon, Smithburg, and Thompson, 1950). Mintzberg (1973) suggests that the constant changes in the external environment are the major sources of influences on planning and that the manager should look to them for planning cues.

Simon and Mintzberg closely relate planning and decision making. All planning includes decision making, but not all decision making includes planning. Mintzberg emphasizes the relationship of plans and decisions through the concept of the manager as a dynamic actor who plans and implements (decides) at the same time. Successful implementation of policy decisions has its roots in strategic planning, but strategic planning is not decision making. Careful strategic planning is only the first step in a series of activities that lead to decisions about the delivery of governmental services. The eventual attainment of a goal or the meeting of an expectation must be based on specific objectives, which are defined or set in relation to overall goals. Planning actions by dynamic or change-oriented managers must still relate to operational decisions aimed at improving the quality of public service through constant adjustment to citizen needs.

Simon sets forth the concept of *satisficing*, which means that managers seek decisions that *satisfy* them and are *sufficient* for the problems at hand (Rehfuss, 1973: 161). Simon also argues that there are limits on any human being's rationality, a proposition that he calls the *principle of bounded rationality* (March and Simon, 1958: 137-171, 203-204). Especially with modern techniques of information production, it is impossible for the manager to gather and assimilate all the available and relevant information for decision making. Therefore, the manager cannot really reach an optimal strategic or implementation decision; it must be a satisficing one.

Nor can the manager clearly obtain a prescriptive or normative decision-making environment in which the manager knows what *ought* to be done. Absolute certainty of the future is simply not possible, and an uncertain future implies risk. Simon recognizes that the practicing manager makes decisions based on limited rationality, often without plans or full information (Simon, 1979).

The satisficing manager is faced with two types of situations that require planning. Simon labels these *substantive* (nonprogrammed) planning and *procedural* (programmed) planning. Substantive planning is a response to new situations; procedural planning is intended to handle recurring problems and to deal with the internal requirements of the organization. Strategic planning is an example of substantive planning or goal setting, while problem solving to find the most effective internal division of work is an example of procedural planning (March and Simon, 1958: 178-182).

In both types of planning, the decision maker *sequentially searches*— that is, examines the options, one after the other, in an effort to find feasible courses of action that will meet the needs defined by a group of organizational actors or by a higher-level manager. When a solution that meets the needs of the manager and the organization (or at least does not conflict with the needs of the organization) is found, the decision maker tends to settle for that solution; typically, no attempt is made to gather additional information—for information is costly—or to search for another decision. In other words, the decision maker satisfies, or settles for the first feasible alternative with the fewest undesirable consequences that can be foreseen at the time (March and Simon, 1958: 180). Satisficing demands more use of short-term plans, but also implies a constant need to replan (although time may not permit that). The satisficing level is influenced by the media, elected officials, the general public, and the manager's staff.

The object of satisficing is to get the job done, perhaps not in the most efficient way but with a minimum number of complications. But plans are potential complications. They take time to complete, and they require negotiation, bargaining, and the resolution of conflict. Many managers are conditioned by their experiences or the experiences of others to avoid conflict, because it tends to reduce managerial effectiveness. Thus, even short-term planning may be avoided by managers or engaged in only reluctantly. March and Simon (1958: 185) refer to this as "Gresham's law of planning"—that is, "daily routine drives out planning."

Mintzberg approaches the problem of planning from the perspective of the environment of the organization and its effects on the working conditions of the manager. Managers, he argues, spend virtually all of their time responding to "high-pressure disturbance situations," or crises, "because 'poor' managers ignore situations until they reach crisis proportions," while " 'good' managers cannot anticipate the consequences of all actions taken by their organizations" (Mintzberg, 1973: 84).

Since the manager is not in complete control of time, managerial planning does not usually take place under routine, regular conditions. Competing tasks often intervene. The manager becomes conditioned to this hectic environment. Without plans and under pressure, the manager is then tempted to make decisions that deal with the situation only superficially and marginally, meaning that just enough additional effort is applied to quiet the problem for a time (Mintzberg, 1973: 171). This allows the manager to move on to the next pressure point, with no real attempt at lasting solutions. If there are enough pressure points, the manager spends all of the time dealing with such "emergencies."

Another aspect of the manager's plight as depicted by Mintzberg is the "planning dilemma," which arises when the manager has a professional planning staff. While the authority to implement plans and the judgment and information necessary to formulate good plans reside within the manager, only the professional planning staff has the time and the training in the techniques required for sound, detailed planning (Mintzberg, 1973: 152). The manager and the planner often have very different ways of looking at problems. Often the manager is a generalist, without training in planning or planning skills; other managers are specialists with a background in professions such as engineering or medicine, with ideas about planning that may be quite different from those that are useful in public organizations.

To Mintzberg, the manager is a victim of the environment; to Simon, the manager is operating within inherent human limitations. The point that both authors make is that comprehensive, foolproof planning is impossible. Plans and decisions will always need improvement. Public managers face a constant insecurity about the success and adequacy of their plans and decisions. Planning staffs may help, but only if the manager is able to relate to their work.

The development and execution of a planning process are a means by which organizations and managers may undertake the improvement of plans, to reduce insecurity and vagueness.

Table 2-1 presents an example of such a process. It is a definition of what planners do as well as an identification of the key elements in the process.

VARIETIES OF PLANNING

The main purpose of planning is to facilitate the accomplishment of organizational objectives (Sisk and Williams, 1981: 62-63). There are four

Table 2-1 A Sample Planning Process

Step Number	Content
1	Description of the needs underlying the plan
2	Preparation of a broad outline of the plan
3	Approval of proposal to plan
4	Designation of planning staff and its responsibilities
5	Definition of strategic, long-run, and short-run elements of plan
6	Acquisition of data
7	Completion of provisional plan
8	Testing and evaluation of plan, discussion, adjustments
9	Preparation of final plan
10	Approval
11	Initiation of continuing planning process

steps essential to a rational planning and managerial process. First, the goals are defined. These goals should reflect the general outcomes or directions toward which the organization is to move. Second, alternative ways of achieving each goal are identified and the estimated costs and benefits (consequences) are calculated for each alternative. Third, choices are made of the alternatives with the most favorable ratio of benefits to costs that can be found. Fourth, the chosen alternatives are translated into clear, operational statements, or what were earlier labeled objectives. Objectives are usually expressed in quantities or other numerical terms, so that they can be precisely measured and analyzed. If that is not possible, qualitative terms are used that may still allow the responsible manager to assess the degree of achievement.

But planning is more than a straightforward, rational process, as we have learned from Simon and Mintzberg. Rather, it is a dynamic process of constant adaptation to changes in the internal and external environments of the organization; in short, it is a political process. Changing environments impose new demands, and organizations cannot keep doing the same things, so that planning must be concerned with change (Kastens, 1979). Changes bring opportunities, but they also bring risks. It is the role of planners to reduce risks while taking advantage of opportunities (Koontz, O'Donnell, and Weihrich, 1982: 73). While planning must constantly deal with change, it also seeks to ensure that the change is controlled and directional and therefore of use to the organization.

Planners must make a continuous effort to analyze events and formulate solutions to the problems that emerge. The planning process is never finished but is the articulation of many phases or steps (Koontz,

O'Donnell, and Weihrich, 1982: 74). Organizational goals are continually being checked against the reality in which the organization operates. Indeed, this checking is another way to describe planning. Managers check on what will happen next, what will happen in the near future, and what will happen later on. These perspectives reflect different measures of the futures that planners envision and indicate the importance of the time span covered by a plan.

THE TIME FRAMES OF PLANNING

Planners confront change by using time as a definition of the range of developments. A plan using the longest time span is called strategic planning; the plan with the shorter time span is called implementation planning. Implementation planning can be further broken into long-range (two to five years) and short-range (about one year) plans. Short-range plans are often called current operating plans.

Strategic planning addresses issues in the overall direction of the organization. Among strategic planning techniques are forecasting, identifying alternative approaches, goal setting, and contingency planning. Ideally, implementation planning takes place under a strategic planning umbrella. Long-range and short-range plans, along with scheduling, are other planning activities that use many of the same techniques as strategic planning. However, although long-range and short-range plans form the basis for managerial decision making, they do not encompass the big picture. Decisions in these nearer time frames require *objective setting* to make the connections between general strategic planning goals and day-to-day operational control.

Strategic planning establishes the major direction of the organization five to twenty years into the future. Strategic plans must be redone regularly (in some organizations, as frequently as every two or three years), as changing social, political, and technological developments make the existing plans obsolete. Even though an organization has been established and has a history to examine, its leaders must constantly ask, "Where should we be going?" Organizational plans must determine what existing products or services will be continued into the future and what new products or services will be offered. It is very important that strategic planners identify target populations and potential political demands or support for future operations.

For the public manager, strategic plans may include such elements as likely changes in jurisdictional boundaries and population composition, economic growth or decay, technological developments, the types of services that will have to be expanded or reduced, the growth or erosion of the tax base, the training needed for employees, expected changes in political opinion, and the interactions among these elements. Strategic planning has also gone under the names of "comprehensive corporate planning, formal planning, comprehensive integrated planning, corporate planning, strategic planning, and other combinations of these words" (Steiner, 1979: 13).

Long-range implementation planning covers a period of two to five years beyond the present and addresses the question, "How will we do what we have decided to do?" Long-range plans are also sometimes called "strategic management plans," since they are formulated to meet strategic objectives. A five-year capital construction plan and a personnel staffing plan are examples. Long-range plans are often discussed within an organization and formally approved by superiors or submitted to a policy-making body such as a legislature or city council for formal action. They are generally reviewed at least once a year in the light of organizational performance and changed conditions.

The long-range plan never comes true in a literal sense; rather, it is like a moving target that is always a few feet out of reach. The long-range plan defines the direction in which the organization intends to move; it is not an exact goal by which to assess individual performance or organizational achievement directly. It is revised regularly to keep the goals up to date. The long-range plan is thus an ongoing, dynamic plan for managerial action. Since we tend to think in term of stages ("if I can just get this done, then I can take a rest!"), it is difficult to adjust to the idea that there is *always* something else to do. But this is a powerful benefit of long-range planning: there is always a defined future for implementation by managers. Since the long-range goals are never precisely achieved (there are too many intervening events and changes), a manager can never rest on past or even current laurels. The long-range perspective provides constant stimuli to creativity and action.

Short-range planning for a period of one year or less is the second implementation stage. It has also been referred to as action planning, situation analysis, and tactical management. Managers and their subordinates formulate short-range objectives within the long-range planning framework to determine annual operating needs. Perhaps the best examples are the annual budget for operations or the annual capital spending plan for physical facilities. Short-term concerns are recurrent, but in a public-sector organization, there may be no specific long-range plan because of changes in political leadership or the loss of political consensus. Decisions based on short-term concerns may therefore assume great importance and generate much public debate. The short-range plan is the one with which we are probably most familiar. It is often the only plan in which legislatures take an interest. Indeed, this focus on short-range plans is the reason why many public policy decisions are characterized as incremental rather than comprehensive.

TECHNIQUES OF PLANNING

As planning is being done, the political (external) and administrative (internal) environments of the organization are undergoing change, and a variety of managerial techniques are employed to deal with these changes. Most of the resulting adjustments, such as attempts to improve productivity and stricter budgeting, are marginal or incremental rather than general or comprehensive. However, there is increasing support for analytic approaches to managing change (McGowan and Stevens, 1983). Planning is an effective tool because it uses methods and techniques based on analysis rather than on intuition, guesses, or feelings.

Planning techniques may be differentiated by their relative reliance on mathematical (quantitative) and nonmathematical (qualitative) analysis. The more precisely defined the goals, the better is the chance that a quantitative technique will be applicable. Reduction of vague, long-range, or strategic goals to mathematical terms may help in their clarification, even if that requires assumptions that are little more than leaps of faith or the judgments of the plan designer. It is important not to resort to too many judgments for the purpose of analysis, however. Dominance by quantitative analysis may strain the political credibility of planners and eliminate from the planning process a consideration of important questions that cannot be framed in other than qualitative terms.

Table 2-2 presents a list of planning techniques, organized according to the time frames in which they are most often used and their relative emphasis on quantitative analysis. The table also includes a brief description of each technique. It is important to point out that the table does not constitute a top ten list from which to choose. The usefulness of a specific approach will vary by the type of problem confronted and the influence of the surrounding situation.

STRATEGIC PLANNING

The keys to effective strategic planning are the amount of coverage and the accuracy of available information (Bozeman and Straussman, 1990). This includes information on the goals of the organization, its structure (levels, products, functions), its resources, and the environment in which it operates. Mintzberg (1973: 178) notes that information means

Table 2-2 Major Planning Techniques

Name of technique	Time frame and analysis type[a]	Description	Selected sources
Regression	S, L-R; quan.	Future values are calculated on the basis of a trend formula	Welch and Comer (1983); Garson (1976)
Delphi	S, L-R; qual., some quan.	Group of experts makes projections about the future; successive projections may also be made	
Brainstorming	S, L-R; qual.	Ideas are discussed in a conference or other open format, sometimes with participation of resource persons	Bryant and Keans (1982)
Econometrics	L-R; quan.	Future values are calculated by the solution of a set of simultaneous linear equations	Klein (1980, 1981)
Leading indicators	L-R; quan.	Uses measures of the economy that anticipate change: average work week, unemployment rate, insurance applications, housing starts	
Simulation	L-R, S-R; quan.	Similar to econometrics, but applied to problems such as housing and solid-waste disposal	
Operational gaming	L-R, S-R; mostly qual.	Determines and explores logic and patterns underlying ideas and concepts	
Scenario forecasting	L-R, S-R; qual.	Describes alternative futures for the organization	Gershuny (1976)

[a] *Key:*
  S   = Strategic
  L-R = Long-range
  S-R = Short-range

  quan. = quantitative
  qual. = qualitative

power, and power is translated into the legitimate authority that managers must have to lead an organization and motivate their employees.

Managers must make decisions that not only keep their organization functioning but also allow it to grow and develop so that it can do more for its clients at less cost and with improved quality. Public managers are faced with constant scrutiny by political forces (legislative committees, budget reviewers, inspectors, auditors), by economic forces (changes in tax revenues, competition with private-sector organizations that provide similar services), and by social forces (the media, public opinion, evaluations by citizens' groups). Public managers have to be strategic managers, if strategic management is defined as a process that ensures that an organization's resources "are adapted to its environment in a way that permits efficient achievement of the organization's goals, using appropriate courses of action with acceptable degrees of risk" (Paine and Anderson, 1983: 6).

A typical approach to strategic planning stresses the process by which the plan is derived. Strategic planning encourages consideration of as many future possibilities as is feasible (Quade, 1982: 107). Initially, it may take the form of brainstorming for ideas and their ramifications. When brainstorming the participants assume that nothing is impossible and that resources are unlimited. Of course, reality eventually forces a comparison with actual possibilities and their relevant limitations.

A usual first step is to take a goal (or goals) that have been agreed on and analyze the programs in each goal area, characterizing them in some fashion such as "programs to be reduced," "programs to be retained as they are," "programs to be retained with modifications," "programs to be expanded," and "possible new programs." This list is usually made through a Delphi procedure (see Table 2-2), using experts drawn from agency and community officials to classify the programs.

Next, each program may be assessed in terms of its major strengths and weaknesses. The actions necessary for each type of program may be examined to determine their external consequences and the ways in which they will affect the organization. Priorities are then set by making a calculation or judgment of the benefits and costs. The priority criteria may be grouped around unifying ideas or general policies, such as support for economic development, potential for approval, or response to a community need. Each of these general policies may be placed on a numerical scale of priorities according to defined criteria, and each program can be scored in terms of each criterion and can then be given a total score based on all criteria. The result of this process is a ranked inventory of existing and proposed programs, which can assist policy makers and managers in making their long-range decisions. Regular updating of the inventory makes it more useful.

DEVISING ALTERNATIVES

Clear definition of planning alternatives is a fundamental step in strategic planning; vague alternatives must be brought into focus if preliminary choices are to be made. Planning for programs aimed at the amelioration of social conditions is just as exacting as planning for the development of physical facilities or of general public services such as police and fire protection. Social programs often fail when they are not based on adequate research into alternatives at the strategic planning stage (Rossi, Freeman, and Wright, 1979: 120). Transforming these possible futures into realistic alternatives is the start of a planning process through which public debate, the policies of elected officials, and the work of government staffs are coordinated.

Realistic future alternatives shape the strategies of an organization. Public debate helps to determine the general direction of a public-sector organization, by indicating, for example, the resource uses preferred by groups and individuals. Public officials translate these comprehensive public objectives into specific programs and policies that identify the responsible public organizations, define their limits, and allocate resources among them. Given these more specific objectives, public-sector managers then assess the long- and short-range consequences of their actions and the requirements for the use of resources in achieving objectives. Each actor influences the work of the others. For example, public officials may use public-sector managers' long-term forecasts as the basis for their resource allocations, and both officials and managers may influence public opinion. It is from these interactions that a politics of public management planning arises.

It is to be expected that not every alternative can produce a viable program, for any of a variety of reasons. At this point, then, a series of questions must be answered in order to select the most appropriate alternatives. One basic question is, "Which alternatives have realistic probabilities of accomplishing the organizational goals?" Answers to this question help managers identify the alternatives that have the best chance of implementation at an acceptable cost. Strategic planners often hypothesize or sketch goals in detail because some objectives will then emerge as more desirable than the others, and on this basis, the manager will develop an action plan (Koontz, O'Donnell, and Weihrich, 1982: 152).

Although strategic planning has been emphasized by business for the last three decades, its importance in the public sector is only now being recognized (Eadie, 1983). However, there remain many barriers to successful strategic planning by public managers. Among them is the overwhelming emphasis on an annual budget, which discourages thinking beyond the range of a fiscal year. Some budget reformers have emphasized improvement of short-range planning, advocating freezes and rigorous principles of budget balancing, while others have placed greater hope in broader reforms, such as the Planning-Programming-Budgeting System (PPBS). In the case of PPBS, typically there was insufficient funding for developing planning skills among employees, as well as a distrust of putting too much power in the hands of appointed officials (the planners). These practices and influences have combined to discourage use of strategic planning, especially at state and local government levels (Halachmi, 1986). The lack of public support for strategic planning may also reflect a general feeling that since the average citizen is not involved in these "blue-sky" or "think-tank" exercises, there should not be any public funding for them.

For the organization, strategic planning allows the development of a sense of direction, a concept of the future, and a way of controlling aspects of it in which the organization has an interest. Whether or not it is pie in the sky, the strategic plan generates the preliminary information with which to move forward into long-range planning for organizational decisions (Pennings and associates, 1985). Strategic planning offers the possibility of significant improvements in management and in programs even without elaborate long-range planning (Eadie and Steinbacher, 1985).

THE TRANSITION TO LONG-RANGE PLANNING

When the preferred alternatives have been identified by organization leaders, an assessment phase follows, leading to the conversion of the larger, strategic concerns into more detailed, tactical steps. The assessment phase involves consideration of such problems as potential side effects or risks, complexities in the actions required, and the impacts on people and resources. Among the questions raised are these:

1. Can the objectives be achieved as they have been defined? Are the definitions accurate? Are the objectives realistic?
2. What are the possible side effects, either positive or negative, of each alternative, including the possible unintended consequences?
3. Are the choices too complex? Will there be problems in availability of resources, costs, or time? Are there undisclosed political objectives of major actors that are important to the strategic plan?
4. Is there flexibility in the alternative strategies? Could some of the strategies be combined? Could machines be substituted for human labor in implementation?

5. Is the existing staff able to implement the alternatives?
6. Is the alternative justifiable in relation to potential risks? How remote or how probable are the risks associated with each alternative?

LONG-RANGE IMPLEMENTATION PLANNING

When the strategic alternatives have been identified and sorted out and a strategic approach determined, long-range forecasts give shape and quantity to the implementation plan. The Delphi technique, already mentioned as an example of a management tool for strategic planning, is equally useful in long-range implementation planning. This method involves consulting with experts in the areas of interest to the organization (see Bingham and Ethridge, 1982: 35-57). The composition of the panel of experts is determined by management, but it usually includes authorities with reputations in the general field as well as persons who are knowledgeable about the specifics of the organization. These experts are interviewed individually, so that they will say what they think, not merely what they hear others say. Because of this absence of interaction among the persons involved, Delphi groups are often called nominal groups.

The initially wide range of opinions is narrowed through subsequent interviews, in which some kind of feedback is given to the experts. Feedback stimulates reconsideration and elaboration of first judgments, in an attempt to channel opinions toward a consensus on the best estimate or forecast. The feedback may consist of rankings derived from a questionnaire or it may use a descriptive approach. Successive interviews, or repeated rounds of feedback, are usually necessary to produce consensus among the experts. The version of the future ultimately reached by the Delphi panel depends on the creativity of its members, which can be a limiting factor (Jones, 1980: 14-20).

Through strategic and long-range planning, an organization seeks to develop and clarify its goals and to define the missions it wants to pursue, in accordance with an analysis of the key factors in the organization's internal and external environments (Tichy, 1982). Strategic alternatives are made more specific as they are translated into long-range plans on the basis of anticipated (forecasted) situations and circumstances.

Long-range implementation planning rests on long-range prediction. A *prediction* is a probabilistic statement, usually with a relatively high confidence level, that a specified event will occur within a specified time (Starling, 1979: 280-285). As the time frame is extended into a more distant future, the chance for error in the prediction increases, because there is more time for unknown events or circumstances to intervene.

A *forecast* or *projection* is an estimate of a future event or environmental influence over which the manager of the organization has no direct control. Forecasts may enable planners to form expectations of what will happen to costs or other relevant variables outside the control of managers (Ascher and Overholt, 1983; Scott, 1972: 2). The usefulness of a forecast is enhanced if the manager who asks for it provides precise definitions of the variables of interests.

There is no one best strategy, formula, or approach in predicting the future. Typically, managers use a variety of forecasting techniques for different sorts of problems (Tersine, 1983). Makridakis and Wheelwright (1978) devised a procedure to analyze data and surrounding circumstances to identify the most appropriate forecasting techniques for a particular problem. The specific techniques to be used depend on such conditions or factors as the time horizon (distance into the future) of the forecast, the cost of calculations, the accuracy needed, and the complexity of the problem. The value of a forecast is also heavily dependent on the skills of the manager in interpreting its contents and applying its findings.

One of the most important problems with forecasting models is the basic assumption that the data used in calculating the models at the start will have the same content as the new data that are acquired in the future. Events never go that smoothly, and the models themselves provide some distortions. A model is like a road map; it gives a driver a general idea of location and directions, but the driver is well advised to recheck the map frequently, in order to verify location, and to keep a constant eye on the road to deal with the unexpected.

THE MAJOR FORECASTING METHODS

Regression analysis is used to describe the values of a "dependent" variable—dependent because its values are influenced by and change in relation to the values of another variable or set of variables in the model, the "independent" variables. Regression finds the linear (straight-line) equation that best weights and sums the independent variables in order to predict the dependent variable most accurately. In the simplest case, only two variables are used, one independent and one dependent. Most statistics books include a discussion of regression and the procedures for its calculation (see, for example, Welch and Comer, 1983: 180-232). If the regression model employs several independent variables, the analysis is

Figure 2-1 Plotting Variant Trend Lines

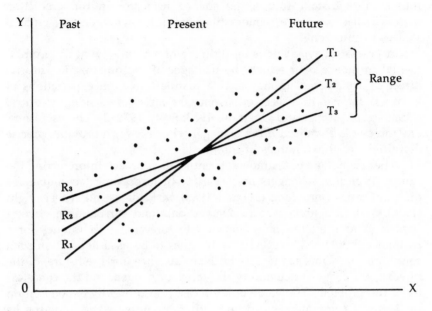

R_1, R_2, R_3 = possible trend lines
T_1, T_2, T_3 = projected future values of Y

more complicated but can be done quite conveniently with computer programs (Welch and Comer, 1983: 200).

Trend extrapolation is a forecasting method related to regression. It is based on the assumption that the direction and magnitude of change experienced in the past will persist into the future. However, actual future values may fall above or below the values projected by the trend line. This creates a problem if a manager depends on a single trend line when actual values vary widely from the projected values.

One way to deal with this problem is to plot several different possible trend lines (Figure 2-1). It is easy to see that one could estimate and draw several lines that seem to fit the data, or this could be done by a computer program that calculated the values for individual lines using data and assumptions of different models. As shown in Figure 2-1, the dependent variable will then take on a range of values. These may be called future or target values.

Even if not always precise, these projections are valuable results. They place limits on the likely futures and thus help the public manager who may want, for example, to plan for future office space, the need for which will depend on the estimated number of employees, or for the acquisition of police cars, the need for which will depend on housing patterns, population, and types of crime, among other factors. Often one value is chosen as the planned target, and the others are designated as the targets in contingency (secondary or back-up) plans.

While the linear model is the most common, not all trends are in a linear form. Some are shaped like arcs (parabolic curves), others like the letter *J* (exponential), still others like the letter *S* (logistical) (Yamane, 1964: 701-729). Each of these leads to a different pattern of future decisions. Nonlinear models are more complicated mathematically.

Econometric models, another important forecasting method, consist of systems of linear or nonlinear equations involving several interdependent variables. They may be static (dealing with one point in time) or dynamic (dealing with changes over time). Dynamic models in particular sometimes have colorful names, such as "explosive cobweb" (Brennan, 1973: 207-255). The models provide a framework within which to analyze systematically the interdependencies among economic phenomena (Howrey et al., 1981).

If a government would like to know the effects of a tax reduction or increase, it would probably use an econometric model. A change in tax rates will have direct effects on personal disposable income and on government revenues, but it may also have indirect effects on prices, employment, savings, capital spending, and other variables. Each of these may in turn influence personal disposable income and therefore tax revenues in subsequent years. In short, through a series of connected reactions, a tax change can affect almost all economic factors. These interdependencies must be considered if the effect of the change is to be anticipated accurately. It may be true that the politics of a tax change are often debated in terms of consequences for a specific industry or interest; nevertheless, econometric models are tools for increasing the understanding of the way an economic system works and for testing and evaluating alternative policy choices (Klein, 1979).

Linear equations may also be used to develop solutions to managerial problems. In this method, a rate for each of several variables is determined, and these rates are then combined into a summary equation. As a single example, unit productivity (P) may be found to improve by 30 percent if employees attend a training course (variable A) but to decline by 20 percent if employee salaries do not keep pace with changes in the cost of living (variable B). A linear equation expressing these relationships would be $P = .30A - .20B$.

One of the major weaknesses of econometric models and linear equations is that satisfactory measures of the variables are often difficult to find. In a service agency, for example, it may be hard to give quantitative expression to the concept of "productivity." Another weakness is the absence of a set of rules that can be applied across different situations. This lack of uniformity makes the application of econometric models and linear equations highly dependent on the specific situation and requires the involvement of skilled and experienced people (Makridakis and Wheelwright, 1978: 230-234). The sophistication of the techniques may make them unusable without computers, although simple models may be solved by hand or with a calculator. Finally, the assumptions on which these techniques depend may require too much abstraction from reality for them to be very useful to the typical manager. Nonetheless, attempts to abstract and formulate the interrelationships among events *do* assist the public manager in dealing with long-range developments.

OTHER FORECASTING METHODS

Another approach to forecasting is the *scenario*, which is a description of a sequence of events that might occur in the future (Gershuny, 1976; Bingham and Ethridge, 1982: 77-89). This method usually proceeds by (1) studying the facts of a situation, (2) selecting a development that might occur, and (3) trying to foresee the results that might follow if it does occur. The advantages of scenarios are that extensive computations or complicated assumptions are not necessary and the costs are low.

Construction of a scenario requires that planners develop descriptions of relevant conditions and events at either a specific point (static scenarios) or over time (transition scenarios). Scenarios are helpful because they allow the planner to examine several general influences at the same time. Furthermore, the exercise provides an opportunity to examine details and to explore combinations of social, economic, and political influences.

Descriptive modeling is the development of a model or representation of a complex functioning system through observing and estimating how its components interact. *Operational gaming* is one approach to model building. The game consists of a series of "transactions" between two or more competitive teams that are assigned conflicting objectives. The teams are made up of the employees of the organization, and they may actually use the results of the game as a plan. There are three phases in the game: preparation, playing, and analysis. In the preparation phase, the purpose of the game is defined in terms that are familiar to the players, the environmental influences are described, rules are set forth for both the model and the players, and the players are briefed on the rules and the situation. During play, each team devises a strategy and plans. Each chosen course of action is evaluated by a game referee or "facilitator," often an outside consultant brought in to conduct the games. The teams may negotiate with each other in several cycles to refine results.

In the analysis phase of the game, the outcomes and the teams' strategies and tactics are evaluated. There may be a follow-up, consisting of either repeat playing of the game or a field test of the results. Operational gaming is not a substitute for true experiments, however, nor does it predict the future. It provides only guidelines and illustrations as an approach to planning.

Other methods of long-range planning utilizing descriptive approaches include contextual mapping (finding out about competitors or influential surroundings), historical analogy (projecting the future from past results in similar situations), and direct consultation with an expert. The usefulness of any of these approaches depends heavily on the guidance of the manager for design and application. Managers do not have to treat descriptive models as predictions or forecasts, but the models do allow the dramatization of alternative courses of action.

The most important factor common to all the methods of long-range planning is that they deal with uncertainty. Part of the responsibility of public managers is to make judgmental decisions about the design and deployment of a specific technique so that the estimated outcomes will have some reasonably close relationship to the realities that the organization will confront.

A number of circumstances may have an influence on the accuracy of a forecast. The quantity and quality of the available information may change, often quite rapidly. There may be changes in economic conditions: the onset of a recession or of a period of inflation. There may be changes within the organization or in demographic factors such as population composition and distribution. Finally, there is no definitive way to determine what technological changes may occur. All of these changes must be accommodated within limited amounts of time. As a rule of thumb, the longer the time frame of the forecast, the greater the amount of error will be. These factors, separately and in combination, limit the utility of any long-range plans (Makridakis and Wheelwright, 1983: 706-792).

To sum up, long-range forecasting is a means of discovering, articulating, and estimating the opportunities and problems that a public-sector organization will encounter at some time in the future. There is great variety in the form of governmental organizations and in the types of programs they operate (Seidman, 1981), but some form of long-range planning is applicable to almost all of them.

SHORT-RANGE OR OPERATIONAL PLANNING

In addition to the larger or strategic concerns, managers also face the smaller or *tactical* problems of making decisions about actions to be

Figure 2-2 A Gantt Chart

Unit Objective					
Schedule Percentage	20	40	60	80	100

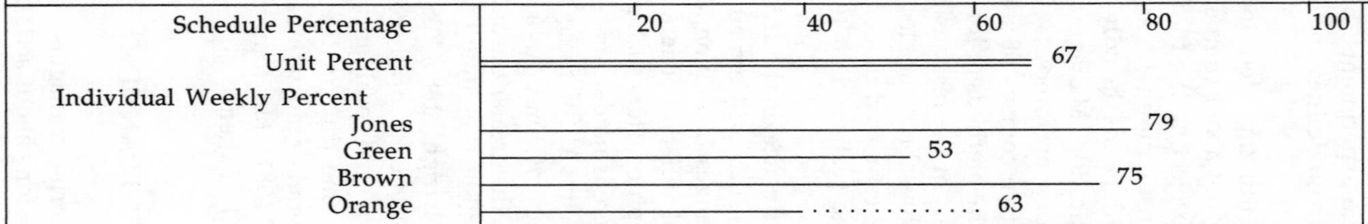

Unit Percent: 67

Individual Weekly Percent:
- Jones — 79
- Green — 53
- Brown — 75
- Orange — 63

Individual Daily Activity	Monday	Tuesday	Wednesday	Thursday	Friday	Hours
Jones	4.5 M	4.5 M	5.5 T	7.5 F	7.5 F	29.5
Green	4 Y	4 Y	4 Y	4 Y	4 Y	20
Brown	5 L	5 L	6 L	6 L	6 L	28
Orange	7.5 F	6 I	6 I	4 I	0 V	23.5

Actions Needed for Improvement:

Directions: Observe worker and write in amount of time employee actually worked each day on activities related to unit objective. Note reason that describes why employee did not meet work schedule. For individual weekly percent, add hours and divide by 37.5 hours. For unit percent, add individual values and divide by number of individuals. Plot bar graph lines according to Schedule Percentage scale.

Reasons for failures to meet daily schedule:

A = absent
G = lack of experience
I = lack of instructions
L = slow operator
R = repairs needed on equipment
M = trouble with materials

T = trouble with tools
V = holiday
Y = work objective achieved
   in less time than scheduled
F = full day of work

Key: |‒‒‒| space between lines is daily time available
               amount of work actually done in a day

        ······· time worked but not scheduled according to
                 unit objective

        ‒‒‒‒ weekly total percent for individual:
                 solid for actual schedule work; dotted for
                 unscheduled work

        ═══ weekly percent for unit

taken during the next month or the next quarter. Indeed, these "microproblems" often occupy most of a manager's time, for what they lack in scope they more than make up for in urgency. While some of the long-range planning techniques can be adapted to the needs of short-range planning, short-range planning requires some distinct techniques.

GANTT CHARTS

Perhaps the most common short-term planning problem is scheduling, and one of the first methods of systematic scheduling was the Gantt chart, named for its developer, Henry L. Gantt, an Army officer. Essentially it consists of drawing a bar chart that compares work actually done with planned objectives (Clark, 1957). A Gantt chart, an example of which is shown in Figure 2-2, presents the facts of unit achievement in relation to planned unit achievement. The very act of recording the plan on a chart where it may be seen by others gives the plan an aura of precision and accuracy. The Gantt chart also facilitates the assignment of clear-cut tasks to individuals.

This approach enables the manager to compare what has been done with what should have been done and so to keep informed about the progress of the implementation of the plan. If progress is not satisfactory, the Gantt chart also gives the manager some clues to the reasons (see Figure 2-3), so that appropriate steps can be taken to deal with scheduling problems. Feedback on the results will then be generated in the next work period. A two-week or one-month charting period may give a broader base to these data without imposing the need for accumulating an amount of data that might become too large to be useful.

Scheduling problems can sometimes involve complicated mathematics. For example, how does a manager schedule street-patching and street-line-painting crews so that the painting crews do not have to spend time waiting for the patching crews to finish their work? One answer might be to have multipurpose crews, but that may mean a reduction in the quality of work or an increase in costs. A technique for handling such problems is the *Johnson solution* (Carlson, 1967: 87-93). A hypothetical Johnson solution is shown in Table 2-3. The situation requires that the street-patching crew finish its work before the lines are repainted. The existing scheduling plan is FiFo—first in, first out. When the paving job is logged in, it becomes the next job to be done. By looking at the results of the scheduling plan, the manager sees that the paint crew is wasting two hours waiting for the patching crew to finish the next job (Table 2-3a). The number of different orders in which the jobs can be done is five factorial, or 120 ($= 5 \times 4 \times 3 \times 2$). To determine

Figure 2-3 Flow-Process Chart for a Supply Requisition

Step No.	Description	Operation	Transportation	Inspection	Delay	Storage	Distance	Time (mins.)
1.	Clerk fills out requisition	●	△	□	D	▽		15
2.	Requisition carried to supervisor	O	▲	□	D	▽	120'	1
3.	Supervisor has on desk	O	△	□	▶	▽		90
4.	Supervisor checks order	O	△	■	D	▽		5
5.	Supervisor initials order	●	△	□	D	▽		.25
6.	In supervisor's out-basket	O	△	□	▶	▽		180
7.	Carried to supply department	O	▲	□	D	▽	1500'	10
8.	In supply in-basket	O	△	□	▶	▽		180
9.	Supervisor assigns job number	●	△	□	D	▽		.5
10.	Supervisor screens order	O	△	■	D	▽		2
11.	Order filed in "To Fill" folder	O	△	□	▶	▽		240
12.	Stock clerk fills order	●	△	□	D	▽		15
13.	Stock clerk files one copy	O	△	□	D	▼		2
14.	Original of order sent to budget department	O	▲	□	D	▽	300'	5
15.	Supplies carried to clerk	O	▲	□	D	▽	1500'	10
16.	Requester files copy	O	△	□	D	▼		1

Note: Step is executed where symbol is blackened.

the effects of every one would be expensive and time consuming, so the manager looks for a satisficing solution: have the patching crew do its shortest job first, then the next shortest, and so on. Table 2-3b shows that waiting time would be reduced to 100 minutes, but a more diligent search finds a scheduling order that would further reduce waiting time to 40 minutes (Table 2-3c). Of that amount, 30 minutes comes at the start of the day, while the line painters are waiting for the patching crew to finish its first job. An imaginative manager might propose that the painters start their workday a half-hour later than the street patchers to further reduce wasted time.

PERT AND CPM

The Program Evaluation Review Technique (PERT) grew out of the Gantt chart and in turn became the basis for a more sophisticated

Table 2-3 A Johnson Solution

	Street Patching		Line Painting		
Job no.	No. of minutes required	Schedule	No. of minutes required	Schedule	No. of minutes lost waiting
			(a) FIFO Job Schedule		
1	80	1-80	120	81-200[a]	80
2	40	81-120	20	201-220	
3	160	121-280	120	221-340	
4	70	281-350	80	381-460[a]	40
5	30	351-380	60	461-520	
Total	380		400		120
			(b) Shortest-Job-First Schedule		
5	30	1-30	60	31-90[a]	30
2	40	31-70	20	91-110	
4	70	71-140	80	111-190	
1	80	141-220	120	191-310	
3	160	221-380	120	381-500[a]	70
Total	380		400		100
			(c) Minimum-Waiting-Time Schedule		
5	30	1-30	60	31-90[a]	30
4	70	31-100	80	101-180[a]	10
1	80	101-180	120	181-300	
2	40	181-220	20	301-320	
3	160	221-380	120	321-440	
Total	380		400		40

[a] Delayed starts.

Source: Format from S. M. Johnson, "Optimal Two- and Three-Stage Production Schedule with Setup Time Included," *Naval Research Logistics Quarterly* 1 (March 1954), as adapted in P. G. Carlson, *Quantitative Methods for Managers* (New York: Harper and Row, 1967), 87-93.

scheduling technique, the Critical-Path Method (CPM). In PERT, the Gantt bars are replaced by a flow-process chart of network analysis. A flow-process chart is a detailed list of the steps required to complete a process, along with a symbolic representation of the sequence of activities and an indication of the time needed for each one (see Figure 2-3).

Network analysis employs the same general technique, but in less detail. The analysis is displayed in diagram or graph form, using circles,

Figure 2-4 Network and Critical-Path Analysis for a Construction
Project

(a) Network analysis

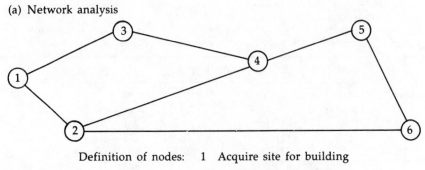

Definition of nodes: 1 Acquire site for building

2 Order prefab building

3 Pour foundations

4 Inspect site preparation

5 Erect building

6 Announce opening

(b) Critical-Path Analysis

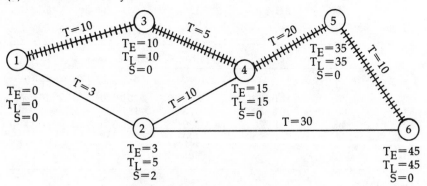

T   = estimated time for each edge
T_E = earliest time event can be completed
T_L = latest time to leave each event
S   = slack time $(=T_L - T_E)$
+++ = critical path

squares, or other symbols to denote the steps in the process, and lines to
show the sequence (Figure 2-4). The circles are called "nodes" and the
lines connecting them are called "branches," "paths," or "edges." The
diagram may be used to determine the *critical path*, which is the longest
sequence of paths between the first and last nodes. Table 2-4 shows how

Table 2-4 Steps in Defining the Critical Path

1. Make three time estimates for each activity: a = most optimistic, b = most pessimistic, m = most likely.
2. Determine the estimated time T for each edge:

$$T = \frac{a + 4m + b}{6}$$

The formula gives the greatest weight to the most-likely estimate. Label each edge with its T.
3. Calculate the earliest expected date by which an event may be completed and label it T_E, starting with T_E = 0 at node 1.
4. Find the latest allowable time for leaving each event (T_L) without delaying completion. Begin at the last event and work backwards. If there are several paths, assign the earliest step identified in the network analysis.
5. Calculate the critical time by summing all $T_L - T_E$. (Note that event 2 in Figure 2-4 has two days slack in it; if it is delayed by that much, the project will still stay on schedule. A delay in any other event, however, will delay the project.
6. Replan and readjust the network to see if slack time can be reduced.

this is done. Since the critical path is the longest, any delay along this route will push back completion of the project. Delays along the other paths are less important, so long as the node times do not exceed the maximums allowed for them. Of course, real network and critical-path analyses are much more complicated than those shown here, to the point where computer assistance is often needed for the calculations.

PERT and CPM are primarily analytic planning tools rather than managerial control or implementation techniques. They are even more useful when costs are calculated together with the time estimates. If a manager found that 50 percent of costs had been incurred when the project was only 20 percent complete, he or she could anticipate a cost overrun and make adjustments in an effort to avoid it. On the other hand, simultaneous cost and time analysis may show that start-up costs are high compared with the costs of later activities, and so they may be averaged over the life of the project in order to keep cost and time on parallel tracks.

OPERATIONS RESEARCH

Operations research (OR) originated in the constellation of methods used by the military in World War II to solve such problems as the best way to use the newly available radar equipment. Businesses adopted the technique as a means of increasing their efficiency, and governments also became interested in it as a way to improve service delivery (Byrd,

1975: 6-8)—for example, in finding optimum routes for public transportation or optimum locations for fire or police stations, or in deciding to enlarge an old jail or build a new one or whether state offices should be located at a central site or in dispersed sites. OR is properly regarded as another form of input into managerial planning. As Morse and Bacon (1967: 2) observed:

> The procedures of operations research are not expected to provide all the bases for managerial decisions; the operations research staff is not expected to take over the administrative function ... there are human aspects of politics or morale which cannot yet be quantified and which the manager must supply from ... experience.

Among the techniques that are included in OR, three are important enough to warrant separate discussion: queuing theory, inventory models, and simulation.

Typically people are irritated if they have to wait in line very long, but increasing personnel or facilities to improve service is costly. *Queuing theory* allows managers to study the trade-offs between investment in greater capacity and the time a citizen has to wait. By properly calculating arrival rates at a service point, total waiting time can be reduced. One application of the principle is the "cattle chute" now commonly used for lines in banks and elsewhere: by having all customers wait in a single line, every teller's time is fully utilized, instead of a situation in which some tellers are doing nothing while long lines wait at other windows. Although some customers may wait a little longer than they might otherwise have to, the total waiting time for all customers is minimized for the given number of tellers. (For further discussion of queuing theory, see Chase and Agrilano, 1981.)

Inventory models use techniques similar to those of queuing theory, but they emphasize exit rather than arrival rates. A mathematical version called the economic order quantity model (EOQ) has a specific application to purchasing decisions. Since the manager can control arrival rates of stock by appropriately timed purchasing decisions, the triggering information in this model is the rate at which supplies are used in (exit from) the system. The purpose of this method is to keep inventories at the lowest feasible volume; large inventories are undesirable because items deteriorate on the shelf or become obsolete, storage space is costly, and there is increased possibility of theft.

When a planning problem is very complex, the choice of an appropriate model may not be clear. In those cases, *simulation* may be used to build several different models, typically mathematical models embodied in a computer program, which will then allow prediction to be made of the consequences of changes in some of the elements of the model. Essentially, simulation maps the statistical likelihood of a chain of related events. If so little is known about the relationships among the elements that they can be considered randomly related, the simulation is called a Monte Carlo model, after the famous gambling resort. (For more on simulations and their application to managerial problems, see McKenna, 1980: 330-368.)

A form of simulation known as dynamic programming is used when a series of multistage decisions are necessary to the achievement of an organizational objective. It leads to what is sometimes called the best one-stage-at-a-time solution (see Carlson, 1967: 68-86). Dynamic programming can also be used to link the results of regression analysis with case-study characteristics (McCaffrey et al., 1985).

Another OR tool is *replacement analysis,* in which a model is used to determine the optimal time for replacement of a physical good by balancing the costs of maintenance against the costs of acquiring a new one.

While all of these techniques and tools can be useful, there are disadvantages to OR. It requires the services of highly trained personnel not usually available on an administrative staff. It is time consuming; a great deal of time must be spent, for example, in informing the specialist researcher of the many details of the organization and its plans and alternatives. However, an investment in OR may be returned to the agency many times over, through more efficient services, lower costs, and improved accountability to legislative bodies.

RISK ANALYSIS

Another planning tool is *risk analysis,* which is the process of developing a statistical model based on the probability distributions of favorable and unfavorable events.

The probabilities in question may be either (1) relative, based on the frequencies of randomly occurring events or on the actual frequencies of observed past events, or (2) subjective, based on the beliefs of the analyst without a theoretical framework or specific historical evidence. When the probabilities have been determined, they are inserted into a "decision tree" (Figure 2-5). Suppose a municipality is going to build a parking garage and has to decide whether to buy insurance against liabilities it may incur for injuries or losses a citizen may suffer in the garage. The responsible administrator estimates that the government will make $50,000 a year in net revenue from the garage. The administrator further assumes that the odds are 999 to 1 against the occurrence of an accident that might result in governmental liability in any one year (subjective probability). However, if there *is* an accident, the

Figure 2-5 A Risk-Exposure Tree

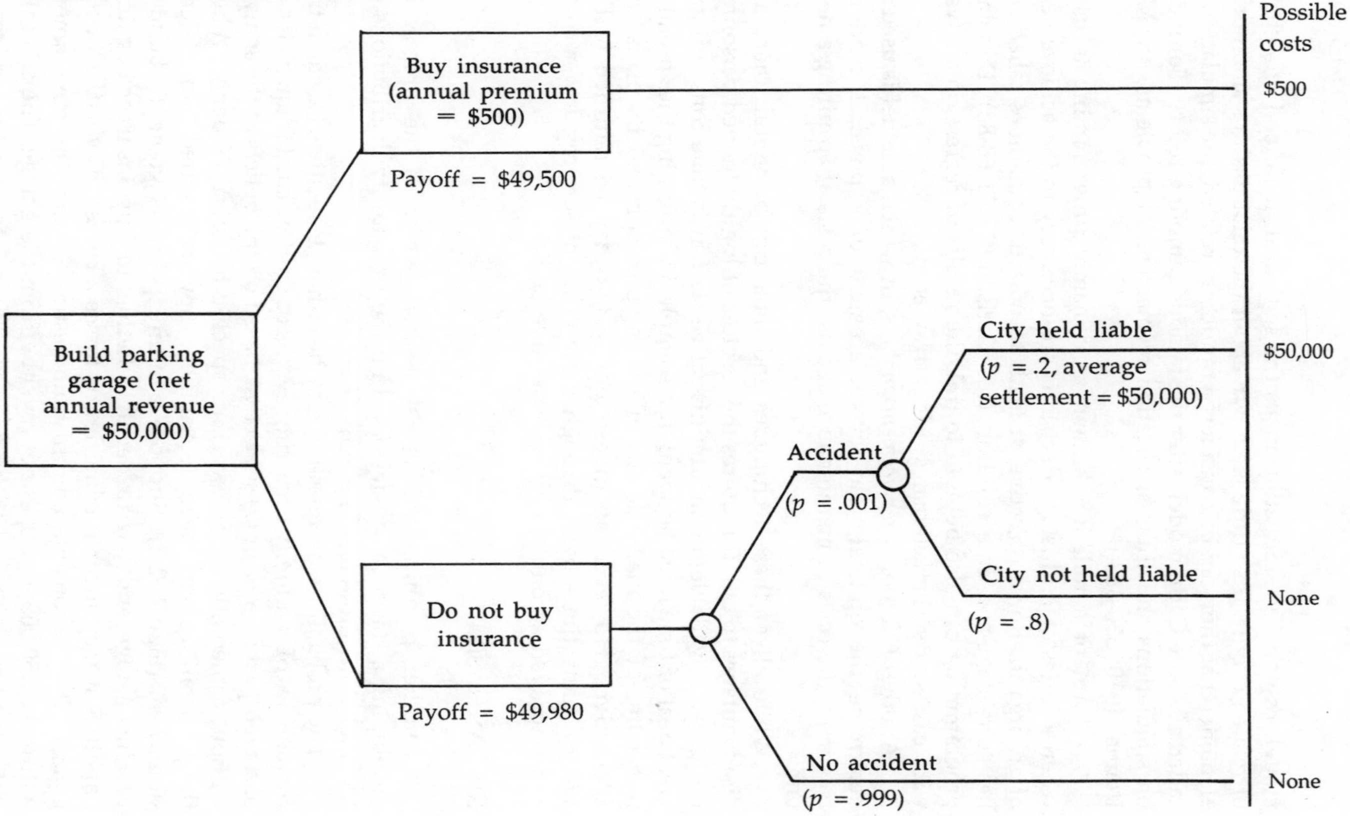

Possible costs	
$500	Buy insurance (annual premium = $500) — Payoff = $49,500
$50,000	City held liable (p = .2, average settlement = $50,000)
None	City not held liable (p = .8)
None	No accident (p = .999)

Accident (p = .001)

Do not buy insurance — Payoff = $49,980

Build parking garage (net annual revenue = $50,000)

probability is 20 percent that the city will be held liable (perhaps a relative probability based on experience in other cities, adjusted for the age of the buildings, changes in the interpretation of the laws regarding municipal liability, and other factors). When cities *have* been held liable, the average settlement has been $50,000; on the other hand, the cost of the insurance coverage is $500. Should the city buy the insurance under these circumstances?

In using the decision tree, the estimated payoff for each branch is calculated back toward the trunk. The payoff for the "do not buy insurance" branch is $[(.8 \times .001 \times \$50,000) - (.2 \times .001 \times \$50,000)] + (.999 \times \$50,000) = \$49,980$. The payoff for the "buy insurance" branch is $49,500. The risk manager may still prefer to buy insurance even though the payoff is less when the probabilities of alternative events are taken into account. The estimated value of the decision to avoid the cost of insurance ($49,980) does not even offset the absolute risk of an entire year's net revenue against just one average $50,000 liability settlement. Calculating payoffs, however, gives the manager more information with which to decide. (For further discussion of decision trees, see Welch and Comer, 1983: 260-266, and Starling, 1979: 278-290.)

Risk analysis serves to improve short-range planning when there are important elements of uncertainty about the consequences of a decision. However, a manager who is "risk aversive" may choose to forgo this kind of analysis and simply follow the safest course of action without regard to the relative payoffs of the risks.

TIME SERIES

The last short-range planning tool that will be discussed here is *time-series analysis*, which is the measurement over time of a variable against the benchmark of a standard defined from the beginning of the activity. The variables to be tracked might be turnover rates, citizens' complaints, crime rates, productivity records, or revenue collections. A regression line may be used to display the trend, or a trend line may be estimated from inspection of the data and drawn with a straightedge (Figure 2-6). Another technique is to use semi-averages: the time series is divided into two parts, the average for each part is calculated, and the two points are connected with a straight line. If the activity is one in which there is much variation from one month to the next, the time series may be made up of "moving averages" to smooth out these variations: first the average of months 1, 2, and 3, then the average of months 2, 3, and 4, and so on. Another refinement is to adjust for seasonal variations by calculating a "normal" ratio of each month to the yearly average (perhaps based on the experience of past years), and then

Figure 2-6 Trend Line Drawn by Inspection

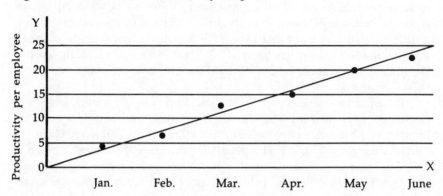

developing a time series that shows how far above or below that ratio the values for subsequent months are.

Given the variety of strategic, long-range, and short-range planning tools at a manager's disposal, the next need is to link the planning process to the other organizational processes in POSDCORB. A technique that meets that need and is popular among governments and businesses alike is management by objectives.

THE MBO TECHNIQUE

Management by objectives, or MBO, is an approach to management that determines (1) what must be done, including establishment of priorities, (2) how it must be done, (3) how much it will cost, (4) when it must be done, (5) what constitutes satisfactory performance, (6) how much progress is being achieved, and (7) when and how to take corrective action. In the absence of a systematic approach of that kind, planning is apt to be done immediately before or concurrently with the activity, if at all; there are frequent changes in plans, because objectives were not articulated beforehand or alternative ways of accomplishing them were not considered; and effort is likely to be measured largely by the effort that is put forth rather than by the results that are produced. In MBO, the manager not only defines in advance the results to be achieved and the program steps required to achieve them, but also provides standards by which to measure the performance of employees.

The development of MBO was accelerated by the work of several individuals and groups. In a landmark book, Drucker (1954) emphasized that objectives must be set in all areas where performance affects the health of the enterprise. The General Electric Company (1954) used elements of MBO in its move toward the decentralization of managerial decision making. The contribution of McGregor (1957) was to criticize programs that used personality-trait criteria for evaluating subordinates and to suggest that the evaluation of performance against measurable objectives was a more constructive way of appraising and motivating employees. Since that time, MBO has found many other advocates (Odiorne, 1965; Raia, 1974; McConkey, 1983) and its application has been extended to governmental organizations (Brady, 1982). The MBO process begins with the establishment of measurable (verifiable) goals by a chief executive, a division head, an operational manager, or a frontline supervisor. These goals may be set for any period—a quarter, a year, five years, or whatever appears desirable in given circumstances. In many cases, the goals are set to coincide with the organization's fiscal year or with the duration of a major project. The length of the period tends to get shorter as one moves down the organizational chain of command.

The goals are expected to be based on an analysis and judgment of what can and should be accomplished by the organization during the given period in the light of the organization's mission, its strategic and long-range plans, and its strengths, weaknesses, and opportunities. They are generally regarded as tentative, and subject to modification as they are translated into objectives further down the line.

Setting these objectives is the next difficult task. The objectives should indicate the quality and the cost of achieving them. The objectives should present a challenge, reflect organizational priorities, and promote personal and professional growth and development. Finally, conflicts among the objectives of different units must be attended to so that *suboptimization* (the maximum achievement of one objective at the cost of minimum achievement of another) or less than satisficing decisions do not occur.

The process of developing objectives must incorporate feedback from each state and level. Feedback gives information for judging the acceptability of the objectives. Compatibility with the organizational mission is the major criterion by which feedback assists in the validation of objectives. Discussion by as many organizational actors as possible gives even those who disagree a sense of being able to agree on the organization's objectives.

There are three classes of objectives, which serve different purposes in the organization. For the most part, these categories are congruent with the types of planning discussed earlier in this chapter. Short-range or *routine* objectives refer to the specific, day-to-day outcomes that are the nuts and bolts of the organization. Long-range or *problem-solving* objectives characterize areas targeted for resolution. Strategic or *innovative* objectives refer to the vision or image that effective managers have of their organizations. This congruence occurs because the MBO process is indeed a planning process. Defining an operational plan through objective-setting converts strategic, long-range, and short-range plans into schedules. A plan without a schedule is a fatally defective concept, like a car without a clutch or a concert without an announced starting time.

Thus, MBO integrates planning and organizational operations. It allows the public manager to specify the standards by which organizational progress will be measured. It allows employees to monitor their own contribution to achievement of the work objectives in their specific units. In this respect, MBO is also a system of motivation. It is not without its weaknesses: it may lead to inflexibility or overemphasis in the short run, and there are intrinsic difficulties in mobilizing the resources and attitudes to complete objective-setting (Koontz, O'Donnell, and Weihrich, 1982: 106-107). Nonetheless, the aims of MBO are generally recognized as heading in a direction toward which public managers should move.

THE BENEFITS OF PLANNING

The ways to determine if an organization is effective, and the very meaning of effectiveness, vary from organization to organization. Cameron (1980: 67) identifies four basic approaches to evaluating effectiveness: (1) how well an organization accomplishes its goals; (2) the extent to which it acquires needed resources; (3) the degree to which it reduces the internal strain on employees; and (4) its success in relating to the major outside groups or strategic constituencies that influence it.

In contrast to effective organizations, "organized anarchies" have ill-defined goals, are loosely connected internally by many different definitions of success, use varying strategies to get the same results, and really do not have an output that can be linked analytically to resources (Cameron, 1980: 70-71).

Even under conditions of vagueness and imprecision, however, planning aids in the struggle for clarity of organizational purposes and for organizational improvement. Plans reflect the information and attention that planning analysts are able to direct toward practical choices of action (Forester, 1989: 19-20). The major benefit of planning is the designation of a future course of action, which promotes coordination of the organization's internal resources with its political and external challenges. The planning process integrates the functions of the organization with its resources toward the end of achieving the objectives of the organization (Sord and Welsch, 1964: 13).

- A second benefit of planning is that it helps public managers make those current decisions that have the best chance of creating the desired consequences—both in the present and in the future. It allows managers to know where the organization is at the present, what its resources are or might be, and where the organization's leaders or policy makers want to go. A long-range perspective, supported by analyses and improved organizational capacities, is required to manage a crisis such as a problem involving the environment and natural resources (Henning and Mangun, 1989).

A third benefit of planning arises out of the assessment of future and actual conditions and the encouragement and support for managers in trying to establish objectives. Rational decisions are enhanced if managers have the enlarged vision of a group of alternatives from which to choose. Emotion, guesswork, and intuitive reactions are reduced. Managers are able to do more than make marginal changes. Planning avoids a perpetual state of emergency and provides guidelines for considered, controlled actions. The organization is consequently in a better position to develop opportunities and avert threats.

A fourth benefit of planning is that it enables managers to decide in advance what to do, how and when to do it, and who is to do it. With plans, managers can ensure that each operation lies in someone's area of responsibility and can determine whether each function is properly placed and whether the responsible individual has and uses the requisite authority. Conversely, planning improves accountability by clarifying organizational functions and defining responsibilities (Reinharth, Shapiro, and Kallman, 1981: 4-5).

Finally, planning provides for organizational control through the establishment of performance standards. Individual and organizational levels of achievement may be compared to these standards, as is commonly done, for example, in comparing expenditures to a budget.

Planning and management are inseparable, because planning decisions provide a point of reference by which subsequent actions, achievements, and realities can be evaluated, and needed corrective actions may then be taken. Even a basic problem such as facilities management shows improvement when a planned approach is used for energy costs and preventive maintenance (Lewis, 1991). Without knowledge of a planned future course of action and events, managers have no basis for decisions. Successful implementation of plans is constantly threatened by problems of organizational control, the behavior of employees in the organization, and the general tendency of an organization to resist change (Gordon, 1992: 410-414).

After planning comes organizing, the second function in the POSDCORB chain. Organizing provides the structural relations between people to translate plans into action. It is the subject of the next chapter.

REFERENCES

Anderson, F. Wayne, Chester A. Newland, and Richard J. Stillman II. 1983. *The Effective Local Government Manager.* Washington, D.C.: International City Management Association.

Ascher, William, and W. H. Overholt. 1983. *Strategic Planning and Forecasting: Political Risk and Economic Opportunity.* New York: Wiley.

Benveniste, Guy. 1989. *Mastering the Politics of Planning: Crafting Credible Plans and Policies that Make a Difference.* San Francisco: Jossey-Bass.

Bingham, Richard D., and M. E. Ethridge. 1982. *Reaching Decisions in Public Policy and Administration.* New York: Longman.

Bolan, Richard S. 1975. "Emerging Views of Planning." In American Institute of Planners, *The Comprehensive Planning Process: Several Views.* Washington, D.C.: AIP. (Reprinted from *Journal of the American Institute of Planners.*)

Bozeman, B., and J. D. Straussman. 1990. *Public Management Strategies: Guidelines for Managerial Effectiveness.* San Francisco: Jossey-Bass.

Brady, R. H. 1982. "MBO Goes to Work in the Public Sector." In *Public Budgeting: Programming, Planning, and Implementation,* 4th ed., ed. F. J. Lyden and E. G. Miller, 169-183. Englewood Cliffs, N.J.: Prentice-Hall.

Brennan, M. J. 1973. *Preface to Econometrics.* 3d ed. Cincinnati: South-Western.

Bryant, Stephen, and Joseph Keans. 1982. "Workers' Brains As Well As Their Bodies: Quality Order in a Federal Facility." *Public Administration Review* 42 (March/April): 144-150.

Byrd, Jack, Jr. 1975. *Operations Research Models for Public Administration.* Lexington, Mass.: Lexington Books.

Cameron, Kim. 1980. "Critical Questions in Assessing Organizational Effectiveness." *Organizational Dynamics* 9 (Autumn): 66-80.

Carlson, P. G. 1967. *Quantitative Methods for Managers.* New York: Harper and Row.

Chase, Richard B., and N. J. Agrilano. 1981. *Production and Operations Management.* Homewood, Ill.: Irwin.

Clark, Wallace. 1957. *The Gantt Chart.* London: Pitman.

Drucker, P. F. 1954. *The Practice of Management.* New York: Harper and Row.

Eadie, Douglas C. 1983. "Putting a Powerful Tool to Practical Use: The Application of Strategic Planning in the Public Sector." *Public Administration Review* 43 (September/October): 447-452.

_____, and Roberta Steinbacher. 1985. "Strategic Agenda Management: A Marriage of Organizational Development and Strategic Planning." *Public Administration Review* 45 (May/June): 424-430.

Forester, John. 1989. *Planning in the Face of Power.* Berkeley: University of California Press.

Garson, G. David. 1976. *Handbook of Political Science Methods*. 2d ed. Boston: Holbrook.

General Electric Company. 1954. *Professional Management in General Electric*. New York: G.E.

Gershuny, J. 1976. "The Choice of Scenarios." *Futures* 8 (December): 496-508.

Gordon, G. J. 1992. *Public Administration in America*. 4th ed. New York: St. Martin's.

Halachmi, Arie. 1986. "Strategic Planning and Management? Not Necessarily." *Public Productivity Review* 20 (Winter): 35-50; reprinted in J. S. Ott, A. C. Hyde, and J. M. Shafritz. 1991. *Public Management: The Essential Readings*. Chicago: Lyceum Books/Nelson-Hall Publishers, 241-254.

Henning, D. H., and W. R. Mangun. 1989. *Managing the Environmental Crisis: Incorporating Competing Values in Natural Resource Administration*. Durham, N.C.: Duke University Press.

Howrey, E. P., L. R. Klein, M. D. McCarthy, and G. R. Schink. 1981. "The Practice of Macroeconomics Model Building and Its Rationale." In *Large Scale Macro-Economic Models*, ed. J. Kmenta and J. B. Ramsey, 19-58. New York: North-Holland.

Jones, Thomas E. 1980. *Options for the Future: A Comparative Analysis of Policy-Oriented Forecasts*. New York: Praeger.

Kastens, Merrit J. 1979. "The Why and How of Planning." *Managerial Planning* 28 (July/August): 33-35.

Klein, L. R. 1979. "Use of Econometric Models in the Policy Process." In *Economic Modelling*, ed. Paul Ormerod, 309-329. London: Heinemann.

_____.1980. *An Introduction to Econometric Forecasting and Forecasting Models*. Lexington, Mass.: Lexington Books.

_____.1981. *Econometric Models As Guides for Decision-Making*. New York: Free Press.

Koontz, Harold, Cyril O'Donnell, and Heinz Weihrich. 1982. *Principles of Management: An Analysis of Managerial Functions*. 5th ed. New York: McGraw-Hill.

Leuchtenburg, William E. 1983. *In the Shadow of FDR*. Ithaca: Cornell University Press.

Lewis, D. L. 1991. "Turning Rust into Gold: Planned Facility Management." *Public Administration Review* 51 (November/December): 494-502.

McCaffrey, D. P., D. F. Andersen, P. McCold, and D. H. Kim. 1985. "Modeling Complexity: Using Dynamic Simulation to Link Regression and Case Studies." *Journal of Policy Analysis and Management* 4 (Winter): 196-216.

McConkey, Dale. 1983. *How to Manage by Results*. 4th ed. New York: American Management Association.

McGowan, R. P., and J. M. Stevens. 1983. "Local Governments Initiatives in a Climate of Uncertainty." *Public Administration Review* 43 (March/April): 127-136.

McGregor, Douglas. 1957. "An Uneasy Look at Performance Appraisal." *Harvard Business Review* 35 (May/June): 89-94.

McKenna, Christopher K. 1980. *Quantitative Methods for Public Decision Making*.

New York: McGraw-Hill.

Makridakis, Spyros, and Steven C. Wheelwright. 1978. *Interactive Forecasting: Univariate and Multivariate Methods.* 2d ed. San Francisco: Holden-Day.

——. 1983. *Forecasting: Methods and Applications.* 2d ed. New York: Wiley.

March, James G., and Herbert A. Simon. 1958. *Organizations.* New York: Wiley.

Mertins, Herman, Jr. 1971. "A Study in Transitions." *Public Administration Review* 31 (May/June): 254-258.

Michael, S. R. 1982. "Organizational Change Techniques: Their Present, Their Future." *Organizational Dynamics* II (Summer): 67-80.

Mintzberg, Henry. 1973. *The Nature of Managerial Work.* New York: Harper and Row.

Morse, P. M., with L. W. Bacon, ed. 1967. *Operations Research for Public Systems.* Cambridge, Mass.: MIT Press.

Odiorne, G. S. 1965. *Management by Objectives: A System of Managerial Leadership.* New York: Pitman.

Paine, F. T., and C. A. Anderson. 1983. *Strategic Management.* Chicago: Snyder.

Pennings, Johannes M., and associates. 1985. *Organizational Strategy and Changes.* San Francisco: Jossey-Bass.

Quade, E. S. 1982. *Analysis for Public Decisions.* 2d ed. New York: Elsevier.

Raia, Anthony P. 1974. *Managing by Objectives.* Glenview, Ill.: Scott, Foresman.

Rehfuss, John. 1973. *Public Administration as Political Process.* New York: Scribner's.

Reinharth, Leon, Jack H. Shapiro, and Ernest A. Kallman, ed. 1981. *The Practice of Planning: Strategic, Administrative, and Operational.* New York: Van Nostrand.

Rossi, P. H., H. E. Freeman, and S. R. Wright. 1979. "Research for Program Planning." In *Evaluation: A Systematic Approach,* ed. P. H. Rossi, H. E. Freeman, and S. R. Wright, 81-120. Beverly Hills, Calif.: Sage.

Scott, Claudia Devita. 1972. *Forecasting Local Government Spending.* Washington, D.C.: Urban Institute.

Seashore, S. E. 1977. "Criteria of Organizational Effectiveness." In *Management Classics,* ed. M. T. Matteson and J. R. Ivancevich. Santa Monica, Calif.: Goodyear, 279-285.

Seidman, Harold. 1981. "A Typology of Government." In *Federal Reorganization: What Have We Learned?* ed. Peter Szanton, 33-57. Chatham, N.J.: Chatham House.

Simon, H. A. 1976. *Administrative Behavior.* 3d ed. New York: Macmillan.

——. 1979. "Rational Decision Making in Business Organizations." *American Economic Review* 69 (September): 493-513.

Simon, H. A., D. W. Smithburg, and V. A. Thompson. 1950. *Public Administration.* New York: Knopf.

Sisk, Henry L., and J. C. Williams. 1981. *Management and Organization.* 4th ed. Cincinnati: South-Western.

Sord, B. H., and G. A. Welsch. 1964. *Managerial Planning and Control As Viewed by Lower Levels of Supervision.* Austin: University of Texas, Bureau of Business Research.

Starling, Grover. 1979. *The Politics and Economics of Public Policy.* Homewood, Ill.: Dorsey.

Steiner, G. A. 1979. *Strategic Planning: What Every Manager Must Know.* New York: Free Press.

Tersine, Richard. 1983. "Logic for the Future: The Forecasting Function." *Managerial Planning* 31 (March/April): 32-35.

Tichy, N. M. 1982. "Managing Change Strategically: The Technical, Political, and Cultural Keys." *Organizational Dynamics* 11 (Autumn): 59-80.

Vieg, John. 1942. "Developments in Governmental Planning." In *The Future of Government in the United States: Essays in Honor of Charles E. Merriam*, ed. L. D. White, 63-87. Chicago: University of Chicago Press.

Welch, Susan, and J. C. Comer. 1983. *Quantitative Methods for Public Administration: Techniques and Applications.* Homewood, Ill.: Dorsey.

Yamane, Taro. 1964. *Statistics: An Introductory Analysis.* New York: Harper and Row.

3

Organizing

In both the popular and professional press, public organizations are commonly characterized as bureaucracies. To most people, this term conjures up images of long corridors, hundreds of little offices, enormous secretarial pools, and, above all, armies of vacant-eyed and humorless bureaucrats who dully perform their daily routines in an environment of detached and dispassionate indifference. When we think of bureaucracy, our minds turn to thoughts of immense, sterile, and inflexible governmental machinery.

Although exaggerated, this popular perception of public organizations often comes uncomfortably close to reality. While bureaucratic tendencies are found throughout both the public *and* private sectors, governments seem to be especially fond of creating hierarchical organizations that lack vitality and spontaneity.

Government's tendency to create bureaucracies is generally attributed to two interrelated advantages that the bureaucratic model theoretically offers over competing organizational formats. This model, which will be discussed more thoroughly later in the chapter, maintains that *efficiency* is best achieved in organizations that are hierarchically structured, monocratic (having one leader), rule-oriented (that is, they rely mainly on rules to get their work done and their members to obey), and impersonal in their behavior toward employees and clients alike. These factors combine to provide the leaders of such organizations with a high degree of control over the actions of subordinates. Second, bureaucracies are able to render public employees accountable to political authorities. Because it offers the complementary benefits of accountability *and* efficiency in the delivery of services, bureaucracy has become the predominant organizational form in governments throughout the industrialized world.

However, bureaucratic structures are not without their disadvantages. As already noted, the work environment within a bureaucracy can be stifling. During the 1930s and 1940s, researchers concluded that the productive and creative energies of workers could be most effectively tapped in organizational structures that allowed a greater degree of individual expression than is typically present in a pure bureaucracy (see Chapter 5). Excessive emphasis on control and centralization of authority was found to contribute to employee apathy, and decentralization of decision-making responsibility came to be viewed as a virtual panacea for nearly all the ills that plagued complex organizations. Although later research findings have discredited the simplistic notion that a bureaucratic framework is inherently destructive of employees' motivation and creativity (see, e.g., Doig and Hargrove, 1987; Perry and Wise, 1990), widespread scholarly uneasiness with the bureaucratic model became an enduring legacy of the organizational studies conducted since the 1930s.

The primary purposes of this chapter are to describe what is now known about organizational structure and to discuss its impact on employee performance and agency effectiveness. Organizing is the term commonly used to refer to the managerial activities concerned with (1) arranging work into logically connected and manageable units; (2) structuring these units in such a manner that work can be accomplished efficiently; and (3) integrating the different units so that they do not work at cross-purposes. Stated more simply, the organizing function is intended to ensure that the various components of an organization are properly designed and structured for maximum productivity.

At first glance, organizing appears to be one of the most straightforward and easily understood management functions. Because it deals with such tangible concepts as organizational charts and department titles, it seems much more real than the more esoteric planning, leading, evaluating, and controlling functions. Furthermore, the other management functions must be performed as ongoing processes, whereas organizing seems to be a one-shot affair. Once you've organized—that is, once you have selected and implemented an appropriate organizational design—you shouldn't have to do it again soon.

While all of this is basically true, it belies the fact that organizing is one of the most difficult concepts for students of public management to comprehend. Organizing is a challenging topic for two very basic reasons. First, it is a subject that has traditionally been either ignored or deemphasized by many students and practitioners of public administration. Most of the theory-building and research in the area of organizational structure and design have occurred in disciplines other than public administration and political science. While any number of possible explanations might be offered for this neglect, the most plausible seems to be that public managers often take organizational structure as a given. External entities (either the legislative body or the executive officer) ordinarily establish the broad structural parameters of most public agencies. Whereas the other management functions are everyday concerns of administrators at all levels, from first-line supervisors to agency directors, only the most influential public managers have any significant input into decisions affecting their organization's designs. For this reason, some managers may feel that there isn't much point in spending too much energy on the topic. Yet, as will be discussed later, decisions concerning the most appropriate structural configuration are becoming increasingly important for managers throughout the organizational hierarchy.

The second factor that makes the discussion of organizing especially difficult is the sheer volume of research and writing that has been directed at the topic in recent years. Scholarly interest and curiosity run high in this area because organizational structure is the bridge by which plans and objectives are translated into action. Moreover, the particular structure that is selected can in some ways determine the nature of other important management functions. For example, the leadership style that is utilized (see Chapter 5) depends in large part on the level of centralization in an organizational structure, and the staffing and control functions (Chapters 4 and 5) are shaped by the extent to which the structure allows lower-level subordinates to exercise decision-making authority. In attempting to fine-tune our understanding of the linkages between organizational structure and the other management functions, contemporary researchers have made many great strides in explaining organizational behavior.

ADVANTAGES AND LIMITATIONS OF BUREAUCRACY

For more than fifty years, the starting point for most introductory courses in public administration has been Max Weber's "ideal-type" bureaucracy. Weber, a German sociologist, became "the founder of the systematic study of bureaucracy" (Merton, et al., 1952: 17) when he published in 1922 a series of essays entitled *The Theory of Social and Economic Organization*. In this masterful work, Weber traced the evolution of modern public administration from its earlier roots. He observed that, as industrialization and capitalism spread, the types of administrative practices that appeared differed in several important ways from those of the past. Chief among the changes was the tendency on the part of modern governments to staff their public agencies with personnel selected on the basis of their technical competence, rather than on such personal criteria as kinship or political patronage. This important development, along with a number of closely related alterations in the ways public agencies went about their business, was viewed as being necessary to sustain the growth of modern industrial societies. In order to flourish, industry needed effective and dependable governmental machinery to deliver the mail, inhibit destructive competition, and perform a myriad of related support functions. At the same time, governments themselves needed to respond to the growing pressures for democratization by opening their doors to a broader spectrum of people. Thus, a new form of public organization, the bureaucracy, emerged. Among Weber's many contributions to the management literature, the most enduring has been the identification of the primary features of the pure form, or ideal type of bureaucracy. These are:

1. *Division of labor and specialization of functions.* Weber observed that, in order for an organization to perform complex tasks efficiently, the work had to be subdivided and the several parts assigned to different people. In so doing, the organization is able to achieve high levels of performance and accuracy, because each worker presumably acquires great skill in performing the same function over and over. Increased specialization also allows the organization to control its workers more effectively because their assigned duties and responsibilities are clearly delineated.

2. *Hierarchy of authority.* All positions (or, as Weber called them, "offices") in a bureaucracy are arrayed in a hierarchical fashion, in which each lower office is under the supervision and control of a higher one. Varying levels in the hierarchy correspond to variations in *authority*, with each higher office carrying more decisional responsibility than lower ones. Hierarchical levels also establish the formal communication network.

3. *Emphasis on rules and procedures.* A primary objective of any bureaucracy is to reduce work to specific rules and operating procedures. In this way, work becomes routinized. The presence of a consistent system of abstract rules reduces employee discretion to "the application of these rules to particular cases" (Weber, 1952: 20), thereby ensuring uniformity and predictability of treatment.

4. *Impersonality.* According to Weber, "the ideal official conducts his office in a spirit of formalistic impersonality, *sine ira et studio,* without hatred or passion, and hence without affection or enthusiasm" (Thompson, 1975: 3). In other words, personal preferences and feelings have no place in a bureaucracy. Instead,

officials are expected to apply the relevant rules to each situation in an impartial manner.

5. *The career system.* In order to attract and retain qualified personnel, bureaucracy offers its employees the advantage of a formalized career system. Among its components are that employees are hired according to their technical qualifications; employment is full time, rather than part time or seasonal; a system of promotions is provided, based on some combination of achievement and seniority; and employees are protected against supervisory actions that are inconsistent with the organization's rules and procedures (that is, supervisors' authority over their subordinates does not extend beyond the work situation, and basic rights of due process are provided to employees to ensure that they are not treated arbitrarily).

Weber describes bureaucracy's advantages over alternative organizational formats in the following way:

> Experience tends universally to show that the purely bureaucratic type of administrative organization . . . is, from a purely technical point of view, capable of attaining the highest degree of efficiency and is in this sense formally the most rational known means of carrying out imperative control over human beings. It is superior to any other form in precision, in stability, in the stringency of its discipline, and in its reliability. It thus makes possible a particularly high degree of calculability of results for the heads of the organization and for those acting in relation to it. It is finally superior both in intensive efficiency and in the scope of its operations, and is formally capable of application to all kinds of administrative tasks. (Weber, 1952: 24)

In effect, Weber's ideal type depicts the organization as a simple tool in the hands of its master. Like a hammer or a screwdriver, the tool does what its owner desires. It does not ask questions, it does not state opinions, and it yields predictable results. It is a cold, depersonalized, objective, and rational instrument that stands ready to do the bidding of the individual in charge. As such, it is an extremely powerful instrument of social control. Recognizing this fact, Weber was careful to note that the ideal type could never exist in the real world. He knew that no set of rules and authority relationships could ever totally eradicate employee discretion and personal considerations, and he was fully aware that bureaucracy contained certain internal limitations and contradictions that weakened its influence. Even so, Weber admitted that he was frightened by the raw power of the bureaucratic organization.

Before going much further with the traditional critique of Weber's bureaucracy, a word of caution is offered. Many of the most notable theorists of public administration have devoted portions of their careers to correcting perceived distortions in Weber's works. Dimock (1959), for example, argues that Weber ignored the role that good leadership can play in altering the impersonality and mechanistic behavior of organizations. Students need to be aware of the fact that Weber's vision is not accepted without debate or modification (see Gulick, 1990; Stever, 1990).

BUREAUCRACY'S WEAKNESSES

If one accepts the premise that organizations are inherently purposive entities that ought to perform exactly as their owners dictate, then Weber's theoretical construct is logically compelling and emotionally pleasing. Isn't it only right and just that organizations respond precisely and efficiently to commands? Nevertheless, it is also true that rigidly bureaucratic structures are likely to possess certain traits that are not especially desirable.

Most of us are quite aware of bureaucracy's failings. Anyone who has ever encountered an officious and self-important civil servant will relate the experience in a story punctuated with such expressions as "red tape" and "paper shufflers." Due to society's low esteem for bureaucracy, the term "bureaucrat" has become almost as insulting as some expletives.

In the traditional view, the particular traits that have contributed to bureaucracy's poor image primarily relate to its emphasis on the impersonal application of rules and procedures. Because all of us have a strong desire to be treated as individuals, we are offended by civil servants who refuse to acknowledge that our problems are somehow special. While we may readily concede that, in principle, fairness and efficiency require that all cases be treated alike, few of us are willing to view our own case as being routine. Yet bureaucrats do tend to treat us as mere problem categories (a welfare claimant, a student on academic probation, a heart-attack victim). This produces the impression that bureaucracy is cold, impersonal, and unconcerned. Compounding this perception is the tendency on the part of many bureaucrats to elevate their rules and procedures into desirable behavior for their own sake, a phenomenon referred to as *goal displacement* or *inversion of ends and means*.

Actually, insensitivity is only one manifestation of much more fundamental weaknesses of bureaucratic organizations. According to many organizational theorists, bureaucracies have two interrelated Achilles' heels. First, bureaucracies tend to be static. This resistance to change stems from their authoritarian and monocratic nature. Because the authority system is entirely "top-down" (that is, all authority is vested in the organization's leader, rather than being shared with subordinates), any change must be initiated from the top. But, again because of bureaucracy's strict hierarchical structure, the leaders often do not receive information suggesting a need for change. As information makes its way up through the hierarchy, it is subject to suppression and distortion at successive levels. Bureaucrats are not prone to pass along information that may be displeasing to their superiors or that does not reflect favorably on themselves. Another major discouragement to innovation and change is that the preoccupation with rules and procedures fosters conformity among employees. Following the rules becomes a ritual.

Bureaucracy's other fundamental flaw is its dehumanizing impact on its workers. The only individual who really seems to matter in a bureaucratic organization is the leader (or owner). As Carl Friedrich noted (1952: 31), "[Weber's] very words vibrate with something of the Prussian enthusiasm for the military type of organization, and the way seems barred to any kind of consultative, let alone cooperative, pattern." Workers in a bureaucracy tend to be thought of—and may even think of themselves—as cogs in a machine. They are expected to surrender their autonomy, to follow the rules, and to be loyal to their supervisor. In exchange for these behaviors, they receive a career and a steady salary. The relationship between worker and organization does not extend beyond this superficial level. In effect, bureaucracy values discipline over morale, rule application over motivation, and impersonality over esprit de corps.

The cold and impersonal portrait of bureaucracy that is embedded in Weber's ideal type served as an intellectual foundation for what became known as the classical school of management. An implicit assumption of this school was that people are economic rationalists who respond only to material incentives. Management's objective was to structure the work situation in such a manner that employees could maximize their income by maximizing their productivity. This view stimulated attempts to reduce management to simplistic formulae and scientific principles, such as the utilization of time-and-motion studies to structure work patterns. Management theorists in the first half of the twentieth century held to such positions as these: piecework was better than a fixed salary; the optimal span of control was five or six subordinates; and work should be specialized according to one of four organizing principles (specialization by purpose, process, clientele, or geographical area).

THE BEHAVIORAL INFLUENCE

The allure of management theories based on Weberian notions of bureaucracy began to diminish after the publication of the results of the celebrated Hawthorne studies. These studies yielded three broad findings that directly challenged the classical school's view of human nature and the "science" of management (Roethlisberger and Dickson, 1939; Etzioni, 1964: 32-35): (1) The level of a worker's production is usually determined by *social norms* rather than by the physiological capacity of the individual worker. (2) Noneconomic rewards and sanctions influence employee behavior and limit the effects of economic incentives. (3) Workers often act and react more as *members of groups* than as individuals.

These findings introduced several new ingredients into Weber's recipe for effective management. Most significantly, the concept of workers as being social animals, rather than automatons responding only to economic stimuli, rose to prominence. Theorists began to recognize the critical importance of employee motivation to the management process (see Chapter 5). Additionally, they came to realize that *informal groups* played an important role in the workplace. Employees, through their informal associations with co-workers and on-the-job acquaintances, establish a social system that can function either as an ally or as an enemy of the formal system (management, as defined by the hierarchy and by the organization's rules and regulations). As Chester Barnard (1938) observed, the informal system can contribute to the organization's mission by providing social support to workers, responding to their needs for status and security, supplementing the formal information system (through the grapevine), and filling in where the rules are silent (for example, when workers decide among themselves how to handle problems and situations that have not come up before). Conversely, the informal system can represent an impediment to management when it engages in such activities as artificially restricting the level of production and blocking the enforcement of worthwhile yet unpopular rules (such as no private long-distance telephone calls during work hours).

Having acknowledged that organizations are composed of more than simply a formal set of rules and authority relationships, theorists began to construct a description of organizational reality that included such concepts as informal groups, employee motivation, and intra-organizational conflict. Almost without exception, the resulting theories were based on a less hierarchical view of organizational structure. Instead of concentrating on control functions, they began to emphasize leadership, organizational communications, and employee motivation and participation. In short, they offered a *decentralized* organizational structure as an alternative to the bureaucratic model.

Decentralization implies that an organization's leaders are willing to share their decision-making authority with their subordinates. The organization has relatively few levels in its hierarchy (it is flat rather than pyramidal) and the communication channels are more open. Information travels more freely in lateral and upward directions than in a bureaucracy. Finally, decentralized organizations are less reliant on rules, procedures, and norms of impersonality. Diversity in thought and approach are (at least theoretically) encouraged, and compliance with organizational directives is achieved relatively informally. Workers comply out of a sense of loyalty and affection for the organization, and because they have internalized the organization's goals as their own. When these conditions are present, the following advantages are thought to accrue to the organization (see Mackenzie, 1978: chapter 6; Morris, 1968: 176-177):

1. The decision load and coordination responsibilities of upper management are reduced, giving them more time to deal with the most significant issues.
2. Decisions are made by those best equipped to acquire the information on which the decision should be based: "the person closest to the problem deals with it most effectively."
3. The time required to reach decisions and implement solutions to problems is reduced.
4. The organization's reactions to changes in its environment are speeded up.
5. Executives moving up through the organization have a wider range of experiences and training.
6. Worker motivation, morale, and commitment are enhanced, leading to greater productivity and reduced turnover.
7. Information is subject to less distortion by virtue of the reduction in the number of levels through which it must pass.

This list of advantages may make it seem that decentralized organizations are better than bureaucracies. Some organizational theorists might agree (though not without a number of qualifications), but neither model is intrinsically superior to the other. In the first place, neither of them exists (or can exist) in a pure form; all organizations contain both centralized and decentralized characteristics. Moreover, *any* kind of organization—centralized, decentralized, or something in between—can be effective, given the right set of conditions. Finally, the choice of organizational structure involves certain trade-offs. A more centralized type will provide control and accountability but will suffer from inflexibility. Conversely, the greater adaptability and responsiveness achieved in a decentralized organization may be offset by a corresponding decline in its ability to control its operations. The major challenge to the organizing function, then, is to gain an understanding of the factors that influence the effectiveness of different organizational structures, so as to make possible the selection of the mix of characteristics most suitable to a given set of conditions.

THE BUILDING BLOCKS OF ORGANIZATIONAL STRUCTURE

Although the science of organizing is in its infancy, complex organizations (some having hundreds of thousands of members) have existed for millennia. Alexander the Great, Genghis Khan, and Julius Caesar were among history's most effective organizers. The organizing problems and choices that they faced were similar in many ways to those that currently confront city managers, agency directors, and governors.

DIVISION OF LABOR AND SPECIALIZATION

Long before Max Weber pointed out its significance, the division of labor was a reality of industrial life. Indeed, ever since people first joined forces to perform purposive activity, work has probably been divided into separate activities and job assignments. The reason for this is obvious: many of the things that people do are too complex to be handled by one individual. Efficiency is increased when work is divided into tasks that can be performed separately by different individuals. Imagine, for example, what a post office might look like without specialization of activities. If the same person sold the stamps, sorted the mail, and brought the letters to their addressees, there would be a great deal of wasted effort.

Another important set of advantages is derived from the specialization that accompanies a division of labor. As was initially pointed out by Adam Smith (1776/1937), specialization allows a task to be learned very quickly. By performing the same task repeatedly, workers gain both speed and expertise. Eventually, the value of output produced by each worker is greater than the cost of additional workers, thereby reducing the price of the goods and services produced. This effect is greatly enhanced when the tasks are simple or repetitious enough to permit automation.

The Need for Coordination. Specialization, however, is potentially troublesome. Suppose, for example, that our hypothetical post office hires several specialists to perform the various steps of the mail-delivery process and that they all perform their tasks without concern for what the others are doing. The delivery personnel may then receive the wrong batches of mail from the sorters, or they may continually bicker over the assignment of routes. Mail intended for

Buffalo may end up in Sacramento, and some delivery trucks may stand idle while others are filled to capacity. The window clerks may all decide to take their breaks at the same time, leaving the service windows unattended. While each specialist may be very speedy and efficient in performing his or her own functions, the post office will operate in a very ineffective manner. This brings out an immensely important rule of organizing: for every degree of specialization that is present in an organization, a corresponding measure of coordination must be provided.

According to Mintzberg (1979: 3) the strategies that are used to coordinate work are "the glue that holds organizations together." He goes on to describe five forms of this adhesive (Mintzberg, 1979: 3-9):

1. *Mutual adjustment.* The most basic form of coordination is derived from the informal communication that occurs in all organizations. The various specialists coordinate their activities by conferring with one another and agreeing on a work plan. As will be noted later, mutual adjustment is used in all organizations, from the simplest to the most complex.
2. *Direct supervision.* Coordination can be achieved by assigning one individual responsibility for the work of others. This involves the establishment of a work plan, the issuing of orders, and the monitoring of activities—in effect, the performance of the planning, leading, and controlling functions of management.
3. *Standardization of work processes.* In order to coordinate work without the need for much direct supervision or mutual adjustment, the work processes can be standardized or programmed. This is easiest to do in the most repetitious types of jobs, in which the tasks can be specified in minute detail. While we generally associate this with assembly-line manufacturing, it also regularly occurs in government agencies. Building inspectors, for example, may work under rules that limit their inspections to 15 minutes and explicitly tell them which items to review and which to ignore.
4. *Standardization of outputs.* In this form of coordination, the results of the work (the product qualities, the level of performance, and so on) are specified. An Office of Intergovernmental Relations, for example, may be held accountable for acquiring a certain amount of grant money each year, or for submitting a certain number of grant applications. The political leaders are not so much interested in how those goals are achieved (except that they might insist that no laws or rules be broken) as they are in *whether* they are achieved.

5. *Standardization of skills.* Once a worker has been trained and has gained sufficient experience, coordination occurs almost naturally. As an increasing number of vocations become professionalized, coordination through the standardization of skills is becoming much more common. When hiring professionals, the organization often doesn't even have to train the workers; they bring their training with them, from years of education and socialization by other professionals. Hospitals, for example, do not have to formulate rules regarding the behavior of surgeons when performing an operation, nor do they need to establish output standards: the surgeons already know what to do. Similarly, university faculty members know what the expectations of universities are with regard to teaching, grading practices, and publications requirements. The work gets accomplished (admittedly, with major variations in quality) with little need for external intervention or other coordination mechanisms.

Conflict between Specialization and Coordination. Even while specialization makes coordination necessary, it also makes coordination difficult to achieve. As specialists interact with each other, they develop similar attitudes, ideas, and jargon. Different specialties thus tend to develop different behaviors, thought patterns, and perceptions of how their jobs should be done and even of what the organization's goals should be. This differentiation can lead to serious misunderstandings and conflicts unless an organization does an effective job of integrating the specialists back into a cohesive work unit (Lawrence and Lorsch, 1967; Walker and Lorsch, 1968).

An interesting example of this problem appeared in the antitrust activities of the Federal Trade Commission (FTC). This organization is dominated by two distinct professional groups, attorneys and economists. According to one study (Katzmann, 1980), conflict between these two groups significantly affected the FTC's enforcement programs. The economists, by and large, wanted to prosecute major "structural monopoly" cases, such as the AT&T and Exxon cases. They believed that the greatest amount of benefit could be achieved for the consumer by putting an end to semi-monopolistic activities, even though such cases are "difficult to prosecute, expensive, technically complex, and uncertain of success" (Katzmann, 1980: 164). The attorneys, on the other hand, were not anxious to prosecute such complicated and time-consuming cases. They were eager to have courtroom experience, and they wanted to make a name for themselves by winning large numbers of cases, so they attempted to get the FTC to concentrate on cases that could be prosecuted and resolved more quickly and with a higher probability of success than those that the economists were interested in. Consequently, the attorneys tended to emphasize so-called conduct cases, which generally involve specific consumer complaints about price-fixing or unfair trade practices (for example, an advertiser's unfounded claim that its product has been proven to be more effective than competing brands). Thus, the specialist's different career paths, coupled with competing professional orientations, produced internal tensions that adversely affected the accomplishment of the organization's goals.

Effects on Motivation. One additional problem that can be laid on the doorstep of the division of labor is what some have called "blue-collar blues." Work that is broken down into very simple, repetitive steps runs the risk of becoming boring, tedious, and monotonous. The theorist who has been most critical of this effect of specialization is Chris Argyris (1957). He argues that excessive specialization prevents workers from achieving their full potential. They are asked to use only a few of their talents and abilities, and they are not provided with sufficient challenges to make the work interesting. The workers are placed in a demeaning environment that stunts their growth personally, intellectually, and professionally, and forces them to act in an immature way. Most theorists now agree with Argyris's basic assessment, and most management literature now emphasizes the need to expand rather than reduce the range of tasks performed by workers. This topic will be explored more thoroughly in the context of the discussion of leadership (Chapter 5).

SPAN OF CONTROL

The second major building block of organizational structure is span of control. The basic premise of this principle of management is that managers are limited in the number of subordinates that they can effectively coordinate and control (Fayol, 1949; Taylor, 1947). If they attempt to supervise too many subordinates (the span is too broad), they will be overextended and their workers will not receive sufficient attention. Conversely, if they are assigned too few subordinates (the span is too narrow), their own talents will be underutilized and their workers will probably be overmanaged.

The problem of the span of control, then, is to determine the optimal number of subordinates that a given manager can supervise. There is a considerable amount of disagreement in the management literature concerning the exact size of this number. Lyndall Urwick, an early authority on public administration, at first maintained that it was four, but later he amended that position to "no person should supervise more than five, or at the most, six direct subordinates whose work interlocks" (1943: 53). Others offered dogmatic numbers ranging all the way up to 20. Urwick's insertion of the phrase "whose work interlocks," however, was a precursor of things to come. There is now general agreement that there is no absolute size for the optimal span of control. Rather, the size varies in accordance with a number of considerations, including:

1. The manager's physical proximity to the subordinates (if they are not in the same location, the span should be narrower).
2. The level of complexity of the work being performed (complex work requires a narrower span than simple tasks).
3. The homogeneity of the subordinates' jobs (if they are performing similar functions, the span can be broader than if their jobs are diverse).
4. The subordinates' level of training, experience, and motivation (highly competent workers should function within a broader span than workers with less ability or motivation).
5. The capabilities of the manager (the more skilled the manager, the more subordinates can be effectively supervised).
6. The availability of clear and precise plans (if the unit's plans specify clear and measurable goals, less supervision will be required, thereby permitting the manager to employ a broader span of control).

Implicit within the concept of span of control are several other important principles of organizing. Obviously, if one manager is put in charge of others, a chain of command is created. This, in turn, implies that a hierarchy of authority is present. These concepts, taken together, give rise to the "scalar principle," using the terminology first applied by Henri Fayol (1949: 53). In essence, the scalar principle is that responsibility and authority flow downward, through an organization, while accountability flows upward. As described by Koontz and O'Donnell (1978: 24), "the more clear a line of authority from the top manager . . . is to every subordinate position, the more effective will be the responsible decision making and organization communication." Thus, the scalar principle suggests that all workers should know their place in the hierarchy. They should know from whom they take their orders, and there should be only one such person, a principle called unity of command; and they should know whom they are responsible for supervising and to whom they must refer matters beyond their own authority.

Another assumption implicit in the scalar principle is that authority can and should be delegated down the hierarchy. Indeed, management theorists have come to accept the non-Weberian idea that decisions should be made at the lowest possible level of the hierarchy. This belief, which some theorists see as indistinguishable from the concept of decentralization, has achieved wide currency as our understanding of worker motivation has improved.

Calls for increased delegation almost always go hand in hand with the argument that spans of control should be much broader than they currently are (see, for example, Herzberg, 1968). A byproduct of any expansion in the number of a manager's subordinates is that those subordinates gain more autonomy. They are permitted to exercise some measure of discretion in decision making and in the interpretation of rules and procedures (provided, of course, that the rules and procedures are sufficiently flexible to allow interpretation).

Given this connection between span of control and delegation, the factors that influence the number of subordinates assigned to a manager should also play a part in determining the degree of decentralization of decision-making authority. But in addition to the manager's proximity to subordinates, the complexity of the tasks being performed, the homogeneity of subordinates' jobs, their level of training and experience, the capabilities of the manager, the existence of unambiguous plans, and the location in the hierarchy, theorists generally agree that the effectiveness of delegation depends on the following conditions:

1. *The subordinates' desire for responsibility.* Despite general acceptance of the proposition that most workers want greater authority and responsibility, there is ample evidence that not all employees are so inclined. Theories of worker personalities often include a personality type characterized by a "risk-aversive" approach to life. Downs (1967), for example, referring to such individuals as "conservers," describes them as people who are primarily concerned with protecting their jobs and being left alone. Presumably, it would be a mistake to delegate much authority to such individuals.

2. *The extent of discretion permitted by the technology.* In some work situations, it is unwise to delegate because the costs of mistakes are so great. For example, the director of a state environmental agency should not delegate the decision concerning the granting of a certificate of operation to a major hazardous-waste disposal facility.

3. *The relative importance of long-term and short-term results.* In general, delegation of authority is a long-term process. It often takes a considerable amount of time for subordinates to learn the ropes sufficiently to handle greater responsibility. Thus, if the orga-

nization is experiencing a crisis, if it is under a stringent deadline, a more centralized administrative arrangement is usually called for, if only temporarily.

TYPES OF DEPARTMENTATION

It should be clear by now that there is no one best way to structure an organization. An organizational structure involves trade-offs between a variety of competing needs. Different organizational configurations make different sorts of trade-offs.

FUNCTIONAL DEPARTMENTATION

For many years, the dominant structural form has been *functional departmentation*, in which activities are grouped around the essential functions of the organization. These may be the basic management functions (planning, finance, personnel), or they may relate to the functions that are peculiar to the specific business. Most production facilities, for example, have such functions as engineering, production, sales, and marketing. Similarly, universities tend to be organized according to the functions of their business (admissions, records, registration, student aid, instructional programs), and hospitals are often structured according to theirs (admissions, nursing services, medical services, food services, maintenance). In a functionally designed organization, each of these activities is assigned departmental status, indicating that it is headed by a manager who is in a direct line of authority to the organization's chief executive officer.

Figures 3-1 and 3-2 show how functional departmentation might appear in state and municipal governments. Both tend to departmentalize by management function and business function. Their management functions are of course quite similar, but their business functions differ in several ways. States are primarily concerned with such activities as education, welfare, and agriculture, while cities place more emphasis on police and fire protection. But both levels of government tend to prefer the functional structure over alternative configurations. This is partly attributable to tradition, but the tradition can be linked to the fact that control is accentuated in organizations that arrange themselves by functional activity, and control has always been important to governmental organizations. In fact, the tendency of state and local governments to emphasize functional departmentation has even accelerated in recent times, due in part to politicians' desires to promote efficiency and executive power (Conant, 1988).

Figure 3-1 Functional Departmentation in State Government

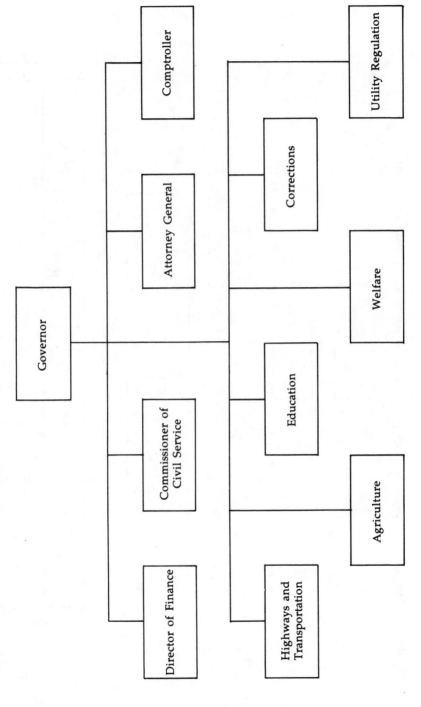

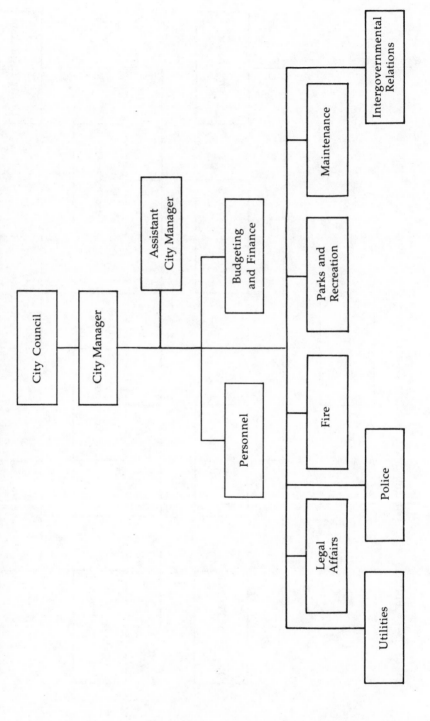

Figure 3-2 Functional Departmentation in a Council-Manager Municipal Government

The main reason that functional departmentation facilitates managerial control is that it is the most centralized of the various organizational types. The direct reporting relationship between department heads and the top manager implies that clearance must generally be sought before any nonroutine actions or decisions are undertaken. Moreover, functional allocation of tasks fixes responsibility: management knows whom to blame if something goes wrong.

Another attribute of this form is that it does the most to allow the organization to reap the benefits of specialization. Because all occupational and professional specialists are in homogeneous departments, they can all represent their own interests vigorously. No specialty is submerged, as often occurs in organizations that are dominated by one particular profession (for example, in hospitals, physicians could overwhelm other professional groups, such as public-health professionals). Moreover, departmentation by function ensures that the specialists can practice their crafts without interruption and without interference from other professional groups: each specialty is thereby able to hone its technical skills. Finally, functional departmentation offers a high degree of economy of scale. Each department offers its services to the entire organization, thus minimizing duplication of effort. By concentrating each activity in a functional department, agencies can have them performed much more efficiently than would otherwise be the case.

On the other hand, functional departmentation tends to spawn a kind of occupational myopia. Of all organizational types, this one generates the highest level of differentiation, the obverse of the high degree of specialization. The outlooks and perspectives of the occupational groups are so strongly shared by their department affiliations that they can almost become organizations within organizations. The various specialists may lose sight of the bigger picture, neglecting the organization's goals in favor of their department's interests. Under such circumstances, it is not unusual to find internecine warfare taking place as each department seeks to gain an advantage over others. Coordination of effort thus becomes a major problem. For the same reasons, functionally divided units are seldom good training grounds for high-level administrators. Because of the emphasis on specialization, few managers are able to acquire the breadth of experience that is necessary to prepare them for high office. Finally, the emphasis on control discourages risk-taking among managers and workers alike.

DEPARTMENTATION BY PROGRAM, PRODUCT, OR SERVICE

Probably the second most common structural form is the *program, product, or service design*. The distinguishing characteristic of this ap-

Figure 3-3 Program Departmentation in a Public-Health Agency

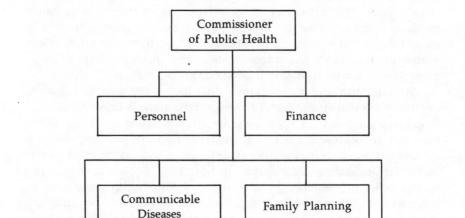

proach is that the departments are constructed around each of an agency's major programs or services. This is accomplished by delegating operational responsibility for the program or service to a program manager (several other titles, such as division director, are also used), who is in a direct line of responsibility to the chief executive officer. The program manager's department contains virtually all of the functional specialties that are needed to deliver the program or service for which it is responsible. This organizational form is often found in social-welfare agencies that, by law, are required to administer distinct programs that are funded separately by the federal government. A state department of public health thus may contain departments charged with such programs as family planning, maternal nutrition, newborn and infant health, and communicable diseases (Figure 3-3). The program manager in each of these service areas will exercise a considerable degree of control over all the specialists (nurses, social workers, health educators, public-health technicians) who are involved in program delivery. The only specialties that may be handled centrally are the so-called staff functions, including personnel and finance, although frequently these functions are delegated to program departments.

The chief advantage of departmentation by program is that it fosters coordination of functional activities. The program director is able to orchestrate the specialists' efforts, because they are all subject to his or her direct supervisory authority. Moreover, since responsibility for each program is in the hands of one person, no program or service is likely to be short-changed. The relevant program director will serve as an advocate, seeing to it that the higher administration is responsive to that program's needs.

Another set of advantages arises out of the effects that program-based structures are likely to have on their members. Employees in such organizations ordinarily have relatively high levels of job satisfaction and motivation because of the decisional autonomy that they enjoy. This effect is heightened by the diverse job experiences that are often available. Because the specialists are required to interact closely with specialists in other fields, they are exposed to a wider range of attitudes and skills than is normally the case in functional departments. In addition to aiding in the integration of the specialists, this provides a rich training ground for future executives.

Program departmentation is usually said to have three major disadvantages (see Dessler, 1982: 45). First, the dispersion of specialists among different program-oriented departments breeds duplication of effort and a diminution in economies of scale. A public-health agency, for instance, might employ five health educators to service each of five programs, whereas under a functional format, one or two might be sufficient. This problem is greatly compounded if staff activities are decentralized to the program units, which is sometimes the case. Second, top management loses a large measure of control over its operations when decision-making authority is delegated to program directors. In effect, management surrenders responsibility for determining methods by which the work will be done, though still maintaining control over the goals and outcomes. Thirdly, organizations that wish to adopt a program format must have an unusually large supply of talented managers. Whereas the functional arrangement requires only the presence of good specialists, program-oriented structures are more reliant on managers who are broadly trained and experienced as generalists. By most accounts, individuals of that kind are in very short supply.

Another, and quite serious, drawback to program departmentation is that submerging specialists in nonspecialized departments places them in a situation in which they can lose touch with those very professional perspectives and work habits that make them valuable to the organization. Located in a work environment that provides little or no contact with members of their own occupational groups, the specialists may internalize values and goals that depart from their profession's norms. An example of this phenomenon is that of physicians who spend many years in hospital management and thus come to accept administrative values even when they conflict with the requirements of good medical practice, as when they discourage the use of expensive diagnostic procedures on grounds of their cost, despite the fact that the procedures may be in the patients' interests.

THE MATRIX ORGANIZATION

To some extent, functional and program forms of organization are on opposite ends of the continuum between specialization and coordination (or, if you prefer, differentiation and integration). Functional departmentation emphasizes specialization but fosters a high level of internal diversity; program departmentation allows for better coordination of specialists' activities but limits the organization's ability to derive advantages from the division of labor.

The matrix form of organization is an effort to combine the advantages of these two other forms by superimposing a program-based organizational structure over one that has been functionally departmentalized.

Suppose, for example, that the city manager in a municipal government already organized along functional lines decides to initiate three programs to attract industry into the municipality. Instead of establishing a new functional department ("Department of Industry Recruitment") or restructuring the government into a program format, the manager might appoint three project leaders (or, as they are often called in the private sector, product managers), who would be given all the requisite authority and responsibility to design and implement the new programs. Specialists from all the relevant functional departments would be assigned to the project leaders, who would assume supervisory responsibility over them as long as they were assigned to that particular project. Thus, the project team might consist of representatives from the departments of public utilities (to ensure that adequate water and electricity will be available to service new industry), legal affairs (to handle such problems as requests for zoning variances), police and fire (to plan for new public-safety needs arising from the population influx), intergovernmental relations (to arrange for industrial revenue bonds and other sources of assistance), and so on (Figure 3-4).

In matrix organizations, the various specialists are joined in a common purpose, thanks to their membership on a team that is supervised and coordinated by an individual with responsibility for achieving a defined set of project goals. Meanwhile, however, their ties to their functional departments are not entirely severed. They operate under a system of dual reporting relationships: they report both to their project leader and to the head of their functional departments. Although

Figure 3-4 Matrix Departmentation in Municipal Government

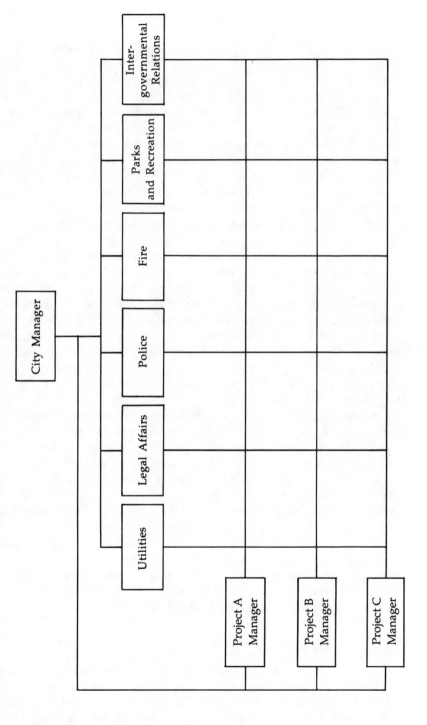

practices vary widely, project leaders generally exercise control over the planning, budgeting, and scheduling phases of the work process, as well as over staffing decisions involving the project's staff (raises, promotions, and so on). Functional department heads, meanwhile, continue to give technical direction and supervision to the specialists representing their departments in the various project teams. In a variation of this format, task forces are formed, in which the leaders have less authority over the specialists; these are typically used for projects that have a shorter life and a changing set of members with relatively informal relationships. Their project leaders coordinate more through persuasion than through the application of formal supervisory authority.

In addition to enabling managers to coordinate specialists more effectively, matrix organizations have achieved a reputation for creating work environments that are highly motivating and productive of innovations. These qualities emerge from the interchange of ideas that occurs when diverse specialists interact, as well as from the inherent excitement of intensely purposive activity. In addition, matrix organizations are commonly used to deal with challenging and difficult tasks, so their members are selected on the basis of very competitive criteria; thus, they provide a rich professional environment that is conducive to creativity and productivity. Many of the technological achievements of the National Aeronautics and Space Administration (NASA) were forged in matrix organizations.

However, while work in a matrix organization may indeed be challenging and exciting, it may also be very risky to one's career. The dual reporting relationships that typify them can be a source of role ambiguity and conflict. Lack of communication and cooperation between the functional and project managers can react to the disadvantage of the worker; decisions about raises and promotions may well be made by a person who is not fully familiar with the professional norms and expectations of the specialized employees within his or her project team. Research has shown that these factors can lead to reduced loyalty of workers to their organizations; heightened anxiety over career opportunities and long-term professional development; and a generalized belief that professional advancement is not proceeding as rapidly as it does for specialists assigned to functional departments (Reeser, 1969).

DEPARTMENTATION BY CLIENT

Another common method of departmentation is to organize activities by client or customer groups. This structure is most likely to be used when the organization services easily identifiable client populations with diverse needs. Subdivisions of major federal agencies, for example, are often organized by client groups. The Veterans Administration uses separate departments to attend to the needs of disabled veterans, GI Bill recipients, and retirees. Indeed, it could be argued that the entire executive branch of the federal government is organized along client lines: witness the Departments of Agriculture, Labor, Education, Health and Human Services, and Veterans Affairs. Many public utilities are organized according to their primary consumer groups (residential, commercial, and industrial), and the instructional programs of many universities reflect their client groups (regular day students, mature students, evening students, graduate students, extension students, and the like).

Most of the attractiveness of client-based departmentation is found in its emphasis on meeting the needs of the particular client group that is being served. The managers of such departments are expected to serve as advocates for their clients, just as program managers act as advocates for their programs. Thus, faster and more efficacious service for the client groups should result. This partially explains the popularity of the technique in public agencies. Given the fact that many government agencies exist precisely to tend to the needs of particular client populations (Thomas, 1990), departmentation by client is a logical feature in government jurisdictions. In addition to ensuring that the client group's interests are served, it offers the advantages of program-based structures, including integration of specialists, decentralization of decision making, and enhanced employee motivation.

If client-based organizations enjoy the advantages of the program format, then one would expect them to fall prey to its disadvantages as well, and this is certainly the case. In addition to reducing top management's control, client departmentation can result in duplication of effort and reduced economies of scale.

Another disadvantage, perhaps peculiar to the public sector, is that the presence of one or more client-centered departments in an agency creates external pressures for more departmentation. Client groups that are not favored with their own departments may clamor for one. They feel that, if a special department isn't created to represent their interests, they may be left out when shares of the public pie are distributed. While their fears may be well-founded, the resulting proliferation of departments can be a serious drain on the agency's resources—and, ironically, can interfere with the agency's ability to serve all of its client groups.

PROCESS DEPARTMENTATION

Public agencies that are involved in the processing of claims, documents, or people often arrange their departments or work groups accord-

Figure 3-5 Process Departmentation in a State Employment Office

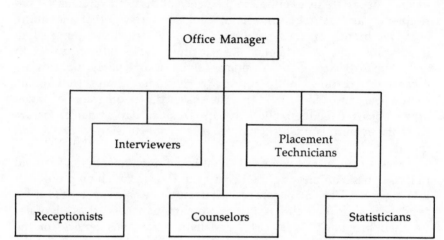

ing to the various stages of the processing cycle. In a state employment or workers' compensation office, for example, clients are moved through the organization in a step-by-step progression. Each employee group that delivers specialized services has departmental status (Figure 3-5).

Process departmentation represents one of the highest forms of specialization. By repeatedly performing one routinized task (interviewing claimants or reviewing grant applications), employees acquire considerable facility and competence. Moreover, communication and coordination within the specialties are enhanced, which may be very important if the workers' jobs require narrow technical skills, such as determining if grant applications meet all procedural and legal requirements. But, by the same token, process departmentation is especially vulnerable to coordination problems between specialties, precisely because it fosters such a narrow view of the unit's work. And again, the highly specialized jobs that are typical in such departments are not conducive to strong employee motivation and high morale. This problem is exacerbated by the fact that, given the restricted range of jobs performed in each department, the workers' career ladders are unusually short, meaning that promotional opportunities are rare.

CONTINGENCIES OF ORGANIZATIONAL STRUCTURE

For much of its short history, the study of management has been susceptible to fads. Public and private managers alike have figuratively swooned over scientific management, human relations, and other grandiose theories, all of which preach a dogma of the one best way. Theoretical principles took precedence over both empirical evidence and common sense, leaving management theory in a sterile state. Practicing managers, forced to work with a limited range of administrative tools and concepts, paid the price, often with costly trial and error experiments.

During the early 1960s, however, a more complex approach to management began to emerge. This approach, called *contingency theory*, is based on two conclusions grounded in empirical studies: "(1) there is no one best way to organize; and (2) any way of organizing is not equally effective" (Galbraith, 1973: 2). The primary focus of these studies was the identification of the factors or contingencies that influenced organizational design (Galbraith, 1973). They led to the discovery of important clues to interrelationships between structure and situation.

ENVIRONMENTAL CONTINGENCIES

Perhaps the most influential contingency study was that of Burns and Stalker (1961). The original intention of their research, involving about 20 British companies, was to "describe and explain what happens when new and unfamiliar tasks are put upon industrial concerns organized for relatively stable conditions" (Burns and Stalker, 1961). Their underlying premise was that an organization's environment, or the rate of change in its environment, is a significant contingency in organizational design and management.

After an intensive analysis of the environments, work processes, and managerial practices of the companies being studied, Burns and Stalker described two types of organizations, the mechanistic and the organic. Although subsequent interpretations have led many people to assume that mechanistic organizations are inherently bad and organic ones are inherently good, the authors actually said:

> *Both* types represent a "rational" form of organization, in that they may both, in our experience, be explicitly and deliberately created and maintained to exploit the human resources of a concern in the most efficient manner feasible in the circumstances of the concern. (Burns and Stalker, 1961: 119)

In other words, whether an organizational type is effective depends on whether or not it is appropriate to its environment.

Organizational environments, in turn, were described in terms of their level of stability or change. Stable environments were characterized by an unchanging set of competitors; a steady demand for the organization's goods or services; and technological innovation that was "evolutionary rather than revolutionary in that required product changes can be predicted well in advance and the required modifications made at a leisurely pace " (Burns and Stalker, 1961: 79). Changing environments, in contrast, are marked by fluctuating demands for the organization's goods or services, relatively high levels of competition for resources, and rapid technological innovation. In one of the most enduring (if not entirely correct) conclusions in the modern study of management, Burns and Stalker maintained that mechanistic structures are most effective in stable environments, while organic structures flourish in changing environments. Major features of these two organizational types are detailed below (Burns and Stalker, 1961: 119-125).

Mechanistic Organizations

Close adherence to the chain of command

Highly specialized tasks

Functional division of work

Reliance on formal hierarchy to foster coordination

Detailed job descriptions that provide a precise delineation of rights, obligations, and technical methods for performing each task

Insistence on loyalty to the organization and to superiors

A higher value placed on internal knowledge, skill, and experience than on more general knowledge, skill, and experience

A tendency for most actions to be governed by the instructions and decisions issued by superiors

Prevalence of vertical communications between superior and subordinate

"A one-to-one leadership style, that is, with most interactions between superior and subordinate occurring in private discussion and an absence or minimal attention to group processes" (French and Bell, 1984: 260)

Organic Organizations

A divisional or project form of departmentation

Less focus on the chain of command

Jobs that are less specialized and are continually adjusted to meet changing circumstances

More extensive communications that occur both horizontally and vertically; consultative information gathering, rather than the dissemination of instructions and decisions

A pervasive commitment to the organization's tasks, which serves an important control function by reducing reliance on rules, procedures, and rewards and penalties

High value placed on expertise that is relevant to the technological environment of the organization

"A team leadership style, with an emphasis on consultation and considerable attention to interpersonal and group processes, including methods of decision making and more frequent decisions by consensus" (French and Bell, 1984: 261)

The argument that the degree of environmental uncertainty is the principal determinant of the effectiveness of organizational structure won numerous adherents; it is now accepted as conventional wisdom that, in uncertain, rapidly changing environments, organically structured organizations are most appropriate (Miles, 1975). Some proponents even go so far as to predict that bureaucracy will disappear altogether as a result of the accelerating pace of change in the environments of all organizations, public and private. Bennis (1966), for example, predicted the rise to prominence of organizations that are temporary, "adaptive" (his term for "organic"), and arranged around problems to be solved rather than around on-going work routines. Interestingly, the emergence of matrix organizations, which *are* generally created to solve specific problems, is viewed by some commentators as a concrete indication of the accuracy of Bennis's prediction. While few other researchers are as intrepid in their prognostications as Bennis, most agree with his fundamental thesis. Almost without exception, management theorists have become advocates of organic, decentralized, and democratic organizational structures (see, for example, Likert, 1967; Wise, 1990).

In one sense, the thought of living and working in a world composed only of organic organizations is exhilarating. But it is wise to recall that no absolute prescriptions have ever survived the test of time. All have run aground on the rocks of empirical research. Thus, any theoretical proposition that purports to be completely generalizable, including the one that "rapidly changing environments require organic structure," must be looked on with some suspicion. While the underlying argument has received considerable empirical support (J. Thompson, 1967; Weick, 1969; Ginsberg and Venkatraman, 1985), its unidimensionality alone is cause for caution. Other research has uncovered additional contingencies, such as the need for organizational stability.

If we apply this analysis to contemporary realities in the public sector, what kinds of environmental contingencies are apparent? The first thought that comes to mind is that, especially in government, there are many employees who interact with the environment without much of an organizational shield. They are front-line troops who cannot be buffered from environmental influences, yet who must act on behalf of the organization when interacting with citizens. For example, police officers, social workers, teachers, regulatory enforcers, and other "street-level bureaucrats" (Lipsky, 1980) exercise considerable discretion over their clients, often with only the most general guidance from their organizations. Michael Lipsky's book on *Street-Level Bureaucracy* (1980) gives an informed analysis of how these workers cope with the environmental stresses of their jobs.

Another important facet of the contemporary management landscape is the elevated level of environmental turbulence. A case could easily be made that this is one of the most unstable and stressful periods in our history. Economic pressures, coupled with widespread public irritation with government, have placed almost unprecedented demands on public agencies. For the first time in decades, most public organizations are either shrinking, or are at a stage of zero-growth. These conditions inevitably generate both internal and external conflict as agencies scramble for pieces of a shrinking resource pie.

There are risks and ironies in governments' responses to these challenges. On one hand, public agencies have a tradition of "battening down the hatches" during storms. Centralization and increased reliance on managerial controls are a comforting way of dealing with stress, since this provides at least the illusion that accountability is fixed and fewer resources are wasted. Politicians, caught in a squeeze between an unhappy public and chronic budget shortages, often opt for the least risky strategy of layering on additional controls to ensure that they are not embarrassed by media accounts of bureaucratic inefficiencies or apparently stupid public expenditures (who can forget Senator Proxmire's "Golden Fleece Awards," or the more recent disputes over the funding choices of the National Endowment for the Arts). Privatization, productivity initiatives, and choices concerning budget cutbacks during government's ongoing fiscal crisis are often conducted in a highly centralized fashion.

Contingency theory, on the other hand, points to a different strategy for adjusting to environmental turbulence. Authority ought to be delegated to the lowest possible level during such times because creative solutions are needed. Public administrators operating closest to the problems are best positioned to experiment and to tailor innovative responses to particular crises. Although this response is not as widespread as one might hope, there are indications that public organizations *are* becoming flatter during this era of economic restructuring. As will be discussed in later chapters, authority over many operational aspects of public management does seem to be shifting to lower levels of the organization. This trend is especially apparent in regard to the personnel function (Chapter 4), but can also be seen in the budgeting (Chapter 6) area as well.

TECHNOLOGICAL CONTINGENCIES

Another contingency was brought to light in a study of 100 British firms conducted by Joan Woodward in the middle and late 1950s. Using Burns and Stalker's research as a model, she attempted to classify each firm as either organic or mechanistic, using information on the companies' manufacturing processes, objectives, rules and procedures, and performance data. However, she found wide and confusing variations in the firms' structural components (such as the number of managerial levels and the spans of control of chief executives) within each type. But she noted that the firms' *technologies* could explain many of the differences. She identified three technological types, ranging from the least to the most complex: *unit and small-batch production,* as exemplified by tailor shops and other facilities that fabricate small numbers of products using a relatively well-defined work method; *large-batch and mass production,* such as is found on assembly lines; and *process production,* the kind employed in the oil-refining and chemical industries. Once the companies were categorized according to their technologies, the researchers were able to detect a large number of commonalities and trends within each type and differences among types. These included the following:

The span of control of chief executives increased with technological complexity, as did the ratio of clerical and administrative personnel to production personnel.

Mass-production firms made fine distinctions between line and staff, whereas unit and process companies did not.

The span of control of *middle* managers *decreased* with increased technological complexity.

Functional departmentation appeared in mass-production firms, while unit and process organizations typically employed project or product departmentation.

Job specialization was higher in mass-production firms than in either of the other types.

Mass-production firms tended to have bureaucratic structures, while process and unit organizations were more organic.

One of Woodward's most significant findings was that organizations whose structural characteristics differed markedly from the norm for organizations of the same technological type tended to be less successful than other companies. She had thus related organizational structure to performance, with technology being the critical variable in the relationship (Woodward, 1965).

While Woodward was unable to offer a completely satisfying explanation for her findings, later analyses provided additional insights. Blau and his colleagues (1976), for example, found that many of the structural characteristics of mass-production forms can be attributed to the routinization of work. Mass-production technology leads to near-complete routinization of tasks, and as a consequence, employees of mass-production companies are not as highly skilled as those in other technological types. Because of their low skill levels, they require close (bureaucratic) supervision. In contrast, the workers employed by unit and process companies are generally more professional and thus do not require a rigid structure for control and coordination. Moreover, they have to adapt more frequently to unpredictable situations, and so they try to achieve responsiveness and effectiveness through a decentralized (organic) organizational structure. (A corollary of Woodward's research, then, is that employee characteristics are another critical contingency. As will be discussed in Chapter 5, an entire set of behavioral and leadership theories has grown up around that proposition.)

Other students of management have viewed technological contingencies in other ways. James Thompson, for example, identifies three varieties. *Long-linked* technology involves serial interdependence, "in the sense that act Z can be performed only after successful completion of act Y, which in turn rests on act X ... the mass production assembly line" (J. Thompson, 1967: 16). *Mediating* technology establishes relationships among clients or customers who are interdependent, as when insurance companies pool those who are exposed to common risks, or when welfare agencies relate taxpayers and welfare recipients. *Intensive* technology is distinguishable by the fact that "a variety of techniques is drawn upon in order to achieve a change in some specific object, but the selection, combination, and order of the application are determined by feedback from the object itself" (J. Thompson, 1967: 17). A familiar example of intensive technology is the hospital, in which the application of any number of technologies to the patient depends on responses (changes in symptoms or conditions) from the patient.

Thompson hypothesizes that each of his technological types generates a different level of interdependence within the organization. In an organization using long-linked technology, for example, workers must perform their functions in a strictly defined sequence, for otherwise the efforts of all will be worthless. Such observations led Thompson to suggest that organizational structure is essentially the outcome of the organization's effort to coordinate its activities. Since technologies vary in complexity, they present organizations with different kinds of coordinational, and hence structural, problems.

INFORMATION-PROCESSING CONTINGENCIES

Despite significant differences in methodology and findings, the research discussed thus far all seems to point to the conclusion that organizational structure varies with uncertainty, either environmental or technological. Environmental uncertainty is fostered by rapid change and by the presence of numerous competitors, while technological uncertainty is defined in terms of complexity and the absence of a clear understanding concerning cause-and-effect relationships. The technology of space exploration, for instance, is especially uncertain, because we can understand the causes and effects only *after* the research has succeeded—and research *is*, after all, the attempt to discover cause-and-effect relationships. Automobile assembly is a relatively certain methodology, because most of the cause-and-effect relationships involved are well understood—though it is less certain than, say, trash collections.

In his synthesis of these concepts, Galbraith (1973) analyzed exactly why and how uncertainty influences organizational structure. "The greater the uncertainty of the task," he theorized, "the greater the amount of information that has to be processed between decision makers" (Galbraith, 1973: 4). He perceived an increased information load coming out of three factors: (1) the diversity of the organizations' outputs (the number of different products, clients, or services); (2) the diversity of input resources utilized (the number of different technical specialties working on a project, as well as the level and nature of demands from external groups); and (3) the difficulty of goal accomplishment (which is tied to the concept of efficiency, or achieving an end for the least possible outlay) (Galbraith, 1973: 5). As the complexities associated with these factors intensify, managers are challenged to monitor the situation more closely and to react more quickly to changing circumstances. With the increments in uncertainty, more problems are passed up the hierarchy for resolution, because no one below has the authority (or perhaps the will) to assume responsibility. The hierarchy exists to handle exceptions—to decide issues that have not been decided below. This requires a highly sophisticated ability to process information.

Galbraith contends that organizations may choose from among four distinct strategies to deal with an increased information load. The first two strategies are intended to reduce the need for information. The creation of slack resources does this by reducing the required level of performance. For example, an agency may hire additional employees rather than improving coordination and control among its existing employees. Other common examples of creation of slack are pushing back deadlines or reducing the expected level of goal performance (as when a tax-collection agency decides to be content with catching a smaller proportion of tax cheaters). The willingness to "satisfice" (see Chapter 2) rather than trying to maximize is the essence of slack, and it greatly reduces complexity by reducing demands on organizations.

The second strategy that might be used to reduce the need for information is to move from a functionally designed organizational format to self-contained units, as in program departmentation. When units are self-contained, the point of decision is moved closer to the source of the information, and consequently less information must be passed up the hierarchy. Additionally, program departmentation reduces the division of labor, thereby obviating much of the information flow that, in functional organizations, is necessary to coordinate the various specialists.

The other two strategies for contending with the information load are intended to enhance the organization's information-processing capability. By the first of these, investment in vertical information systems, the organization makes use of data-processing and computer technology to collect and digest large volumes of information. Another consequence of information technology is its tendency to disseminate information more widely in the organization, almost inadvertently leading to decentralization. When a greater number of people have quicker access to information, the authority to make decisions tends to descend the hierarchy. Individuals who were once out of the loop are now included. Offices that are networked through greater communication enjoy a higher level of coordination without the intervention of management, thereby expanding the span of control. In a sense, the free flow of information is an expedient means of decentralizing, whether or not management intends to promote a flatter organizational structure.

If the introduction of information systems proves inadequate, the fourth and most sophisticated strategy may be invoked—the creation of lateral relations, whereby the organization decentralizes decision making without creating self-contained (program) units. Instead of relying on the hierarchy to coordinate and orchestrate work activity, the organization turns to what Mintzberg called mutual adjustment, the coordination of efforts through informal communications and accommodations. The most basic form of lateral relations and communications is direct contact between managers, followed by the use of special liaison personnel to coordinate tasks, and then by committees, temporary task forces to accomplish one-time goals, and special integrating networks. At the apex of this hierarchy of lateral relations is the matrix organization, which Galbraith considers to be the most advanced structural form for dealing with uncertainty.

Galbraith's theory is quite consistent with the findings of most other contingency researchers. Indeed, there seems to be a widespread consensus on the following points concerning the interplay of organizational structure and contingency variables:

1. As technology becomes more sophisticated and uncertain, organizations need to decentralize their decision making in order to enhance their productive capability.
2. As environmental complexity and turbulence increase, organizations again need to decentralize their decision-making processes in order to respond effectively to changes and challenges from external sources.
3. Functional departmentation, emphasizing control and specialization, tends to be most appropriate in situations characterized by stable environments and relatively certain technologies.
4. The more decentralized forms of departmentation, such as program and matrix organizations, are best suited to changing environments and uncertain technologies.
5. As the level of uncertainty in organizations increases, the use of formal coordination and control mechanisms decreases substantially, while the use of informal and lateral communications to achieve coordination rises.

On other points, there is less agreement. The size of organizations, for example, is thought by some to have a direct effect on the degree of formality of their structures; the number of levels in the hierarchy and the degree of specialization are seen as increasing with size. Other theorists, however, contend that it is technology that tends to determine an organization's size—that what the organization does, and how it does it, dictate the number of employees it will have. A few theorists argue for the importance of the locus of power as a contingency. Mintzberg, most notably, asserts that organizations that are controlled by outside forces (which would include all public agencies) tend to be highly centralized and place great reliance on rules and regulations for internal control (Mintzberg, 1983: 146). However, although this seems plausible, there is not yet sufficient empirical evidence to assert it as fact.

Another hypothesis is that organizational structure is related to certain human factors, such as the skill and knowledge levels of the organization's staff. As will be discussed in Chapter 5, knowledgeable and motivated workers generally perform better in a decentralized setting, while unskilled workers often require more structure and control. If this is true, it follows that agencies employing large numbers of professional workers should make heavy use of matrix or program-based organizational designs, especially in organizational settings characterized by rapid change and technological complexity—conditions that exist in many public agencies. Since almost 40 percent of the nation's professional workers are employed by government, and since a growing proportion of all civil servants occupy professional or technical positions, one could infer that highly centralized bureaucratic structures are disappearing (Rouse, 1990). While that certainly is not the case, flatter organizations do appear to be more prominent in the future. As was mentioned earlier, the fiscal pressures of the 1990s are stimulating decentralization in many areas of public management. Other forces that point in the same direction include a greatly increased information burden and ever-accelerating technological advances.

Given the ferment now occurring in the field, students intending to pursue careers in public administration are due for an exciting ride. The challenges have never been greater; it is hoped that they will be matched by an equal number of opportunities. The stresses are sufficiently acute to ensure that the old ways of doing things will no longer suffice. Reorganization, experimentation, and innovation will almost certainly be a major part of the future. We can only hope that the lessons learned thus far concerning the relationships between organizational structure and design contingencies will be put to good use. Advances made in the design of public organizations could mean a brighter future for managers, the people they supervise, and the public they serve.

REFERENCES

Argyris, Chris. 1957. *Personality and Organization.* New York: Harper and Row.

Barnard, Chester. 1938. *The Functions of the Executive.* Cambridge, Mass.: Harvard University Press.

Bennis, Warren. 1966. *Changing Organizations.* New York: McGraw-Hill.

Blau, Peter, Cecelia M. Falbe, William McKinley, and Phelps Tracy. 1976. "Technology and Organization in Manufacturing." *Administrative Science Quarterly* 21 (March): 20-40.

Burns, Tom, and G. M. Stalker. 1961. *The Management of Innovation.* London: Tavistock.

Conant, James K. 1988. "In the Shadow of Wilson and Brownlow: Executive Branch Reorganization in the States." *Public Administration Review* 48 (September/October): 892-902.

Dessler, Gary. 1982. *Organization and Management.* Reston, Va.: Reston.

Dimock, Marshall. 1959. *Administrative Vitality.* New York: Harper and Brothers.

Doig, Jameson W., and Erwin C. Hargrove, ed. 1987. *Leadership and Innovation.*

Baltimore: The Johns Hopkins University Press.

Downs, Anthony. 1967. *Inside Bureaucracy*. Boston: Little, Brown.

Etzioni, Amitai. 1964. *Modern Organizations*. Englewood Cliffs, N.J.: Prentice-Hall.

Fayol, Henri. 1949. *General and Industrial Management*. London: Pitman.

French, Wendell L., and Cecil H. Bell. 1984. *Organization Development*. Englewood Cliffs, N.J.: Prentice-Hall.

Friedrich, Carl. 1952. "Some Observations on Weber's Analysis of Bureaucracy." In *Reader in Bureaucracy*, ed. Robert K. Merton et al., 27-33. Glencoe, Ill.: Free Press.

Galbraith, Jay. 1973. *Designing Complex Organizations*. Reading, Mass.: Addison-Wesley.

Ginsberg, Ari, and N. Venkatraman. 1985. "Contingency Perspectives of Organizational Strategy: A Critical Review of Empirical Research." *Academy of Management Review* 10 (3): 421-434.

Gulick, Luther H. 1990. "Reflections on Public Administration, Past and Present." *Public Administration Review* 50 (November/December): 599-603.

Herzberg, Frederick. 1968. "One More Time: How Do You Motivate Employees?" *Harvard Business Review* 46 (January/February): 53-62.

Katzmann, Robert A. 1980. "Federal Trade Commission." In *The Politics of Regulation*, ed. James Q. Wilson, 152-187. New York: Basic Books.

Koontz, Harold, and Cyril O'Donnell. 1978. *Essentials of Management*. New York: McGraw-Hill.

Lawrence, Paul R., and Jay W. Lorsch. 1967. *Organization and Environment*. Boston: Harvard Business School.

Likert, Rensis. 1967. *The Human Organization*. New York: McGraw-Hill.

Lipsky, Michael. 1980. *Street-Level Bureaucracy*. New York: Russell Sage Foundation.

Mackenzie, Kenneth D. 1978. *Organizational Structures*. Arlington Heights, Ill.: AHM.

Merton, Robert K., Ailsa P. Gray, Barbara Hockey, and Hanan C. Selvin, ed. 1952. *Reader in Bureaucracy*. Glencoe, Ill.: Free Press.

Miles, Raymond. 1975. *Theories of Management: Implications for Organizational Behavior and Development*. New York: McGraw-Hill.

Mintzberg, Henry. 1979. *The Structuring of Organizations*. Englewood Cliffs, N.J.: Prentice-Hall.

———. 1983. *Designing Effective Organizations*. Englewood Cliffs, N.J.: Prentice-Hall.

Morris, W. T. 1968. *Decentralization in Management Systems: An Introduction to Design*. Columbus: Ohio State University Press.

Perry, James L., and Lois R. Wise. 1990. "The Motivational Bases of Public Service." *Public Administration Review* 50 (May/June): 367-373.

Pfeffer, Jeffrey. 1978. *Organizational Design*. Arlington Heights, Ill.: AHM.

Reeser, C. 1969. "Some Potential Human Problems of the Project Form of Organization." *Academy of Management Journal* 12 (December): 459-467.

Roethlisberger, F. J., and W. J. Dickson. 1939. *Management and the Worker*. Cambridge, Mass.: Harvard University Press.

Rouse, John E. 1990. "Perspectives on Organizational Culture: An Emerging Conscience for Public Administrators." *Public Administration Review* 50 (July/August): 479-485.

Smith, Adam. 1776/1937. *An Inquiry into the Nature and Causes of the Wealth of Nations*. New York: Random House.

Stever, James A. 1990. "Marshall Dimock: An Intellectual Portrait." *Public Administration Review* 50 (November/December): 615-621.

Taylor, Frederick. 1947. *Scientific Management*. New York: Harper.

Thomas, Christine L. 1990. "The Policy/Administration Continuum: Wisconsin Natural Resources Board Decisions." *Public Administration Review* 50 (July/August): 446-449.

Thompson, James D. 1967. *Organizations in Action*. New York: McGraw-Hill.

Thompson, Victor. 1975. *Without Passion or Enthusiasm*. Tuscaloosa: University of Alabama Press.

———. 1976. *Bureaucracy and the Modern World*. Morristown, N.J.: General Learning Press.

Urwick, Lyndall. 1943. *The Elements of Administration*. New York: Harper.

Walker, Arthur H., and Jay W. Lorsch. 1968. "Organizational Choice: Product versus Function." *Harvard Business Review* 46 (November/December): 130-142.

Weber, Max. 1947. *The Theory of Social and Economic Organization*, trans. A. M. Henderson and Talcott Parsons. London: Oxford University Press.

———.1952. "The Essentials of Bureaucratic Organization: An Ideal-Type Construction." In *Reader in Bureaucracy*, ed. Robert K. Merton et al., 18-27. Glencoe, Ill.: Free Press.

Weick, Karl E. 1969. *The Social Psychology of Organizing*. Reading, Mass.: Addison-Wesley.

Wise, Charles. 1990. "Public Service Configurations and Public Organizations: Public Organizational Design in the Post-Privatization Era." *Public Administration Review* 50 (March/April): 141-155.

Woodward, Joan. 1965. *Industrial Organization: Theory and Practice*. London: Oxford University Press.

4

Staffing

If one were to ask a sample of public and private administrators to identify the management function in which flexibility and discretion are most desirable, the majority would almost certainly specify staffing. Whereas limitations on a manager's range of choice in the areas of planning and organizing can prove to be troublesome (see Chapters 2 and 3), unnecessary restraints on staffing decisions can invite disaster. Imagine, for example, a situation in which the chief executive officer of a major corporation is unable, without clearing numerous procedural hurdles and warding off intrusions from her board of directors, to hire, train, promote, transfer, demote, and fire her subordinates. Under such conditions, could we have expected Thomas Watson to create IBM? Nevertheless, many public managers operate under precisely those handicaps.

The seeds of staffing inflexibility were sown in the nineteenth century, during the so-called spoils or patronage period. In attempting to democratize the civil service—in other words, opening it up to the common person—Andrew Jackson introduced *rotation in office* as the major premise of public-sector personnel management. This practice, which meant that newly elected politicians could clean house on assuming office and install their own party loyalists in government jobs, soon resulted in some of the worst corruption and incompetence in American political history (see Hoogenboom, 1968; Van Riper, 1958). Finally, when President James A. Garfield was assassinated by a disappointed office-seeker, reformers forced a reluctant Congress to pass the Civil Service Act of 1883 (Pendleton Act). The provisions of this act were the basis for what has become known as the merit system, whose main elements are:

1. *Competitive examinations:* Entry into the public service is by examinations open to any qualified member of the public.

2. *Lateral entry:* Entry into the civil service may occur at any level, meaning that candidates for upper-level jobs need not start at the bottom and work their way up.
3. *Insulation from political pressure:* Several measures—including the establishment of an appointed, bipartisan commission to police the merit system and stern restrictions against political coercion of public workers—were designed to ensure that the spoils system would not resurface.

Introduction of the merit system was unquestionably one of the most transforming and positive events in the maturation of American political institutions. Without a competent and neutral civil service, the movement toward an industrialized society would surely have been impeded.

Despite this fact, however, the merit system was accompanied by a managerial philosophy that produced some negative consequences. One unfortunate legacy of this first civil-service reform movement was the perception that politics are somehow bad. Reform came about as a crusade against the evil of the spoils system, thereby leaving a lasting imprint on the public's view of the civil service and the role of the staffing function in public organizations (Mosher, 1984). In effect, the public came to associate goodness with insulation from political influence. This later led to a plethora of statutory, judicial, and administrative initiatives that were intended to protect public employees from the political bosses. The scope of the merit system was expanded from 10 percent of the employees in federal service in 1883 to 90 percent by the 1930s, and the depth of the system was increased by additional measures to insulate public employees from arbitrary personnel actions. For example, the Lloyd-La Follette Act of 1912 required that civil servants be given an opportunity to rebut charges against them before removal, and judicial decrees effectively shifted the burden of proof from the employee to the public manager who was attempting to remove or discipline an employee. Personnel professionals contributed to this trend by devising increasingly sophisticated staffing techniques that further reduced management's ability to influence personnel decisions.

The consequences of these inflexible staffing practices became a major political issue over time. Prompted by fiscal crises and corresponding tax increases, the public's general irritation with big government found expression in attacks on the merit system, which was perceived as a major cause of the government's inefficiency and unresponsiveness. This theme became a major backdrop of both the 1976 and the 1980 presidential campaigns, providing the candidates with ample opportunities to attack the most vulnerable aspects of public staffing practices. The drawbacks of the merit system were brought to light. It was widely publicized, for example, that more than 99 percent of all federal workers regularly received merit raises and that less than 300 federal employees (out of about 2.9 million) were terminated in any given year. Similar statistics concerning state and local merit systems were paraded before the public, resulting in great pressures for response by politicians at all levels.

These forces ultimately stimulated the most widespread reform of public personnel management since merit systems were first introduced in the United States. Ironically, the primary thrust of this reform has been to put the *merit* back into the merit system. In order to accomplish this goal, the staffing practices of business and industry are being emulated on a broad scale.

The private-sector staffing characteristics that are most attractive to public managers are *decentralization* and an emphasis on *performance*. A decentralized administrative format is valued because it permits the line managers, the individuals who are closest to the work situation, to make those staffing decisions that directly influence their unit's productivity and morale (Ingraham and Rosenbloom, 1989). Emphasis on performance as a major criterion for allocating rewards and punishments provides managers with an effective motivational tool. Public-sector staffing has made little use of either of these orientations. Decentralization has traditionally been avoided because it is not conducive to control; if staffing decisions were delegated to line managers, the difficulties in guarding against political corruption would be compounded. Likewise, concern for the quality of performance was an early casualty of the effort to neutralize the civil service; with seniority as the basic rationale for placement and promotion decisions, supervisors could not punish or reward subordinates on the basis of political (or other irrelevant) considerations. While relatively effective in safeguarding the civil service from excessive political interference, these staffing strategies eliminated much of the spontaneity and responsiveness that had proven valuable in private-sector personnel management.

This chapter provides an overview of the government staffing function within the context of these changing orientations. Because these changes represent a significant redefinition of the role of staffing in public agencies, more of the chapter is devoted to broad questions of scope than to discussions of specific staffing techniques. However, certain newly popularized staffing strategies that have appeared as outgrowths of the movement toward increased flexibility and responsiveness are described and are contrasted with the techniques that they are meant to supplant.

THE STAFFING FUNCTION IN GOVERNMENT

Of the numerous definitions that have been made of the staffing function, the one that best captures its essence is also the simplest: "to hire good employees and make them better" (Riggs, 1985: 58). Given the fact that salaries and fringe benefits constitute between 75 and 80 percent of all nonfederal government expenditures, one would think that public administrators expend enormous energies attracting qualified applicants, upgrading their skills, and weeding out incompetents. In reality, however, the typical manager rarely devotes much attention to these activities. Indeed, it can legitimately be argued that staffing is one of (if not *the*) most neglected administrative functions among line managers.

In fact, the responsibility for staffing activities has gradually shifted away from line managers. As public agencies grew in size and complexity, economies of scale demanded that certain routine staffing functions be assigned to centralized staff units. In place of the anarchy in which each line department handled its own recruitment, testing, and classification, specialized personnel departments were created to ensure a degree of uniformity and economy. A logical (yet unfortunate) consequence of this movement toward departmentalization was that staffing came to be viewed as the function of those specialized units, rather than as a critical management function that required the attention of all supervisory personnel.

This perception was reinforced by the actions of the professional employees who staffed the newly created personnel departments. In response to the public sector's desire to neutralize the civil service, these personnel administrators (or "personnelists") devised a whole range of procedures that were intended to make all staffing decisions "objective" (in other words, nonpolitical). In many jurisdictions, the personnelists were aided by overly enthusiastic civil-service commissions, which imposed additional layers of cumbersome staffing requirements and which, in some locations, exercised unchallenged control over all personnel policy. By continually pressing for greater degrees of standardization and uniformity, personnelists and civil-service commissions moved most staffing decisions "into the cold objective atmosphere of tests, scores, weighted indices, and split-digit rankings" (Clapp, 1941: 291). With each successive step along the road to objectivity, staffing lost more of its relevance to line managers. The result is neatly summarized in Wallace Sayre's classic statement that public personnel management represents "a triumph of techniques over purpose" (1948: 134).

Examples of this phenomenon abound in the literature of public administration. A study by Savas and Ginsburg (1973) revealed that applicants for civil-service positions in New York City could not be considered for an opening unless they specifically identified the *exact* position for which they were applying. Further, if a required number of applications was not received for an opening, the position had to be readvertised and the individuals who responded to the first announcement had to re-apply. Because of such requirements, warfare often erupted between line managers and personnel departments. Managers found they were unable to hire replacements expeditiously, to reclassify or promote employees when warranted, and to take appropriate disciplinary actions. Staffing procedures were regarded as obstacles to getting the job done rather than as tools for effective management.

Although taxpayer revolts are often credited with prompting major changes in the organizational role of the staffing function, significant reforms were afoot as early as the 1940s. City and county managers, in particular, served as catalysts for change. These new urban professionals found themselves in a predicament: elected officials held them responsible for the actions of their subordinates, yet their authority over those subordinates was severely constrained by the civil-service commissions. In effect, a city manager could be dismissed because of the ineptitude of employees who had been hired, evaluated, and rewarded according to procedures over which the manager exercised little or no influence. Deeply disturbed by the flawed logic of this situation, various professional associations mounted attacks on the civil-service commission form of personnel management (Municipal Manpower Commission, 1962; National Civil Service League, 1970). These efforts were ultimately successful. By 1990 only two states and less than 10 percent of all local jurisdictions that had formal merit systems continued to use civil-service commissions. In their place, *executive personnel systems* had become the predominant organizational arrangement for conducting the staffing function.

In executive personnel systems, the jurisdiction's chief executive is directly responsible for the operation of the merit system. Staffing functions are generally performed by a separate personnel department that is headed by an appointee of the chief executive (governor, mayor, city manager, and so forth). Thus, responsibility and authority are combined in one office.

THE PERSONNELIST'S ROLE IN THE ORGANIZATION

The changes in staffing procedures that are under way are the outgrowths of a series of developments that repeatedly jolted this function of management. The first major tremor was felt during the 1960s, when the push for social equity in the form of demands for equal employment opportunity and affirmative action required managers to reconsider most of their assumptions concerning the proper ways of testing, selecting, and otherwise managing the work force. This was followed by the growth of public unionism, huge increases in government payrolls, and precipitous declines in the rate of productivity growth. These phenomena provoked increasingly intense searches for new ways of dealing with old and new problems. Thus, when the wave of fiscal conservatism struck, carrying with it an epidemic of governmental budget crises, public managers had long since begun to redefine many of their customary roles and responsibilities.

More recently, added pressure for greater staffing flexibility and effectiveness has come from the perceived challenges of *Workforce 2000* (Hudson Institute, 1987) and the troublesome, predictable conclusions of the National Commission on the Public Service (1989). The *Workforce 2000* projections highlight demographic changes that will characterize the work force of the future. Most notable among the trends identified is the fact that *most* of the new workers will be minorities, immigrants, and women. The forecasts raise serious questions about the readiness of employers to accommodate child care needs, insurance costs, and a plethora of related challenges.

The National Commission Report (also called the *Volcker Commission Report*) paints an even more troubled picture of the realities of public personnel systems. Lamenting such trends as "bureaucrat bashing," inadequate salaries, and ineffective political leadership, the *Report* draws attention to a "quiet crisis" in the civil service. Low morale, high turnover, and a corresponding reduction in the talent level of public workers constitute a few of the more disturbing findings. The Commission's recommendations include a *strengthened personnel function* in government. Recruitment practices need to be simplified, training opportunities must be expanded. Further, staffing decentralization should be permitted, and the civil service system's entire culture needs to be transformed (Wildavsky, 1988).

In fashioning responses to budgetary pressures line managers have been forced to engage in a dialogue with personnelists. Most managers are coming to realize that the staffing function generally, and personnel departments specifically, will be in the forefront of public administration's struggle to respond to current problems. As a former (and, incidentally, the last) chairman of the U.S. Civil Service Commission noted, the challenges "beamed a powerful spotlight into that erstwhile backwater, the personnel office" (Campbell, 1977: 1).

Perhaps the most important lesson that has been learned during this tumultuous era is that, in order to be effective, staffing must be a *continuous* concern of all managers and supervisors. It must be viewed as a pervasive activity that transcends departmental boundaries. This point is best demonstrated by pointing out the numerous linkages that staffing has to some of the other major management functions (Teasley and Williams, 1991).

Planning. No systematic planning program can be effective without taking into consideration the future availability of skilled workers and managers. Planning for staff involves an inventory of individuals and skills currently on hand, projections concerning future personnel costs, and the identification of excesses and shortages in particular skill categories.

Organizing. The nature of an organization's work force should be matched to the organization's structure. As was pointed out earlier (see Chapter 3), unskilled workers may require a more structured environment than skilled workers. Thus, before implementing any structural changes, steps must be taken to ensure that the employees are properly prepared for (or capable of handling) the revised organizational format. Some workers, for instance, may need additional training in advance of any move to decentralize decision making. Moreover, organizational structure directly influences job design, the classification system, and the reward structure. Due to these close linkages, many business-oriented textbooks discuss staffing within the context of the organizing function.

Budgeting. As has been discussed, the public sector has emphasized one side of the budgeting function (keeping the civil service neutral so that it can be controlled) to the detriment of other considerations. Staffing aids organizational budgeting activities by recruiting and selecting capable and dedicated workers, providing them with necessary skills (orientation and training), detecting and remedying performance deficiencies (performance evaluation and employee development), and weeding out malcontents and incompetents. In effect, all staffing activities influence the budget function either directly or indirectly, given the fact that approximately 75 percent of any jurisdiction's expenditures consist of employee salaries and benefits.

Leading. The goal of leadership is to motivate workers to achieve organizational goals. As will be discussed in the next chapter, the leadership process requires certain prerequisites in order to be effective. Among these are that workers have appropriate expectations about the nature and purpose of the work they are performing, that they have the capabilities for accomplishing the work that is assigned to them, and that a suitable range of incentives be provided to reward successful effort. Obviously, the staffing function is instrumental to all of these activities.

For public managers to reap the full benefit of staffing's potential role in the management process, close collaboration between personnel departments and line managers is necessary. One of the most important developments in this regard is the tendency on the part of some personnelists to assume a *proactive* role in helping line managers to deal with their problems. Instead of emphasizing control to the exclusion of any other considerations (a *reactive* approach), these individuals become intimately involved in the realities of work situations in order to be able to develop strategies that can directly enhance the effectiveness of other managers.

Various authors have identified three specific types of activity that characterize the proactive approach to staffing (see Hays and Reeves, 1984: 83-85). The first, termed the advisory role, emphasizes the personnelists' responsibility to counsel and advise line managers on such matters as employee development, incentive programs, and the like. The diagnostician role (Dillon, 1975) envisions the personnelist as the focal point for information that will be used to formulate recommendations to other managers. By systematically collecting and analyzing data concerning agency operation and performance, the personnel department can diagnose such diverse problems as improperly defined job descriptions, inappropriate allocations of authority, and poor morale. Once problems are accurately diagnosed, the policy initiator and implementer role comes into play. This involves responsibility for proposing, drafting, and implementing policies and procedures to remedy recurring problems or to prevent anticipated ones (Beach, 1967: 56). Implicit within these staffing roles is an overarching perception of the personnelist as a trouble-shooter who teams up with line managers to improve organizational performance.

SPECIAL CHARACTERISTICS IN PUBLIC ORGANIZATIONS

Although there are many similarities between the staffing practices of government and industry, several important differences combine to make the public manager's task more complex than that of his or her private-sector counterpart. These differences can be roughly divided into three kinds: the lack of an economic imperative; the idea that public jobs are public resources; and what may be called "tradition."

Lack of an Economic Imperative. The private sector's biggest advantage over government is its unambiguous reason for existing. Business and industry use profit as the basic yardstick for all that they do. Public agencies, in contrast, are provided with relatively vague missions, such as "regulate in the public interest" or "improve public health and safety." As a result of such unspecific goals, there is no clear standard by which to judge their performance. This deprives public agencies of a major incentive to staff efficiently. With no generally agreed-upon definition of what constitutes efficient performance, they often have little reason to avoid overstaffing, or otherwise to guard the public's purse strings. Moreover, even if they do perform the staffing function with the utmost care and professionalism, few payoffs are likely to be forthcoming. Most legislatures are less concerned with efficient management (which is not widely visible to themselves or to the public) than they are with public approval, conformity with statutory requirements, and other less tangible measures of output.

Government's monopolistic character constitutes another major disincentive to efficient operation. Because there is no ready substitute for the services that most public agencies provide, their survival is virtually assured (see Kaufman, 1976). To some degree, this insulates government from the market forces—the competitive price, quality, and availability of the goods and services produced—that make most businesses keep close watch on their internal operations.

With the advent of privatization, some public jurisdictions have found themselves in a competitive environment. "Load-shedding" to the private sector (Morgan and England, 1988) through contracting, vouchers, and expanded use of volunteers is beginning to reshape the traditional economic insulation of the civil service. Whether or not this phenomenon will become sufficiently widespread to alter long-standing personnel practices is debatable. Yet, the fact is undeniable that in some areas of government activity—notably garbage collection and prison administration (Wollan, 1986)—the term "monopoly" no longer applies.

Public Jobs Are Public Resources. Although some public managers may view partial insulation from market forces as something akin to a fringe benefit, they pay a high price for this privilege. In exchange for the public funds that they receive, civil servants are subjected to a much wider range of controls and cross-checks than stockholders are apt to impose on their corporate employees. As was noted earlier, many of these controls take the form of procedures that reduce the staffing flexibility of public managers. To make matters worse, many important staffing decisions are not made by the managers themselves. For example, legislatures in many locations are directly responsible for decisions covering such topics as pay scales, benefit packages, raise and promotion criteria, reduction-in-force policies, transfer restrictions, and personnel ceilings. And because these issues are hammered out in the crucible of public opinion and political dialogue, staffing policy often becomes a political football that contending groups use to further personal or partisan interests. In addition to the potential damage to employee morale (for example, from seeing a cost-of-living raise traded away by the legislature in exchange for a new prison), external influence over basic staffing policies has a more serious and immediate consequence. The inability to control such decisions robs public managers of an important source of authority over their subordinates. If a supervisor cannot directly influence the size of his or her workers' raises or the level of their classifications, important sources of reward and punishment that are generally available to business managers are lost.

Tradition. After more than a century of experience with merit systems, government has developed certain standard operating procedures that have come to be sanctified by tradition. Although subject to occasional criticism and attack, these practices have a way of perpetuating themselves merely through the force of inertia. While each jurisdiction has its own unique variety, a few representative types seem to appear with regularity. The most pervasive of these is probably the "rule of three," which permits an appointing authority to select any one of the top three candidates of a civil-service register. Other examples include the federal government's attempt to achieve "regional representation" in its appointments of civil servants and the widespread practice of providing preference to military veterans when they compete for public jobs, regardless of the nature or duration of their service. There are also certain informal norms that constitute powerful staffing policies, even though they have not been sanctioned by statutes or procedural manuals. There is a strong propensity in most jurisdictions, for instance, to avoid the use of external searches (lateral entry) to fill most managerial vacancies, even when the pool of internal candidates is weak. These and other staffing maxims will be addressed a bit more thoroughly in later sections.

RECRUITMENT AND SELECTION

It is a truism that an organization's performance is largely dependent on the quality of its workers. Although training and intensive supervision can transform some less than desirable employees, it is easier to hire employees who are already capable and enthusiastic. Managers can save great amounts of time, energy, and aggravation by placing the right person in the right position. Among the probable benefits of a proper match of employee abilities to particular work situations are enhanced job satisfaction, greater productivity, lower turnover, and a reduction in the number of "problem" employees.

The level of line-manager involvement in recruitment and selection activities varies dramatically among jurisdictions. In the smallest personnel systems, as well as in some larger ones that are highly decentralized, almost all phases of the staffing process are controlled by the managers who will eventually supervise the employees being recruited. Centralized personnel systems, in contrast, may deprive line managers of any active role in the process, except perhaps to allow them to make the final selection from a handful of candidates.

Although most recruiting activities have traditionally been administered by central personnel offices, there is a definite trend toward the decentralization of many recruitment and selection functions. This phenomenon is especially pronounced at the federal level, where the Civil Service Reform Act of 1978 (CSRA) mandated a major delegation of recruiting authority to line managers. The Volcker Commission also emphasized this trend, with an apparent intent to make federal recruiting practices similar to corporate practices by allowing agencies to conduct their own recruitment efforts and examinations.

Some level of centralized involvement is also advocated, due to the increasing difficulties that are encountered in identifying and attracting talented applicants in a decentralized format (National Commission on the Public Service, 1989: 24-27). At present, hiring within the civil service is accomplished in three distinct ways. The traditional approach, *centralized certification*, is used for positions that occur government-wide. For these, it is viewed as most efficient to use a central point-of-entry for screening and referral. For positions that predominantly exist in one agency, such as air traffic controllers, *delegated examining* is often used. Here the central office (OPM) delegates authority to the agency to recruit and screen applicants, subject to OPM guidelines and approval. Under the most decentralized arrangement, *direct hire*, the agency is given authority to directly receive applications, to examine qualifications, and to make selections. This format is most often used in situations involving difficult-to-find personnel, such as engineers and nurses. Due to the paperwork and resulting delays associated with the first two approaches, the use of direct hire has exploded in recent years. By 1990, it accounted for 29 percent of all federal hires, as compared to 40 percent through delegated examining and 31 percent through central certification (U.S. General Accounting Office, 1990a).

STEPS IN THE RECRUITMENT PROCESS

In a decentralized recruitment setting, the following steps are performed with the active participation of line managers.

1. *Deciding where to search.* Once authorization has been obtained to fill a vacant position, the first issue to be confronted is whether

the agency will seek candidates from within the organization, go outside, or accept both internal and external applicants. The difficulty of making this decision can be greatly reduced if an effective human-resources planning program has been in operation. Where this is the case, a staffing inventory has been made before a vacancy occurs, from which it can be determined whether qualified candidates exist within the organization. This is accomplished by assessing the skills, abilities, and qualities of the current work force, comparing them to anticipated staffing needs, and deciding if training or other employee-development strategies are needed to enhance the promotional potential of particular candidates.

If, as is often the case, the decision is made to give preference to internal candidates, the manager may choose between transferring into the vacant position an employee who currently performs similar duties and promoting a lower-level worker into it. In any event, the outcome of the internal-external decision will greatly influence the remaining steps in the recruitment process. If internal selection is management's choice, then the other recruitment activities will probably be much less elaborate and formal than if an external search were to be conducted.

2. *Preparing the announcement.* Using the position's job description as a reference, a job announcement (or "position guide") is drawn up for use in advertising the opening. This announcement typically includes a description of major duties and responsibilities, a list of the requirements that candidates are expected to meet (*job specifications* or *job qualifications*), and other relevant information such as a brief description of the agency or the locale of employment. While designing the job announcement, managers may also seize the opportunity to alter the existing description of the position in order to accommodate changed circumstances. In the absence of an incumbent, it is relatively easy to downgrade a position that has become classified at too high a level or to upgrade a position that has acquired additional responsibilities.

3. *Advertising the vacancy.* Once the job announcement is written, the vacancy must be advertised in a manner consistent with both federal Equal Employment Opportunity guidelines and relevant policies in the agency and jurisdiction. Most merit systems operate (at least on the surface) according to the philosophy that employers should cast the widest possible net. In other words, they should advertise in as many locations and outlets as possible in order to attract the greatest number of applications. Many

agencies and jurisdictions maintain consolidated job listings, recruiting bulletins, or other centralized sources of information to assist potential job candidates. Others conduct recruitment campaigns at selected colleges, trade schools, and similar locations.

Increasingly, computers are utilized to provide applicants with information concerning job openings, *and* to assist managers in identifying and tracking those who have qualified for various types of positions. Through automation, on-line access to applicants' test scores, qualifications, and professional objectives gives managers an expedient way of targeting prospective employees. OPM's Automated Applicant Referral System, for instance, handles 600,000 applications per year, and has trimmed the processing time from twelve to three days since the mid-1980s. Much of the system is "paperless," permitting all entries and updates to be made on-line (U.S. General Accounting Office, 1990b: 39).

4. *Screening the applicants.* For most lower-level positions, civil-service applicants are required to take examinations that measure job-related knowledge and skills. Applicants for midlevel positions (managerial as well as most technical jobs) may also be evaluated by paper-and-pencil tests but more commonly are subjected to a less formal assessment. Ordinarily, this consists of a systematic (or, in many cases, a not-so-systematic) analysis of the candidates' education and experience through a review of their resumes or application forms. Candidates who achieve a satisfactory score are certified as eligible and placed on a register. Then, when a vacancy occurs in the job or job-category for which the candidates applied, the names of the highest-standing candidates on the register (the short list—usually three, but sometimes up to twenty, names) are referred to the appointing authority, generally the manager of the unit in which the vacancy exists. The manager is normally required to interview all of the candidates on the short list and to select from that group. Additional discretion is provided to managers in jurisdictions that permit "name requests," in which the appointing authority submits the name(s) of specific candidate(s) for inclusion on the certification register.

PROBLEMS IN THE PROCESS

Recruitment and selection procedures contain many pitfalls and imperfections. Sometimes these flaws make government recruitment activities appear to be haphazard, if not completely corrupt. Although there is not sufficient space for a thorough analysis of all of these problems, brief treatments of the most common and potentially damaging ones follow.

Preference for Internal Candidates. Many public agencies have a strong tendency to favor internal candidates over external ones, regardless of their relative qualifications. This predisposition is easily understandable, given the realities of organizational life. Elevating internal candidates maintains the morale of the other workers by supporting their belief that, through dedicated service, they too will be rewarded with promotions. Indeed, a single promotion will often set off a ripple effect in which many other workers move up their careers, thereby pleasing large numbers of them at one time (this is called the ladder effect). Moreover, internal candidates are likely to be viewed as safe bets, in that their strengths and weaknesses are already fairly well understood. External applicants, in contrast, are unknowns. In addition to threatening everyone's promotional opportunities, candidates from outside the organization are less likely to prove successful; their turnover rate is generally many times that of internal promotes. They may also be very expensive to attract and to train.

Although very compelling, these reasons are counterbalanced by certain important advantages of outside recruitment or "lateral entry," as it is sometimes called. If an agency has not been performing up to expectations, or if major change is in the offing, the new blood provided by lateral entry can be immensely helpful. If there is no clearly superior internal candidate, lateral entry can provide an escape from the bruised pride and charges of favoritism that may accompany the decision to promote a particular individual from within.

Thus, while a strong preference for internal recruitment may be defensible, it is not the best course of action in all circumstances. Agencies that eschew lateral entry entirely run the risk of becoming paralyzed by inertia. In the metaphor suggested by Anthony Downs (1967), an agency that has had no new blood to rejuvenate it ages by becoming more rule-bound and conservative. Similarly, an agency that fails to use vacancies as opportunities to recruit needed skills and abilities available only from outside candidates may end up simply rewarding existing mediocrity.

Most merit systems require that all vacancies be publicly announced and that all qualified applicants both from inside and from outside be considered—that is, an *open* recruitment process, which may be the optimal strategy. Nevertheless, many agencies never make a real effort to attract outside applications. In fact, it is widely acknowledged that many selections have already been made before the job announcements are written or the vacancies advertised. This situation can be exceedingly irritating to outside candidates who, until they realize what is happening, repeatedly apply for positions for which they are never seriously considered.

Recruitment Stereotyping. As was mentioned previously, vacancies represent important opportunities to public managers. The departure of an incumbent can prompt a needed reassessment of the vacated position and may lead to a reclassification or other significant redefinition of the job's scope and content. More commonly, however, in its haste to locate and hire a replacement, the agency seeks someone who is "just like" the original employee, and the only noticeable change is a new nameplate on the office door.

Other manifestations of recruitment stereotyping are equally common. Many applicants are the victims of stereotypes governing the appropriate characteristics for proper performance of the job for which they are applying. Male nurses, for example, do not fit the model that nurses are "supposed to be" female. This type of employment discrimination is now illegal except in the case of characteristics held to be bona fide occupational qualifications (BFOQs). Since almost all BFOQs stemming from race, sex, age, handicap, and the like have been ruled out as BFOQs either by legislation or judicial decrees, employment decisions cannot be based on such factors. Regrettably, however, their illegality does not necessarily mean that these criteria have ceased to play a role in the recruitment and selection process.

Shortcomings in the Exams. Until recently, the public sector relied heavily on paper-and-pencil examinations to screen prospective employees. This reliance dates back to the Pendleton Act, which also required the exams to be "practical in character." Succeeding generations argued over whether civil-service exams should even emphasize practical (job-related) abilities or general aptitude and intelligence, but the utility of examinations themselves was never questioned. However, in the early 1970s, confidence in the examinations was shaken by the shock waves of the movements for equal opportunity and affirmative action. The most severe blow came in the decision in the celebrated case of *Griggs v. Duke Power Company* (401 U.S. 424, 1971), in which the Supreme Court ruled that employment practices that had the effect of excluding minorities "must be shown to be related to job performance" in order to be valid. This ruling meant that entry and promotional examinations, as well as "credentialism" (educational and experience requirements), could not be used unless they were shown to be directly related to effective performance on the job.

For what was essentially the first time, therefore, public managers were required to take a critical look at civil-service examinations. What they saw was not very encouraging.

> Civil service examination validity coefficients are typically at about the .25 level and seldom greater than .50. In other words, performance on civil service examinations usually explains about 6 per cent of the variation in job performance and rarely more than 25 per cent. (Rosenbloom, 1973: 102)

Thus, a lengthy search has been under way for more reliable selection strategies. In 1982, the federal government abolished its standard exam for selecting college graduates for entry-level positions. The Professional and Administrative Career Examination (PACE) was found to be culturally (racially) biased, thereby precipitating a move toward specialized written examinations that could more easily be linked to job characteristics (Lanouette, 1981).

Without a centralized entry point such as PACE, federal agencies have subsequently relied on decentralized, noncompetitive hiring methods that emphasize specialized skills rather than general aptitude. This process has resulted in expanded minority hiring, but has potentially exposed the selection process to inappropriate (non-merit) criteria (Ban and Ingraham, 1988). O. Glenn Stahl alleges that the elimination of PACE is partly to blame for the "subversion" of the merit system, and thus calls for a "reinvigorated recruitment and competitive selection process" through a single point of entry system (1990: 318).

Amidst this uncertainty, the types of examinations that appear to be emerging as the new favorites among both public and private users are unassembled examinations, performance tests, and assessment centers (see Table 4-1). *Unassembled examinations* are commonly used in selecting the managerial and professional employees who once were required to pass general aptitude tests. This exam consists merely of a systematic—that is, scored—review of the applicants' education and experience, as reflected in resumes and job applications. Although quick and cheap, this type of exam has been criticized as being too subjective and prone to evaluator error (Levine and Flory, 1975). *Performance tests* include work samples (for example, candidate typists are required to type), physical achievement tests (for example, candidate firemen must carry a "body" down a ladder), and situational tests, in which candidates for managerial positions display their skills in handling common job situations or problems. These tests are generally regarded as being highly valid, but their major drawbacks are that they are often expensive to administer and that they are not applicable to many job categories. *Assessment centers* consist of a battery of test exercises, including in-basket simulations, oral presentations, leadership games, group discussions, and essay writing (Howard, 1974). The performance of candidates on these exercises is evaluated by "assessors," who hold positions comparable to the one being sought; the resulting evaluations are pooled and analyzed and an overall rating is assigned. Because this technique uses multiple forms of evaluation and multiple raters, it is thought by some to be the most reliable testing strategy available. Thus, its use is spreading rapidly (Ross, 1985), despite the fact that assessment centers are very expensive ($400 to $600 per applicant) and time consuming.

Determining the validity of any type of examination—that is, learning how well it actually predicts job performance—is also an expensive and time-consuming process, yet it cannot be avoided. Unvalidated exams are vulnerable to legal challenge. Moreover, unless high scores on an exam have been shown to be statistically correlated with good job performance (this is called "criterion-related validation"), the exam instrument can never really be trusted to perform its intended function. Today, *all* screening techniques, from minimum educational requirements to the most sophisticated performance appraisals, are legally regarded as tests and must be validated accordingly. By this standard, it is reasonable to assume that a large portion of the staffing decisions made daily throughout the nation are based on unvalidated or faulty evidence.

Circumvention of Selection Procedures. While inappropriate or ineffective staffing techniques account for most of the breakdowns in recruitment and selection, some of the most egregious departures from accepted staffing principles are intentional. When tedious procedures inhibit their staffing flexibility, many public managers simply go around the merit-system requirements. If, for instance, the manager wishes to assist one special applicant over all others, a variety of handy techniques is available. As Shafritz (1974: 487) has pointed out, some public managers will pressure their personnel offices to "reduce the qualifications for a specific position, or to lower the pass point on an entry or promotional exam." Or, if the opportunity presents itself, the position may be redesigned with the favored applicant in mind. In a process called "creative position description," a list of job requirements is drawn up that effectively excludes other applicants. For candidates who have already been certified but who are not included on the short list, "waiting out the register" may be the circumvention strategy. This is accomplished by waiting patiently until everyone above the preferred candidate on the register has either dropped off or been selected for another position, at which time the manager announces the vacancy. Finally, most merit systems permit managers to make appointments to

Table 4-1 Newer Types of Public-Sector Examinations

Exam Type	Description	Advantages and Disadvantages	Primary Uses
Unassembled examination	Evaluation of applicants' training and experience as determined from their resumés and completed applications; comparison of training and experience to the job requirements listed in the position announcement	Very inexpensive to design and administer; candidates not required to be present, so wider pool of applicants can be attracted. Requires excessive number of judgments on the evaluators' part, often leading to overemphasis on quantitative rather than qualitative factors ("credentialism"); low validity due to "fudge factor" and evaluator error	Selection of professional workers; may be coupled with oral interviews for lower-level jobs
Performance tests	Measures of workers' ability to *do* rather than of what they know; includes tests of physical and verbal skills	Inexpensive to design, although may be relatively expensive to administer due to need for proctors or evaluators; are well-liked by applicants because they are easy to understand and feedback is immediate; validity easy to establish. May be applicable only to lower-level workers; can be very expensive to design and administer if applied to professional or managerial workers	Selection of clerical and technical workers and of workers in jobs requiring physical agility or strength

Oral examination	Structured interview administered by a panel or single evaluator; job-related questions are asked in a predetermined format and sequence; responses are scored numerically	Popular among managers because they can see applicants "in action"; may reveal shortcomings in applicants that are not brought out by other instruments. Unreliable, time-consuming, expensive, and inefficient; excessively subjective, yield inconsistent results, and often do not probe job-related knowledge sufficiently	Selection of high-level and mid-level managerial personnel and professional employees
Assessment centers	Applicants proceed through a series of individual and group exercises that are evaluated by a team of raters; overall scores are determined by rater discussion and consensus	Very reliable because raters are trained prior to participation; test emphasizes behavior, not irrelevant factors; provides multiple measures. Very expensive; limited applicability to lower-level workers	Promotion decisions for managerial and some professional workers
Self-selection	Applicants are provided with detailed description of job requirements, including perhaps videotaped displays of typical and unpleasant aspects of the job; applicants then judge their own ability and desire to perform the job	Discourages frivolous applications; screens out possible "turnover" prior to training and orientation; very acceptable technique from the applicants' perspective; highly valid. Very expensive to design and administer; applicability limited to jobs that experience constant turnover and that are characterized by unpleasant working conditions or strenuous physical requirements	Selection of police, fire, and correctional personnel

Sources: Steven W. Hays and Richard C. Kearney, "Examinations in the Public Service," in *Centenary Issues of the Pendleton Act of 1883*, ed. David H. Rosenbloom (New York: Marcel Dekker, 1982), 25-44; R. D. Arvey, *Fairness in Selecting Employees* (Reading, Mass.: Addison-Wesley, 1979); W. F. Cascio and N. F. Phillips, "Performance Testing: A Rose among Thorns?" *Personnel Psychology* 32 (1979): 751-766.

temporary positions. Because these jobs are not supposed to last for more than a few months, they are exempt from almost all competitive procedures; but once employed, occupants of temporary positions have an advantage in competing for permanent openings. Some studies have also shown that "temporary" employees sometimes (even if illegally) hold their jobs for decades (Tolchin and Tolchin, 1971; Freedman, 1988).

Patronage. Often, the impetus for violating merit requirements can be traced to elected officials who seek to use public positions to fulfill partisan objectives. By pressuring well-placed civil servants to cooperate, politicians can find jobs for friends and supporters and further the careers of those who are already employed in particular agencies. Even the most professional and virtuous public manager will be tempted to accommodate to such pressure, for to do otherwise might lead to greater damage to the agency (for example, a reduction in its budget or weakening of its statutory authority). Conversely, even the most ethical politician may feel the need to engage in patronage activities. As Tolchin and Tolchin (1971: 41) have described so eloquently, John Lindsay, while mayor of New York City, was transformed from a fervent opponent of patronage to one of its worst abusers when he realized, after many bitter experiences, that he could not govern the city *without* patronage. He needed it to overcome political opposition, to keep the labor unions peaceful, to cultivate good relations with business, and to maintain his own political-party following.

In reality, then, it is naive to expect patronage to be completely eradicated. Public managers who enter office thinking otherwise are normally (and quickly) disabused of any notions to the contrary. However, it must also be pointed out that patronage considerations touch only a tiny percentage of public positions in all but the most politicized environments. Favoritism exhibited by public managers themselves is a far more common enemy of staffing by merit. From the perspective of citizens, especially those who are seeking public employment, this realization is likely to have two related effects. Many will attempt to exploit the situation by gaining access to influential public managers or elected officials, while virtually all may come to believe that, at least in some public agencies, the most important guideline in seeking employment is: "It's not *what* you know but *who* you know!"

Inadequate Systems. Finally, while many jurisdictions possess sophisticated personnel systems that rival those of major corporations, many more have merit systems that are very poorly structured and operated. For example, one report found that in 172 large city and county jurisdictions that were surveyed only 48 percent used competitive examinations, only 30 percent maintained civil-service registers, and only 49 percent engaged in any systematic recruitment activities. Even these data fail to communicate the true seriousness of the problem, for they apply to *large* jurisdictions, while most civil servants are employed by smaller governmental units that are even *less* likely to operate sophisticated personnel systems. Indeed, most studies have shown that it does not become cost-effective even to create a separate personnel department until the jurisdiction employs more than 200 workers. It can therefore be assumed that a large portion of the public managers who exercise staffing responsibilities do so without the assistance of a full-time personnel office. This situation may be conducive to a desirable degree of flexibility, but it can also represent a severe impediment to effective recruitment and selection. The absence of centralized personnel services means that the manager must either perform all routine staffing functions personally (and probably very informally) or delegate them to someone who may lack any relevant professional training. It can thus be conjectured that the personnel systems in most of these jurisdictions fall far short of the textbook description of how a personnel system ought to be maintained.

EMPLOYEE UTILIZATION

Once recruitment and selection have been (for the time being) completed, the primary concern of most managers is to ensure that the employees who have been hired are effectively utilized. Ever since the scientific management movement during the first few decades of this century, *position classification* has governed employee utilization in most public agencies. Called the "central hub" of public personnel management (Mosher, 1984: 79), position classifications provide the foundation on which almost all other staffing decisions are based. They consist of a sequence of activities in which: (1) all jobs in the organization's personnel system are defined in terms of their duties and responsibilities; (2) the jobs are compared with one another in order to establish a hierarchy of classes based on their relative levels of importance; (3) a standardized set of job titles is assigned; and (4) the resulting classes are used as the basis for determining salary levels or ranges (taking into account the salaries and fringe benefits among comparable employers in the same geographical area). By this procedure, organizations theoretically reap the following benefits:

Objective definition of the content of all jobs
Establishment of clearly defined career ladders

Control of pay levels and assurance that employees performing
　　comparable work are receiving comparable pay
Creation of a uniform job terminology
Establishment of experience and education requirements that
　　are clearly linked to job characteristics (thereby aiding
　　recruitment and selection)
Identification of inconsistencies and duplications in work as-
　　signments
Protection against political or personal preference in the deter-
　　mination of salary levels and career paths

Although they are essential elements of nearly every modern
personnel system, position classifications seldom arouse enthusiasm
among line managers. They do make possible rational career ladders and
indeed are the basis for *rank-in-job* career systems, but managers object to
their rigidity; indeed, they are often cited as one of the chief impediments to managerial flexibility. Career ladders based on job classifications amount to closed systems. Once an employee is assigned to a job,
he or she is in many ways pigeonholed. The particular duties of that job
come to be perceived as being that person's specialty. Subsequent moves
up the career ladder will ordinarily be confined to similar positions in
the classification series. Moreover, the rules of the classification system
ordinarily preclude managers from giving duties to the individual job-
holder that are not included in the formal position description. Thus, for
example, a word-processing specialist may be formally ineligible to
supervise other workers, even if capable of doing so. If a supervisor
wants to reward the word-processing specialist for outstanding performance, the ability to do so is constrained by the salary levels that are
attached to the employee's classification. Employees at the top of their
pay grades cannot receive any increases beside cost-of-living adjustments (COLAs); other employees are limited to a raise determined by a
set percentage, a pay step, or some similar rule.

From the perspective of line managers, then, rank-in-job career
systems limit their flexibility. Most jobs are so narrowly defined
("overspecialized") that their occupants are not able to use their talents
and capabilities fully. Employee morale suffers because many workers
are trapped in dead-end jobs that may or may not accurately reflect their
interests. Because managers are generally unable to provide substantial
rewards to deserving employees, work initiative and productivity may
suffer. For these reasons, alternative career systems have become attractive.

Rank-in-person (or *rank-in-corps*) career systems stress managerial
flexibility rather than organizational control. Instead of the narrow

functional specialties of rank-in-job systems, employees are grouped into broad, generalist-oriented pools. Two common examples are university faculty and the military. In these systems, most employees enter at the bottom and work their way up the career ladder. Few jobs are exclusively reserved for individuals with specialist skills (other than subject-matter areas, in the case of faculty), so most employees perform a wide variety of tasks during their careers. Salary and rank have much more to do with a person's competence and length of service than with the particular tasks being performed, and assignments are normally based more on general aptitude than on any other criterion.

Although not applicable to all public-sector positions, rank-in-person career systems are being increasingly utilized. Their recent popularity is largely attributable to an important experiment launched by the federal government in 1978. As part of the government's attempt to reform its personnel system, the CSRA provided for the creation of a Senior Executive Service (SES). This is a separate personnel system for managers who had formerly been classified within the top three grades of the General Schedule of civil-service classifications (GS-16 through GS-18). The stated purpose of this rank-in-person career system is to provide top federal managers with increased discretion over their administrative corps. Classification-based distinctions within this group were abolished, and senior executives were instead placed in a general pool of managers. All occupants of the pool are subject to assignment, reassignment, and removal on the basis of their aptitude and performance. Unencumbered by classification restrictions, the senior executives can be placed wherever their talents are most needed; thus, they can be moved from job to job and from agency to agency, depending on the desires of their superiors. This situation contrasts with the previous system, in which federal employees were insulated from both unwanted *and* desired reassignments and transfers.

Enticed by the promise of greater managerial flexibility, many state and local governments have instituted their own versions of the SES (Dresang, 1982; Abramson, 1987). Like the federal system, most of the new rank-in-person career systems are confined to the upper reaches of bureaucracy. But as experience with the new systems is gained, further extensions of their coverage are likely to occur, despite mixed reviews from those who have analyzed the state SES experience to date (Sherwood and Breyer, 1987). The federal government, for instance, has considered moving the SES down to the level of GS-12.

Before position classifications are scrapped altogether, however, the reverse side of flexibility should be examined. The implementation of a rank-in-person career system has the effect of diminishing the jurisdiction's control over its work force. Although numerous checks and balances can be built into the system, the level of control that is available through a classification scheme can never be fully restored. The federal government's experience with the SES has suggested that, despite the presence of safeguards, the civil service has become more vulnerable to political manipulation. Since most SES members work directly for political appointees, rather than for other career employees, political criteria have crept into many staffing decisions. As a result of this and other problems, the morale of SES members is reported to be quite low, and an exodus of talented senior executives is underway (Ingraham and Barrilleaux, 1983: Lewis, 1991). Despite this negative side, however, the SES has also been found to have "solid managerial potential" (Perry and Miller, 1991). Over 75 percent of the SES members report that the system has worked "well or very well," although complaints persist about inadequate pay and political intrusions (Goldstein, 1989; Huddleston, 1991).

It appears, then, that neither of these systems is uniformly superior; each one involves certain trade-offs. A career system that relies entirely on position classification reduces flexibility, while one that is purely rank-in-person lays itself open to political exploitation. For this reason, most career systems try to combine the two models, although the rank-in-job type is certainly predominant in most jurisdictions. Reforms like the SES are likely to continue, however, and the forces that prompted them will not go away. Because the pressures for flexibility and productivity are so pervasive, other methods of using public employees more effectively will attract increasing attention. Two of these are briefly discussed below.

JOB DESIGN STRATEGIES

Depending on the character of a jurisdiction's personnel system, certain job design strategies can increase employee motivation while also solving other staffing problems. Although the goal of job design was once to break jobs down into their most basic parts so that they could be routinized (an outgrowth of time-and-motion studies), it has since come to mean the opposite. Today, the term is used to refer to strategies that expand the variety and complexity of tasks associated with a job so that it becomes more challenging and fulfilling for its occupants. The three most common of these strategies are job rotation, job enlargement, and job enrichment.

As the name implies, *job rotation* calls for the movement of workers from one job to another. When workers sample the tasks performed by their co-workers, the technique's proponents argue, boredom will decline, workers will gain a better understanding of their role in the organization, and motivation consequently will increase. Its detractors, however, maintain that job rotation merely exposes workers "to a different series of monotonous and boring jobs" (Ivancevich, Szilagyi, and Wallace, 1977: 148). Despite this uncertainty over its effects, the strategy is widely used in both public and private organizations, though less as a motivational tool than as a means of preparing workers for promotions or to fill in for other employees who become temporarily absent.

Job enlargement (which is sometimes referred to by a particularly ugly jargonistic term, "horizontal job loading") involves an expansion in the number and variety of tasks that a particular worker performs. It is distinguished from job rotation by the fact that the wider range of duties is permanently affixed to the position; the worker does not have to go from job to job in order to experience a variety of tasks. Public-sector examples of job enlargement are often found in departments of public safety. Many jurisdictions "cross-train" public-safety personnel to serve in both police and fire capacities. Some pay certain personnel more money if they acquire the ability to take on added responsibilities; police officers who learn how to give crime-proofing demonstrations, for instance, receive a salary supplement. Although the available empirical evidence is inconclusive, there is some indication that job enlargement reduces absenteeism. Additionally, Korman (1977: 301) reports that the quality and level of employee performance are positively affected by job-enlargement programs.

Job enrichment is the most sophisticated of these three design approaches. Whereas the other two strategies are intended to expand the variety of the worker's *tasks,* job enrichment is concerned with increasing the employee's *responsibility and authority.* An invention of Frederick Herzberg (whose work is discussed in the next chapter), this motivational strategy is based on the belief that most workers desire autonomy and responsibility more than anything else. Also referred to as vertical job loading, job enrichment requires managers to surrender some of their traditional decision-making prerogatives to their subordinates. Workers are to be provided with greater authority over resource allocations, standards of performance, and problem solving. The manager thereby demonstrates faith in the workers' ability, which heightens their sense of accomplishment, autonomy, and self-worth.

Perhaps the best-known public-sector foray into job enrichment was the experience with management by objectives (Jun, 1976; see also Chapter 2). Although not a pure form of job enrichment, MBO was based on most of the same assumptions about human motivation and the desire for autonomy. Under MBO, managers and subordinates jointly established performance objectives, after which little overt control was exercised over the workers. Instead, each work group operated much like a small business (a "profit center"), with a relatively free hand in decision making, resource allocation, scheduling, and work distribution. Thus the workers were endowed with increased responsibility, authority, and latitude of action. The manager, meanwhile, performed the role of a coach, assisting the work team when necessary but not taking an active part in day-to-day operations. Managerial control was supposed to be achieved through pursuit of the objectives that had been jointly established; theoretically, the sole concern of the organization was the unit's performance, as measured by the degree to which its goals were achieved.

Despite its appeal, MBO was a failure in the thousands of jurisdictions in which it was attempted. Among the many explanations that have been offered for its demise, the one that is most widely accepted is also the most disquieting: public managers simply were unable and/or unwilling to permit meaningful employee participation in decision making. Whether this phenomenon was attributable to the managers' insecurity or to an artifact of the system is unclear. Its significance, however, will become even more pronounced in the discussion of employee motivation in the next chapter. As will be noted, the fundamental assumptions of job enrichment have been supported by empirical research, suggesting that managers would be well served if they were to delegate more authority to their subordinates.

SCHEDULING STRATEGIES

Compared to changes in job design, alterations in work schedules seem somewhat pedestrian. In actuality, however, new scheduling strategies are one of the most interesting frontiers in the staffing field. They have caused managers to question some of their traditional assumptions about the nature of work, and they have proved to be remarkably effective at improving employee productivity.

The traditional concept of a standardized work week is nothing more than a creation of the industrial revolution, which aimed at providing managers with greater control over their work force. While the standard work week—today, typically a five-day week of seven or eight hours a day—may still be applicable to some industrial situations (assembly lines, for example), it is not generally required by the needs and technologies of public agencies (Committee on Alternative Work Patterns, 1976). It has survived primarily through inertia, though in the case of public employment, it is reinforced by the Supreme Court's recent decision in *Garcia v. San Antonio Metropolitan Transit Authority* (469 U.S. 528, 1985), which held that the Fair Labor Standards Act was applicable to government agencies.

With the advent of *Workforce 2000,* the changing character of the American labor force has led managers to search for alternative schedules that are better suited to today's employees. Working mothers with dependent children, employees who are reliant on public transportation, and other workers with a variety of external responsibilities and constraints frequently find it difficult to conform to the standard work week. Low morale, high absenteeism, tardiness, and short-term leaves have all been attributed to inflexible schedules (Committee on Alternative Work Patterns, 1976). It is also important to realize that, in state and local governments, part-time employment is growing at a faster rate than full-time employment, thereby creating additional pressures for scheduling changes (Long and Post, 1980).

By far the most promising and widely used nontraditional scheduling strategy is *flextime* (or flexitime). Sometimes termed "variable work scheduling," flextime breaks the work day into "core time" and "flexible time." Core time is the portion of the day when all workers are required to be present. Employees are permitted to choose the times when they will work during the remainder of the day—the flexible hours. As applied in most organizations, flextime allows employees to start work any time between 6:00 a.m. and 10:00 a.m. and to leave between 3:00 p.m. and 7:00 p.m. The period from 10:00 a.m. to 3:00 p.m. is the core time. Other organizations schedule flexible hours in the middle of the day to accommodate professional development activities or to allow employees to attend to personal business.

Flextime has received numerous testimonials from public managers who have observed its effects in the improvement of productivity. In one notable experiment (a regional office of the Social Security Administration), flextime was found to have increased productivity by 12 percent and to have eliminated tardiness, reduced the short-term leave problem, and improved employee morale by "letting the employees know they're adult enough to make their own decisions" (Committee on Alternative Work Patterns, 1976: 3). Other benefits that have been cited include more effective use of equipment and facilities, lower absenteeism, fewer overtime expenses, a decrease in rush-hour traffic, and greater success in affirmative action efforts (owing to the fact that a large percentage of minority families are one-parent households and therefore benefit from flextime). The major complaints about flextime are that it disrupts telephone coverage, interferes with employee availability for meetings, and limits face-to-face contacts between employees and their supervisors.

Compressed time, under which employees work fewer but longer days, has long been used in police and fire departments. The most common format is to allow employees to work four consecutive ten-hour days, thus entitling them to a three-day weekend. A more recently introduced scheduling approach is *job sharing,* in which one job is divided between two employees. This strategy is especially helpful in the employment of working parents, older employees, and the physically handicapped (Long and Post, 1980). Many jurisdictions are making liberal use of *part-time* work schedules because of the cost savings and scheduling flexibility that they offer. Part-time workers do not ordinarily receive fringe benefits, and their schedules can be changed at will. Finally, the technological revolution is leading to something that might be called freestyle scheduling. Some workers are permitted to work at home, using modems and other computer hookups as their links to the office. If this practice becomes widespread, the traditional work week will be bid a not-so-fond farewell.

TRAINING, EMPLOYEE DEVELOPMENT, AND RELATED SERVICES

Training is another staffing function that is undergoing a major transformation in the face of changing technology and work force characteristics. The Hudson Institute's (1987) forecasts concerning the future labor force presents a critical challenge to employers. Workers in the future will be drawn predominantly from sectors of the labor pool with the *least* education and work experience. Meanwhile, the employers' need for workers with specialized skills and technological sophistication will inexorably increase. The obvious result is that employers will have no choice but to invest in training and development opportunities for their workers.

Training within public agencies is already big business. The need to emphasize "the lifelong acquisition of new information" has long been recognized (Sylvia and Meyer, 1990: 132). The governmental response has generally been impressive, with a proliferation of training and employee development programs occurring in recent years. As long ago as 1958 the federal government's Employee Training Act provided for systematic and continuing education programs focusing on technical and management skills. Additional programs were added over the years, leading to exponential increases in the number of workers trained, and in the array of topics that are discussed in the on-going programs.

Similar growth occurred at the state level, spurred in part by federal initiatives. Federally funded programs, for instance, must be administered within clearly defined limits and guidelines. To ensure program compliance, most states developed training programs for state and local workers administering federal funds (Sylvia and Meyer, 1990). Another boost to state and local training efforts came through the Intergovernmental Personnel Act (IPA), which was intended to expand and upgrade merit systems in state and local government. Many states used the bulk of those new resources to establish training centers, most of which survived the demise of the IPA program.

Today, training is directed at any one of four broad goals: production (to improve the delivery of services by upgrading technical and managerial skills); adaptation (to assist employees in adjusting to the changing demands of their environment); socialization (to shape workers' values and perceptions, and to orient them regarding rules and assignments); and coordination (to reduce internal conflict, establish a team orientation, and enhance communication) (Sylvia and Meyer, 1990). These objectives are pursued through a variety of training formats focusing on such subjects as technical skills (for example, computer technology), managerial competence (decision-making strategies, delegation), problem-solving, planning, conflict management, goal-setting, team-building, and the like. Although most training is managed by each agency or department, the federal government and most states also maintain centralized training facilities and programs. The federal efforts are concentrated in four regional training centers, and at the Federal Executive Institute at Charlottesville, Virginia.

An important phenomenon in the training field is the symbiosis that exists between employee development objectives and the rapid push toward professionalization. Many groups wishing to elevate their professional qualifications and reputations have organized continuing education efforts, and a few (such as government finance officers) have even initiated certification examinations in some states. This movement is likely to continue, and is clearly spreading into the more "generic" management disciplines. Nearly twenty states, for example, now run Certified Public Manager Programs (CPM) that specify continuing education requirements for mid-level and upper-level administrators. Although these programs are almost always voluntary, there is little doubt that there is a gradual movement toward making the certification process a formal requirement.

The underside of employee development, dealing with the addictions and emotional problems of today's work force, is also generating a concerted response within public agencies. According to most sources, approximately 20 percent of all workers suffer from alcohol and/or drug addiction, or nervous disorders that diminish their productivity and contribute to health care costs. This problem is expected to worsen as the demographics of the labor pool changes. Minorities suffer disproportionately high rates of addiction, and the incidence of other forms of personal stress (marital discord, family problems, financial hardship) are increasing in all employee groups.

Employee Assistance Programs (EAPs) are becoming a common organizational response to the stresses of modern life. EAPs are viewed as "a management tool, a service to the troubled employee, and a strategy to fight rising health care costs and insurance premiums" (Johnson and O'Neill, 1989: 68). Their purpose is to identify, diagnose, counsel, and refer employees with personal problems (Johnson and O'Neill, 1989: 69). More than one-half of all public employers currently manage EAPs, which is significantly more than are found in the private sector (Foster-Higgins and Company, 1988).

EAPs exist in many diverse forms. They may be provided in-house, or contracted out. They may focus on only a small number of problems (addiction, most commonly), or on the full range of maladies (Johnson and O'Neill, 1989). Some provide treatment and counseling within the agency's own personnel office, while others refer cases to external medical care workers.

Whatever forms they take, EAPs are becoming one of the most important benefits available to civil servants. They function in a non-threatening manner, in that workers with problems are not dealt with punitively. Self-referrals are most common, although supervisors are encouraged (and in many instances, trained) to constructively confront employees who are thought to be impaired in some way. EAPs thus join training as another employee development tool that is used to enhance the capability and productivity of today's public worker.

PAY FOR PERFORMANCE

It has long been one of the most frequent complaints of public managers that their inability to reward good performance obstructed effective supervision. As one major study noted, "Existing procedures make it extremely difficult to provide a meaningful reward for high quality performance or to withhold pay increases for low quality performance. This situation tends to foster mediocre performance" (President's Reorganization Project, 1977: 147). Because most compensation systems provide employees with automatic annual step (longevity) increases, about the only requirement for a raise has been that the worker be warm and breathing at the end of the year.

Given the obvious dysfunctions of this method of salary administration, longevity-based raises have become a favored target of today's civil-service reformers. In their place, *pay for performance*, often called *merit pay*, has become popular. Spurred on by the promise of increased output and greater accountability, the federal and many state governments have made pay for performance a cornerstone of their civil-service reform programs (Argyle, 1982). Yet after several years of experience with merit-pay systems, grumbling can be heard among both managers and employees. One author has called pay for performance "an expensive, complicated and inequitable" program (Silverman, 1982: 29), and others have blamed it for high turnover and low morale (Reese and Ma, 1981). Despite this, pay-for-performance systems had been created in nearly one-half the states by 1990, and their popularity showed no signs of easing (U.S. General Accounting Office, 1990b).

In order to implement a merit-pay system, jurisdictions typically begin by eliminating fixed pay increases. Employees no longer receive automatic longevity raises but instead are assigned salaries within specific pay ranges. These ranges consist of the minimum and maximum salaries allowable for particular positions, as determined by their classification and accompanying pay grade. Thus, the pay range for a grade 25 might be $15,000 to $22,000. Merit raises within the range are determined in one of several ways. Some jurisdictions provide the manager with almost unlimited discretion, setting only a cap (20 percent is common) on the magnitude of a merit raise in any one year. Others provide as many as 35 small steps within the pay range, thereby encouraging managers to make very fine distinctions among employees in the same classifications (Van Adelsberg, 1978). Still other jurisdictions establish fixed raises for various levels of performance: minimally competent effort may be rewarded with a 2.5 percent increase; competent performance receives 4.0 percent; and exceptional performance might earn the worker 6.0 percent. Yet another strategy is to provide workers with bonuses that are allocated according to a formula, either a percentage of savings attributable to employee productivity gains, or a set amount for each level of performance. Bonuses are becoming popular because they limit the growth of salary expenditures. Since bonuses are not added to base salaries, they do not influence the size of future raises that are computed on a percentage basis (COLAs, for example).

Regardless of a jurisdiction's specific approach to merit pay, line managers are ultimately responsible for making the program work. Some pay-for-performance systems require them to make only yes/no decisions (does an employee deserve a raise or not?), while others demand that managers assess relative performance (how do various employees compare with one another?). In either case, managers are obliged to monitor and evaluate employee performance. Obviously, these are not simple tasks. A review of the recent literature points to the following pitfalls along the path to a properly functioning merit-pay system:

1. *Lack of legislative cooperation.* In order to work, a merit-pay system must be properly funded. If it isn't, the entire program is perceived as a sham. Unfortunately, many legislative bodies have

enacted merit-pay plans but have then neglected to provide the requisite funding. This has been notably the case at the federal level, where only a small percentage of the promised funding ever materialized. Additionally, some legislatures are fond of setting arbitrary salary or increase ceilings that inhibit managers' ability to give adequate rewards for outstanding performance (Godwin and Needham, 1981; Perry, 1990).

2. *Difficulty of allocating increases.* Unless the merit pool is generously funded, the granting of a sizeable raise to one worker implies the denial of raises to others. Thus, if a merit pool of $4,000 is available to provide raises to four workers, the manager is presented with a distasteful choice: give a substantial raise to one or two workers and little or nothing to the others, who may well be competent, if not outstanding; or simply give all of them the same amount. Rather than punish several workers to reward a few, many managers select the latter option.

3. *Adverse motivational effect.* Many authors argue that pay for performance places undue emphasis on rewards and punishments and that this is not an effective way to motivate today's workers (Thayer, 1978). Indeed, merit pay may even be a *disincentive* to improve performance and may adversely affect employee morale. (For further discussion, see Chapter 5.)

4. *Measurement problems.* Merit-pay systems lead managers to emphasize the kinds of performance that can be measured quantitatively, because a quantitative criterion for salary determinations renders them less vulnerable to charges of subjectivity and favoritism. However, the performance of public workers often is not easily measured, and many of the goals that are identified often have little to do with the employees' performance (Perry, Petrakis, and Miller, 1989). For example, how does one measure "industrial compliance with state health and safety codes," and to what extent can regulatory employees be held responsible if industries violate those codes? A related problem arises from the fact that, since goals are often amorphous, employees may be motivated to look good, irrespective of their actual performance. Similarly, reliance on quantifiable goals may lead employees to emphasize measurable output (the number of cases cleared or clients interviewed) over qualitative concerns (proper handling of the cases or obtaining needed information).

5. *Unfavorable effects of interpersonal relations.* Merit-pay programs place both managers and employees in uncomfortable situations. Managers may be required to make fine distinctions among the performances of employees, perhaps on the basis of very superfi-

cial evidence. Breaking the bad news to a worker who is not receiving a raise can be a very emotional and unpleasant experience for both parties. Moreover, workers who are deprived of merit raises often attribute that fact to favoritism or other non-performance-based criteria. Finally, few managers and workers enjoy the evaluation process. Great interpersonal skills, as well as much time and scrupulous impartiality, are necessary to perform the task effectively (O'Toole and Churchill, 1982).

Is pay for performance then, anything more than an elusive fantasy? More specifically, what can be done by line managers to make merit-pay systems viable? Although there is no magic formula, there are a few indications that pay for performance *can* be made to work if adequate resources are provided. Since most of these positive signs have appeared in regard to the performance evaluation process, they will be discussed in that context.

PERFORMANCE APPRAISAL

The critical importance of performance appraisal to the staffing process was widely recognized long before pay for performance thrust it into the limelight. In fact, the performance-appraisal process has probably been the subject of more discussion, argument, and research than any other facet of staffing. This high level of professional interest is attributable to the many purposes that performance evaluation serves: (1) to communicate management goals and objectives to employees, (2) to distribute organizational rewards such as salary increases and promotions equitably, (3) to motivate employees to improve their performance, and (4) to facilitate personnel-management research (Klingner, 1980: 227-228). In addition, performance appraisals provide a validity check for all other staffing functions. They allow line managers to assess, among other things, the effectiveness of recruitment and selection practices, training activities, and promotion and transfer decisions (Lovrich, 1990).

This diversity of uses is reflected in two empirical examinations of performance appraisals in state governments. Feild and Holley (1975) reported that performance appraisals are used for the following decisions, in descending order of importance: promotions, demotions, and layoffs; staff planning; salary adjustments; communication between supervisors and subordinates; determination of management development needs; updating of position descriptions; and validation of selection and promotional procedures. The study by Tyer (1982) yielded similar results, except that "communication between superiors and subordinates" and "salary adjustments" were the top of the list. In all, nearly 40 states reported that performance appraisals were "very important" sources of information for a wide range of staffing decisions (Tyer, 1982: 203).

Nevertheless, there is very little agreement within the staffing community concerning the optimal strategy for performance appraisal. During the past 40 years, public managers have experimented with literally hundreds of different approaches. More often than not, the results were disappointing. Although a best appraisal strategy has not been (and probably will not be) discovered, a great deal of information has been collected concerning more and less effective procedures.

THREATS TO VALIDITY

Some of the most valuable lessons have come through the identification of several types of threats to the validity of the appraisal process. The first type of threat is through errors in appraisal instruments:

1. *Use of irrelevant variables.* Some appraisal instruments focus almost entirely on "proxies of performance," such as initiative, enthusiasm, dependability, and loyalty (Robbins, 1978: 216-243). While these may be interesting traits, they generally have little to do with job performance and are exceedingly subjective factors. Different evaluators will use different definitions and standards when assessing them. Moreover, since they relate to factors that are seldom directly observable, raters (almost always the employees' direct supervisor) must make inferences before they can evaluate (Feild and Holley, 1975).
2. *Giving equal weight to all factors.* Many widely used appraisal instruments assume that every item evaluated has the same importance. "Learning ability" may be given the same weight as "dealing with people" even if 95 percent of the person's time is spent meeting the public. Thus, undeserved emphasis is given to some factors, while others are slighted.
3. *Use of inappropriate instruments.* Perhaps the most widespread evaluation error in government is that of using the same variables to assess workers performing widely divergent jobs. Managers, clerks, laborers, and technical specialists may all be evaluated on the same form, using the same criteria. Tyer (1982) found that 34 states used the same form to evaluate supervisory and nonsupervisory personnel, though it should be obvious that different behaviors are required from the two groups.

The other common threat to appraisal validity is error on the part of the evaluator:

1. *Inflation.* The most recurrent error of evaluators is their tendency to rate employees more positively than they deserve ("positive leniency"). This tendency is attributable to the anxiety that accompanies the evaluation process; managers want to avoid the unpleasantness associated with a negative appraisal. Additionally, positive evaluations "require less time to explain" (Prather, 1974: 739).

2. *Halo effect.* This occurs when the rater generalizes from one component of the evaluation to the entire evaluation. For example, if "quantity of work" is the first factor on the evaluation instrument and the employee's performance is particularly good on it, all the subsequent factors may be given higher ratings than they would be otherwise. Conversely, if the rater's overall impression of the worker is "average," all the factors on the evaluation form may be given "average" ratings, irrespective of the worker's actual performance on each one. A variation of the halo effect is the "recency" effect, in which ratings are based chiefly on the performances immediately preceding the appraisal review.

3. *Variable standards.* No two evaluators are likely to apply identical standards to every factor; and of course, the more that judgments are called for, the more likely it is that disparities in standards will lead to different evaluations. Some raters are notoriously soft, while others are overly critical. Researchers have also found that managers sometimes rate subordinates according to their own self-perceptions; thus, a supervisor who prides himself or herself on being a workaholic will give high ratings only to other workaholics ("similarity error"). Finally, some raters tend to give all employees essentially the same rating, irrespective of variations in performance levels ("central tendency").

4. *Prejudices.* A large number of empirical studies have shown that racial, sexual, and other stereotypes and prejudices can corrupt performance appraisals (Glueck, 1978: 292). In general, women and members of minority groups receive somewhat lower evaluations than white Anglo males performing comparable functions (Schneier, 1978). Managers who have a personal dislike for certain workers frequently give those individuals poorer ratings than their performance warrants (Jones, 1973).

TECHNIQUES

Once these threats to validity were perceived, it became possible to evaluate the strategies of evaluation more effectively. Table 4-2 lists the

Table 4-2 Types of Performance Appraisals.

Evaluation Method	Operational Considerations	Error Susceptibility	Vulnerability to Challenge
Rating scale	Inexpensive to design and administer; easy to evaluate results; promotes comparisons among employees; emphasizes performance of employees in present position; lacks future orientation; emphasizes traits over performance	Susceptible to halo effect, recency effect, leniency error; central tendency, prejudice, and perceptual variations; variables not weighted; validity varies from job to job; ambiguous criteria for evaluation	Very high
Behaviorally anchored scale	Relatively inexpensive to design; promotes comparisons among employees; can be clearly tied to performance, thus putting less emphasis on traits	Emphasis on statements of fact helps reduce kinds of prejudice; difficult to standardize and compare results	Moderate
Checklist	Inexpensive to design; easy to administer; more performance-oriented than simple scales	Susceptible to recency error, leniency error, personal biases, and inconsistent standards	High
Critical incidents	Moderately expensive to design; very time-consuming to administer; supervisors must be trained in use; useful in comparing employees; can produce dysfunctional behavior	Subject to interpretational variations by supervisor; reduces recency effect, halo effect, central tendency, and leniency error	Very low

Forced comparison	Expensive to design; outside professional help usually required to design; easy to administer; results need machine grading; difficult for supervisor and subordinate to understand results; little value in counseling and improving performance	Reduced leniency error; somewhat effective in reducing recency, halo, and central tendency errors; moderately subject to prejudice error	Moderate
Forced distribution	Very inexpensive to design and administer; provides graphic representation of employee's relative ranking; nearly useless in counseling and improving performance; may produce morale problems; assumes normal distribution of employees in every unit	Subject to recency effect and personal bias; reduces leniency error	Very high
Management by objectives	Expensive to design and administer; time-consuming; may threaten some employees; may be positively linked to improved performance	Less subject to common evaluation errors; may result in distortions of goals	Very low

Source: Reprinted from Steven W. Hays and Charlie B. Tyer, "Human Resources Management: The Missing Link," *International Journal of Public Administration* 2 (1980): 324-325. Courtesy of Marcel Dekker, Inc.

major types of evaluation strategies and summarizes their error susceptibility. Further details are provided in the discussion that follows.

Rating Scales. For many years, rating scales of various types were the predominant form of evaluation in both the public and the private sectors. By far the most widely used was the "graphic rating scale," which consists of a list of factors that the evaluator scores by checking boxes, circling numbers, or placing marks along a line representing a continuum. Ordinarily, rating scales include both job-related and personality-related factors. For example, "quantity of work" and "knowledge of job" appear on most rating scales, but so do such proxy traits as "judgment," "enthusiasm," and "initiative." The biggest attractions of rating scales are that they are inexpensive to design and that they take little time to complete. Moreover, by having the rater assign points for each factor evaluated and then adding up the total, managers can arrive at a single quantitative score for each worker, thus allowing them to make fine distinctions among their subordinates. However, of all the evaluation methods, the traditional rating scale is the most susceptible to almost all forms of error. Rating scales are often insufficiently related to job performance, they weigh all factors (even irrelevant ones) equally, they force the rater to make many judgments and inferences, and they are very prone to halo, recency, and similarity errors.

For these reasons, *behaviorally anchored rating scales* (BARS) have received increasing attention. The major feature of this relatively new type of rating scale is that the rater is provided with narrative explanations of both the behaviors being evaluated and the standards that are to be used. For example, if "knowledge of job" is being assessed, the rating form includes a definition of the term and descriptions of the types of behaviors that exemplify "inadequate," "average," and "superior" job knowledge. "Inadequate" knowledge, for instance, might be described as "consistently asks for assistance from others; cannot be trusted to provide the right information to clients." BARS are usually designed by personnel experts, who arrange the various measures into "psychometrically organized scales" (Berger, 1983: 25), which greatly enhance their statistical validity. Thanks to these improvements, as well as to the fact that they are often specifically constructed for the jobs or classifications being evaluated, BARS are much superior to the older form of rating scales. However, they still suffer from a few of their predecessors' failings. Although they are much less prone to subjectivity, they are not immune from racial and sexual biases, or from recency, leniency, and other errors.

Evaluation instruments that use rating scales often also contain other types of measures. One type commonly included is the *checklist*, which consists of a list of statements about performance. The rater is asked to check those statements that are characteristic of the employee being evaluated. Another common inclusion is a *forced distribution.* In order to combat positive leniency error, raters are required to rank employees according to a predetermined distribution. For example, a supervisor with ten subordinates might be told to rate only one worker as superior, two as above average, four as average, and three as below average. Obviously, this technique may force the evaluator to fit square pegs into round holes; it assumes that there is a perfect "bell curve" distribution of performance levels in every work group. A similar criticism applies to *rankings* or *forced comparisons,* which require that workers be ranked individually in order of their performance level or by groups (for example, assigning each member of the work group to one of four performance levels, such as superior, above average, average, and poor).

Critical Incidents. One approach to performance appraisal has been devised that aims at reducing the amount of inference and judgment required by focusing entirely on observable performance. It is known as the *critical incidents* technique, and it begins with the preparation of a "dynamic job description" (Levinson, 1976). This consists of a list of the major performance requirements of the job, stated in terms of the types of behaviors or incidents that reflect both very good and very bad behavior. The evaluator then records actual work incidents as they occur. If, for example, the employee is a grants coordinator, a critical incident might include "processing major grant applications within one week of receipt." The employee would be monitored by his or her supervisor to determine if this goal is consistently met. A grant application that has still not been completely reviewed six weeks after receipt would be an unsatisfactory "critical incident."

Because this evaluation technique focuses on specific events, it has a much higher level of validity than do most other approaches. It is not subject to recency error, halo effect, or most other rater-induced problems. Similarly, it is widely acclaimed as being an effective means of reducing racial and sexual biases ("EEO reliability") in the evaluation process, even if not eliminating them altogether. Moreover, it aids the supervisor in carrying out the task of counseling employees. When supervisors can bolster their evaluations with specifics concerning both the accomplishments and the failures of their subordinates, the appraisal interview is apt to be less anxiety-provoking for both parties.

But the critical incidents method has a few important drawbacks. The most serious are that the instrument is expensive to design and time consuming to monitor. Managers must invest a great deal of energy preparing the log, as well as updating it and counseling the employee. Additionally, it can lead to certain perverse consequences. Because it forces supervisors to search for especially good and bad behaviors, it can lead them to overemphasize atypical work habits. Finally, many workers may become somewhat paranoid whenever they see their supervisors scribbling in "little black books." In effect, the technique might strike some workers as being too Orwellian.

Coaching Techniques. Another increasingly popular group of evaluation strategies emphasizes the counseling and coordinating role of the supervisor—that is, places the supervisor in the position of a coach. By far the best-known of these is management by objectives, which has already been discussed in terms of planning (Chapter 2) and employee utilization (earlier in this chapter). When used as an evaluation strategy, MBO consists of the following steps: (1) The worker and supervisor jointly discuss the worker's duties and responsibilities and identify those that are most important. (2) The subordinate establishes measurable performance targets for each of his or her major responsibilities. (3) The supervisor reviews these targets and makes suggestions for revisions or clarifications. (4) Checkpoints are established for evaluation of the subordinate's progress. (5) The worker and the supervisor meet at the end of the review cycle to discuss the worker's performance and various means of improving it (Kindall and Gatza, 1963: 157).

Two characteristics of this process are especially noteworthy. First, the participatory nature of the goal-setting stage helps both parties to the agreement understand and support the performance standards that will be used. Second, if the supervisor takes the role of coach seriously, evaluation is a much less threatening and uncomfortable situation than it is under any alternative appraisal strategy. The manager's responsibility in an MBO system is to provide guidance when necessary, to acquire relevant resources for subordinates, and to be available as needed. Most authorities agree that, given these conditions, MBO can be an effective tool for motivating, evaluating, and developing workers.

Because MBO offers these considerable advantages, its use in public agencies is spreading. Although MBO is not widely applied to planning and budgeting activities and has been a disaster as a job-design technique, its potential as an evaluation strategy is just now beginning to be tapped on a wide scale (Ammons and Rodriguez, 1986). Much of this rising popularity is undoubtedly linked to the interest in pay for performance, to which MBO is especially well suited. The technique is also regarded as being effective at avoiding rater errors and biases. Thus, even though it is somewhat time-consuming to design and administer, increasing numbers of jurisdictions can be expected to turn to MBO as they continue their efforts to implement pay for performance and other staffing reforms.

REMAINING CHALLENGES

Despite its impressive potential as a generally reliable appraisal strategy, MBO alone will not magically transform the evaluation landscape, nor will it automatically make merit pay a reality. Before we can be optimistic about either performance evaluation or pay for performance, a number of additional changes will need to be made in the way most staffing systems are operated. In effect, these changes represent what has been learned about performance appraisal over the past four decades. They include the following:

1. *Employees must be given a real chance to participate in the evaluation process.* Employee participation should occur not only at the goal-setting stage but also as a continuous relationship between supervisor and subordinate. Instead of annual reviews, semiannual or quarterly evaluations should be instituted. The most consistent finding of the research on performance evaluation and merit pay is that frequent and meaningful participation in the process increases employees' faith in and satisfaction with the process (Lovrich and others, 1981; Thompson, 1982). Moreover, research has indicated that frequent feedback and supervisor-subordinate contacts can reduce many of the rater errors in evaluation and minimize the influence of racial and sexual stereotypes (Ford and Jennings, 1977).

2. *Standards of performance should focus on objective and measurable criteria rather than on personality traits and other proxies of performance.* An evaluation program that fails to do so will be prone to evaluator error and will risk being voided in any judicial challenge in which racial or sexual discrimination is alleged (Thompson, 1982).

3. *Evaluations, like all other supervisory decisions, should treat all employees equally.* The quickest way for an evaluation program to lose its credibility, and the surest way to lose any grievances or lawsuits, is to penalize some workers for actions or inactions that other employees are allowed to get away with. Thus, it is operationally and legally, as well as morally, essential that all managers apply the same standards of performance and enforce the same rules in an objective and neutral fashion.

4. *Evaluator training is crucial to the effectiveness of any appraisal program.* If evaluators are adequately trained in the proper methods of evaluating subordinates, and if they are informed about the various pitfalls that reduce the reliability of evaluation decisions, their ability to render objective and informed apprais-

als is greatly enhanced. Research has strongly suggested that the halo effect, the recency effect, and the application of inconsistent standards of performance can all be virtually eliminated if raters are properly trained. Even sexual and racial biases appear to be reduced by adequate training (Schmidt and Johnson, 1973).

Thus, it is probably fair to say that we now know how to make the evaluation process much more effective than it has ever been before. Unfortunately, knowing something is not the same as practicing it. What appear to be simple rules, such as allowing employee participation and treating all workers equally and consistently, are exceedingly difficult to follow in the day-to-day management of an organization's affairs. In the continuing struggle to deal with the minutiae of administrative life, it is easy to lose sight of these rules. This is probably the primary reason for the failure of most staffing reforms. For this reason alone, it is a useful expenditure of time for managers to remind themselves periodically of the rules and their purposes.

DISCIPLINARY AND GRIEVANCE PROCEDURES

Another set of rules that is essential to the success of modern managers is that of dealing with the treatment of problem employees. As any practicing manager will readily concede, one problem employee can easily consume far more managerial time and energy than ten non-problem workers. The presence of one incompetent or disgruntled worker can disrupt the work flow, antagonize other employees, and jeopardize whatever esprit de corps may be present. Public managers occasionally find themselves in trouble with their own superiors when they bungle an attempted disciplinary action, and they may now suffer adverse legal and financial consequences. With the appearance of the concept of tort liability for malpractice, managers may actually have to pay financial damages to subordinates whose constitutional or statutory rights have been invaded at the workplace (Ball, 1982).

Almost every jurisdiction in the United States has a statutory grievance procedure by which employees can challenge adverse actions or other decisions of their supervisors. An adverse action is a staffing decision that works to the disadvantage of the employee, such as a demotion, dismissal, suspension, forced resignation, transfer beyond a specified distance (15 miles in most states), or reprimand. Some states permit grievances to be filed over such issues as wages and pay plans, performance evaluations, and job classifications, although many of them specifically exclude these matters from their grievance procedures (White, 1981).

Common sense dictates that the best way to deal with grievances is to prevent them from arising. A grievance should be seen as a failure on the part of the supervisor to detect and remedy a problem before it reaches the point at which only legal remedies are available. Perceived somewhat differently, a grievance is often a good indicator that there has been a breakdown in the staffing process. Most grievances result from one of the following causes: improper selection and placement of employees; inadequate training of workers or supervisors; lack of communication between supervisors and subordinates (so that, for example, subordinates are unaware of important rules or managerial expectations); and management practices that give some employees preferential treatment.

Most public personnel systems mandate a *progressive discipline* procedure. Such a procedure is grounded on the assumption that employees are entitled (both legally and morally) to be informed of their failings and given an opportunity to improve before a serious adverse action is taken. Progressive discipline generally includes such steps as these:

1. *Diagnosis:* The supervisor identifies the problem.
2. *Discussion:* The employee is confronted with the problem in a discussion that is timely and to the point; the manager should be prepared to provide specific examples of unsatisfactory behavior or performance.
3. *Establishment of goals for improvement:* The supervisor and the employee agree on a plan of improvement, preferably one stated in terms of quantifiable or easily observable goals.
4. *Follow-up:* The supervisor monitors compliance with the plan for improvement and counsels the worker if improvement does not take place.
5. *Disciplinary action:* If there is not sufficient improvement, specified adverse actions are taken, with the employee being informed in writing.

If a dispute arises in the course of these procedures, the employee may file a grievance, and for this, too, there is normally a step-by-step progression: (1) A discussion is held between the supervisor and the subordinate. (2) The grievance is submitted in writing to the supervisor. (3) If there is no satisfactory resolution at this stage, the grievance is submitted to the supervisor's supervisor, and appeals may be made to higher levels of supervision. (4) There may also be provision for submission of the grievance to a formally constituted grievance panel (White, 1981: 315).

Although there is little systematic evidence on the kinds of actions that influence the outcomes of grievance procedures, there is enough anecdotal evidence to permit a few conclusions to be drawn. First, the supervisor must be able to show that he or she has followed the agency's procedures; otherwise, the ruling will go against the supervisor, regardless of the substance of the dispute. Second, the grievance will be settled in favor of an employee who demonstrates that the treatment received was not consistent with that of other employees; thus once again the importance of treating employees objectively and uniformly is emphasized. Third, the supervisor will be required to document his or her contentions. The most critical piece of documentation is the employee's performance appraisal, and if the alleged misconduct or lack of performance is not reflected in the appraisal itself, then the supervisor's complaints will lose much of their credibility. Finally, the supervisor must be able to demonstrate that the worker was adequately informed about relevant rules and requirements and was provided with the necessary skills, equipment, and training to perform the job competently. In effect, then, the grievance process actually originates on the day that the employee is first hired.

REFERENCES

Abramson, Mark A. 1987. "Executive Personnel Systems in Government: How Are They Doing?" *Public Administration Review* 47 (July/August): 360-363.

Ammons, David, and Arnold Rodriguez. 1986. "Performance Appraisal Practices for Upper Management in City Government." *Public Administration Review* 46 (September/October): 460-467.

Argyle, Nolan J. 1982. "Civil Service Reform: The State and Local Response." *Public Personnel Management* 11 (Summer): 157-164.

Arvey, R. D. 1979. *Fairness in Selecting Employees*. Reading, Mass.: Addison-Wesley.

Ball, Howard. 1982. "Toward a Constitutional Law of Torts: The Burger Court and Official Liability." *Southern Review of Public Administration* 6 (Spring): 7-25.

Ban, Carolyn, Edie N. Goldenberg, and Toni Marzotto. 1982. "Firing the Unproductive Employee: Will Civil Service Reform Make a Difference?" *Review of Public Personnel Administration* 2 (Spring): 87-100.

Ban, Carolyn, and Patricia W. Ingraham. 1988. "Retaining Quality Federal Employees: Life after PACE." *Public Administration Review* 48 (May/June): 708-718.

Beach, Dale S. 1967. *The Management of People at Work*. New York: Macmillan.

Berger, Leonard. 1983. "The Promise of Criterion-Referenced Performance Appraisal (CRPA)." *Review of Public Personnel Administration* 3 (Summer): 21-32.

Campbell, Alan. 1977. "Revitalizing the Federal Personnel System." (Speech delivered at the International Personnel Managers Association International

Conference, Chicago.)

Cascio, W. F., and N. F. Phillips. 1979. "Performance Testing: A Rose among Thorns?" *Personnel Psychology* 32: 751-766.

Clapp, Gordon. 1941. "The Rule of Three, It Puzzles Me." *Public Administration Review* 1 (Spring): 287-293.

Committee on Alternative Work Patterns. 1976. *Alternatives in the World of Work*. Washington D.C.: Government Printing Office.

Dillon, John S. 1975. "The New Role for Personnel: Monitoring Superchange." *Personnel Administrator* 20 (November): 20-22.

Downs, Anthony. 1967. *Inside Bureaucracy*. Boston: Little, Brown.

Dresang, Dennis. 1982. "Diffusion of Civil Service Reform: State and Federal Government." *Review of Public Personnel Administration* 2 (Spring): 35-47.

Feild, Hubert, and William Holley. 1975. "Performance Appraisal: An Analysis of State-Wide Practices." *Public Personnel Management* 4 (May/June): 145-150.

Ford, Robert, and Kenneth Jennings. 1977. "How to Make Performance Appraisals More Effective." *Personnel* (March/April): 51-56.

Foster-Higgins and Company. 1988. *Foster-Higgins Benefits Survey*. Princeton, N.J.: Foster-Higgins.

Freedman, Anne. 1988. "Doing Battle with the Patronage Army: Politics, Courts, and Personnel Administration in Chicago." *Public Administration Review* 48 (September/October): 847-859.

Glueck, William. 1978. *Personnel: A Diagnostic Approach*. Dallas: Business Publications.

Godwin, Phil, and John Needham. 1981. "Reforming Reform: Challenging the Assumptions for Improving Public Employees' Performance." *Public Personnel Management* 10 (Summer): 233-243.

Goldstein, Mark. 1989. "Happy Birthday SES." *Government Executive* (July): 12-17, 59.

Hays, Steven W., and Richard C. Kearney. 1982. "Examinations in the Public Service." In *Centenary Issues of the Pendleton Act of 1883*, ed. David H. Rosenbloom, 25-44. New York: Marcel Dekker.

Hays, Steven W., and T. Zane Reeves. 1984. *Personnel Management in the Public Sector*. Boston: Allyn and Bacon.

Hays, Steven W., and Charlie B. Tyer. 1980. "Human Resources Management: The Missing Link." *International Journal of Public Administration* 2: 297-330.

Hoogenboom, Ari. 1968. *Outlawing the Spoils*. Urbana: University of Illinois Press.

Howard, A. 1974. "An Assessment of Assessment Centers." *Academy of Management Journal* 17 (March): 115-133.

Huddleston, Mark. 1991. "The Senior Executive Service: Problems and Prospects for Reform." In *Public Personnel Management*, ed. Carolyn Ban and Norma Riccucci, 175-189. New York: Longman.

Hudson Institute. 1987. *Workforce 2000*. Indianapolis: The Hudson Institute.

Ingraham, Patricia W., and Charles Barrilleaux. 1983. "Motivating Government Managers for Retrenchment: Some Possible Lessons from the SES." *Public Administration Review* 43 (September/October): 393-402.

Ingraham, Patricia W., and David H. Rosenbloom. 1989. "The New Public

Personnel and the New Public Service." *Public Administration Review* 49 (March/April): 116-125.

Ivancevich, John, Andrew Szilagyi, and Marc Wallace. 1977. *Organizational Behavior and Performance*. Santa Monica, Calif.: Goodyear.

Johnson, Arthur, and Nancy O'Neill. 1989. "Employee Assistance Programs and the Troubled Employee in the Public Sector." *Review of Public Personnel Administration* 9 (Summer): 66-80.

Jones, Stephen. 1973. "Self- and Interpersonal Evaluation." *Psychological Bulletin* 79 (March): 185-199.

Jun, Jong S. 1976. "A Symposium: MBO in the Public Service." *Public Administration Review* 36 (January/February): 1-45.

Kaufman, Herbert. 1976. *Are Government Organizations Immortal?* Washington, D.C.: Brookings Institution.

Kearney, Richard C., and Steven W. Hays. 1985. "The Politics of Selection: Spoils, Merit, and Representation." In *Public Personnel Policy: The Politics of Civil Service*, ed. David Rosenbloom, 60-80. Port Washington, N.Y.: Associated Faculty Press.

Kindall, Alva, and James Gatza. 1963. "Positive Program for Performance Appraisal." *Harvard Business Review* 41 (November/December): 153-167.

Klingner, Donald E. 1980. *Public Personnel Management: Contexts and Strategies*. Englewood Cliffs, N.J.: Prentice-Hall.

Korman, Abraham. 1977. *Organizational Behavior*. Englewood Cliffs, N.J.: Prentice-Hall.

Lanouette, William J. 1981. "Reagan's Team Agrees with Carter's: The Government Can't Keep PACE." *National Journal*, March 7, 394-396.

Levine, E. L., and A. Flory. 1975. "Evaluation of Job Applications: A Conceptual Framework." *Public Personnel Management* 4 (November/December): 378-384.

Levinson, Harry. 1976. "Appraisal of What Performance?" *Harvard Business Review* 54 (July/August): 30-44.

Lewis, Gregory B. 1991. "Turnover and the Quiet Crisis in the Federal Civil Service." *Public Administration Review* 51 (March/April): 145-155.

Long, Marion, and Susan Post. 1980. "The State and Local Experience." *Intergovernmental Personnel Notes* (January/February): 9-12.

Lovrich, Nicholas P. 1990. "Performance Appraisal." In *Public Personnel Administration: Problems and Prospects*, ed. Steven W. Hays and Richard C. Kearney, 91-103. Englewood Cliffs, N.J.: Prentice-Hall.

_____, and others. 1981. "Participative Performance Appraisal Effects upon Job Satisfaction, Agency Climate, and Work Values: Results of a Quasi-Experimental Study in Six State Agencies." *Review of Public Personnel Administration* 1 (Summer): 51-73.

Meyer, Robert. 1976. "Personnel Directors Are the New Corporate Heroes." *Fortune*, February, 163-170.

Morgan, David R., and Robert E. England. 1988. "The Two Faces of Privatization," *Public Administration Review* 48 (November/December): 979-987.

Mosher, Frederick. 1984. *Democracy in the Public Service*. 2d ed. New York: Oxford University Press.

Municipal Manpower Commission. 1962. *Manpower for Tomorrow's Cities.* New York: McGraw-Hill.

National Civil Service League. 1970. *A Model Public Personnel Administration Law.* Washington, D.C.: National Civil Service League.

National Commission on the Public Service. 1989. *Leadership for America: Rebuilding the Public Service.* Lexington, Mass.: Lexington Books.

O'Toole, Daniel, and John R. Churchill. 1982. "Implementing Pay-for-Performance: Initial Experiences." *Review of Public Personnel Administration* 2 (Summer): 13-28.

Perry, James L. 1990. "Compensation, Merit Pay, and Motivation." In *Public Personnel Administration: Problems and Prospects,* ed. Steven W. Hays and Richard C. Kearney, 194-115. Englewood Cliffs, N.J.: Prentice-Hall.

Perry, James L., and Theodore K. Miller. 1991. "The Senior Executive Service: Is It Improving Managerial Performance?" *Public Administration Review* 51 (November/December): 554-563.

Perry, James L., Beth Ann Petrakis, and Theodore K. Miller. 1989. "Federal Merit Pay, Round II: An Analysis of the Performance Management and Recognition System." *Public Administration Review* 49 (January/February): 29-37.

Prather, Richard. 1974. "Extending the Life of Performance Appraisal Programs." *Personnel Journal* (October): 739-743.

President's Reorganization Project. 1977. *The Composition, Dynamics, and Development of the Federal Work Force.* Federal Personnel Management Project, Option Paper no. 3. Washington, D.C.: Government Printing Office.

Reese, M., and C. Ma. 1981. "The Federal Brain Drain." *Newsweek,* June 1, 97.

Riggs, James L. 1985. *Productive Supervision.* Englewood Cliffs, N.J.: Prentice-Hall.

Robbins, Stephen. 1978. *Personnel: The Management of Human Resources.* Englewood Cliffs, N.J.: Prentice-Hall.

Rosenbloom, David. 1973. "Public Personnel Administration and Politics: Toward a New Public Personnel Administration." *Midwest Review of Public Administration* 7 (April): 98-110.

Ross, Joyce D. 1985. "Update on Assessment Centers: Implications for Public Sector Selection." *Review of Public Personnel Administration* 5 (Summer): 1-8.

Savas, E. S., and Sigmund G. Ginsburg. 1973. "The Civil Service: A Meritless System?" *Public Interest* 32 (Summer): 70-85.

Sayre, Wallace S. 1948. "The Triumph of Techniques over Purpose." *Public Administration Review* 8 (Spring): 134-137.

Schmidt, Frank, and Raymond Johnson. 1973. "Effect of Race on Peer Ratings in an Industrial Setting." *Journal of Applied Psychology* (June): 237-241.

Schneier, Dena. 1978. "The Impact of EEO Legislation on Performance Appraisals." *Personnel* 55 (July/August): 24-34.

Shafritz, Jay. 1974. "The Cancer Eroding Public Personnel Professionalism." *Public Personnel Management* 3 (November/December): 486-492.

Sherwood, Frank, and Lee Breyer. 1987. "Executive Personnel Systems in the States." *Public Administration Review* 47 (September/October): 410-416.

Silverman, Buddy R. 1982. "The Merit Pay System: A Prognosis." *Review of Public Personnel Administration* 2 (Summer): 29-34.

Stahl, O. Glenn. 1990. "A Retrospective and Prospective: The Moral Dimension." In *Public Personnel Administration: Problems and Prospects*, ed. Steven W. Hays and Richard C. Kearney, 308-321. Englewood Cliffs, N.J.: Prentice-Hall.

Sylvia, Ronald D., and C. Kenneth Meyer. 1990. "An Organizational Perspective on Training and Development in the Public Sector." In *Public Personnel Administration: Problems and Prospects*, ed. Steven W. Hays and Richard C. Kearney, 132-144. Englewood Cliffs, N.J.: Prentice-Hall.

Teasley, C. E., and Lee Williams. 1991. "The Future is Nearly Now: Managing Personnel in the 21st Century." *Review of Public Personnel Administration* 11 (Spring): 131-138.

Thayer, Frederick. 1978. "The President's Management 'Reforms': Theory X Triumphant." *Public Administration Review* 38 (July/August): 309-314.

Thompson, Frank. 1982. "Performance Appraisal of Public Managers: Inspiration, Consensual Tests, and the Margins." *Public Personnel Management* 11 (Winter): 306-313.

Tolchin, Martin, and Susan Tolchin. 1971. *To the Victors. . . .* New York: Random House.

Tyer, Charlie B. 1982. "Employee Performance Appraisal in American State Governments." *Public Personnel Management* 11 (Fall): 199-212.

U.S. General Accounting Office. 1990a. *Federal Recruiting and Hiring*. Washington, D.C.: General Accounting Office.

———. 1990b. *Pay for Performance: State and International Public Sector Pay for Performance Systems*. Washington, D.C.: General Accounting Office.

U.S. Merit Systems Protection Board. 1981. *Status Report on Performance Appraisal and Merit Pay among Mid-Level Employees*. Washington, D.C.: Merit Systems Protection Board.

Van Adelsberg, Henri. 1978. "Relating Performance to Compensation of Public Service Employees." *Public Personnel Management* 7 (March/April): 72-79.

Van Riper, Paul. 1958. *History of the United States Civil Service*. Evanston, Ill.: Row, Peterson.

White, Robert N. 1981. "State Grievances and Appeals Systems: A Survey." *Public Personnel Management* 10 (Fall): 313-323.

Wildavsky, Aaron. 1988. "Ubiquitous Anomie: Public Service in an Era of Ideological Dissensus." *Public Administration Review* 48 (July/August): 753-755.

Wollan, Lavrin. 1986. "Prisons: The Privatization Phenomenon." *Public Administration Review* 46 (November/December): 678-681.

5

Leadership

If management is an art, as has often been suggested, then the specific administrative function that demands the highest level of artistic sensitivity is leadership. This is true simply because the leadership function is more *interpersonal* than any other management responsibility. It requires the manager to direct and coordinate the behavior of many diverse individuals toward the achievement of a common goal. An appropriate metaphor, one that is frequently applied to the leadership function, is that of the orchestra leader who must see to it that the end result does not sound like a cacophony of disorganized and independent-minded instrumentalists. In the process, the orchestra leader may be required to beg, threaten, or cajole any number of temperamental musicians. Thus, in addition to artistic and technical expertise, the task requires a considerable amount of interpersonal skill. Although most orchestra leaders probably do not think of themselves in such terms, they are performing all of the management duties that ultimately comprise what we term leadership. They are directing the efforts of subordinates, coordinating their activities (the D and C in the original POSDCORB acronym), and otherwise using various forms of influence to reach some set of objectives.

Implicit in this view are certain assumptions about the content and character of the leadership function. First, it is clear that the leader must have the attention of his or her followers—they must perceive the leader as the person who is waving the maestro's baton. Power and authority are the attention-getters upon which leaders in all organizations rely. Variations in the types of power and authority, and in how they are acquired, are the topic of the first section in this chapter. Second, in order to motivate their subordinates, leaders need to know what their aspirations and dissatisfactions are. Hence, the next section,

"Employee Motivation," addresses such topics. Finally, the leader is likely to be called on to deal with great variations in talents, personalities, and egos. The alternative leadership styles from which leaders may choose in responding to such differences among their employees are discussed in the third section of the chapter.

POWER AND AUTHORITY

Power has been defined in various ways: "A has power over B to the extent that A can get B to do something that B would otherwise not do" (Dahl, 1957: 205) or power is "the ability to employ force" (Bierstedt, 1950: 730) or "to get a person or group to do something—to change in some way" (Luthans, 1977: 459). The common thread that runs through these definitions is that power *forces* or *compels*. More often than not, the force behind power comes from the organization's control over resources. By rewarding those who comply with the organization's wishes (by granting raises, promotions, or high status) and by punishing those who disobey (by withholding rewards or threatening dismissal), the organization fosters the discipline that is a prerequisite to goal attainment. However, the continual exercise of power has a severe limitation. Employees who are endlessly manipulated by their leader's use of power are likely to become alienated. Instead of being the enthusiastic employees that every leader hopes for, alienated workers may conform in order to avoid punishment or reap rewards. Lacking enthusiasm for the job, they are unlikely to display much initiative or to conform to rules and regulations when they are not being closely monitored by management. Ultimately, they may try to manipulate their bosses to make themselves look good, regardless of the reality of the situation, as a way of striking back at what they feel is an unjust system.

How, then, can power be exercised in a manner that does not alienate workers? A partial answer is that the power that is applied to workers must be *legitimized*; that is, the leader must be viewed as having the *right* to use power to manipulate and direct organizational members, and the workers must see the exercise of power as being in line with their own values and expectations. When those conditions exist, the workers internalize the organization's rules and regulations (Etzioni, 1964: 51). Once internalized, the rules become all the more potent, because the workers, viewing the organization's demands as being right and just, will conform even when to do so is personally repugnant (for example, bringing a nonconforming fellow worker into line) or not essential to avoid punishment (as when the boss is not monitoring compliance). Power that has been legitimated is called authority.

SOURCES OF LEGITIMATION

Although some authors downplay the distinction between power and authority (Mintzberg, 1983), it has long been central to the discussion of leadership. Indeed, the process by which power becomes legitimated, and thus converted into authority, has preoccupied theorists for more than a century. The three perspectives that have commanded the greatest amount of attention are those of Max Weber, George Simmel, and Chester Barnard.

Weber's most enduring contribution to the management sciences was his description of bureaucracy as an ideal type (see Chapter 3). But he was also the originator of a typology of authority that has made its way into the common vocabulary. Weber identified three types of authority: traditional, charismatic, and rational-legal. *Traditional* authority arises from historically established relationships between the leader and the led. The followers perceive the leader's power as being justified by virtue of custom and tradition, as in the relationship that exists between a monarch and the monarch's subjects and between parents and their children. *Charismatic* authority is accepted by followers because of the force of the leader's personality and unique qualities. They obey because the leader's charisma induces a sense of trust, respect, and perhaps admiration. *Rational-legal* authority (sometimes called *bureaucratic* authority) derives its legitimacy from the follower's perception that it is based on generally accepted standards of behavior. Through social interaction, certain rules of conduct assume a mantle of legality and correctness. Two frequently mentioned examples include the law (which most people obey even when the chances of getting caught are remote) and the abstract rules enforced by bureaucratic organizations ("a rule is a rule").

In describing the effects of these different types of authority, Weber offered a few insights that are particularly relevant to modern organizations. First, he observed that social systems grounded in traditional authority tend to be susceptible to nonrelevant considerations that inhibit the rationality of any bureaucratic structures that happen to be present. Status, kinship, or other personal consideration might dictate the selection and utilization of personnel and the distribution of resources, thereby reducing the effectiveness of the bureaucratic apparatus. Because many public jurisdictions can be said to exist within traditionalistic power structures (see Elazar, 1972), their bureaucracies do not necessarily function according to any preconceived notions of rationality or efficiency.

Second, Weber recognized that workers in bureaucratic organizations would have difficulty maintaining an emotional commitment to abstract rules and regulations. Despite their perceived legitimacy, the rules would ultimately begin to wear down the workers. But, he observed, bureaucracies tend to be headed by nonbureaucratic leaders— individuals who are appointed or elected to their positions (presidents, governors, mayors, cabinet members, and the like). These leaders provide a psychological release to the workers "that reinforces abstract commitment to the rules . . . by providing a more concrete and 'warm' image with whom it is easier to identify" (Etzioni, 1964: 55). Bureaucratic workers *want* to ascribe positive traits to their leaders and experience positive feelings such as admiration and affection toward them because to do so makes the formal network of rules and regulations less onerous.

Finally, Weber noted that organizations face a "succession crisis" at the death or departure of their leader. Although this problem is especially serious when a charismatic leader has been in charge, it also arises in bureaucratic organizations when the leader is especially popular with subordinates (that is, when the workers' commitment to the leader is more personal than rational). However, Weber believed that, despite this trauma, the succession crisis was also an opportunity for the organization to alter its practices and otherwise to innovate (see Gouldner, 1954; Hirschman, 1970). Contemporary research on leader succession has generally confirmed these assumptions, yet tends to indicate that the transition period between leaders is much smoother than Weber hypothesized (Farquhar, 1991).

Simmel was a contemporary of Weber's. He postulated that there are only two major sources of authority, personal and organizational (Simmel, 1950). *Personal* authority is acquired by an individual who displays virtues and strengths that are valued and admired by the group. *Organizational* authority is conferred on leaders because of the positions that they occupy in a hierarchy (and so it is sometimes called positional authority). Later theorists have observed that some leaders possess high levels of both types of authority, while others are weak in both. But many individuals who lack any significant positional authority can attain great personal authority through the force of their personalities, expertise, contributions to the organization, or related avenues (such people are generally referred to as informal leaders). Simmel also maintained that, since leadership is an interactive process, authority cannot rest on coercion alone. This led him to the very prescient argument that leaders are to some extent *controlled by* their followers. Simmel saw leaders both as "the unitary expression" of the group will and as "a target for the challenging of power in order that authority should be put in perspective" (Hunt, 1984: 159). Thus, he was one of the first theorists to recognize the extreme significance of the *led* in relation to the *leader*.

The contribution to the understanding of power and authority made by Barnard (1938) was to refine and expand on many of the ideas contained in Simmel's work. The thrust of Barnard's work is summarized in his definition of authority as "the character of a communication (order) in a formal organization by virtue of which it is accepted by a contributor to or 'member' of the organization as governing the action he contributes; that is, as governing or determining what he does or is to do so far as the organization is concerned" (Barnard, 1952: 180). This definition explicitly reflects Barnard's conviction that authority within the organization *flows upward*. This is in contrast to Weber's conception of bureaucratic authority moving from the top downward. Barnard (1952: 181) argued that authority rests on the *acceptance* or *consent* of the individuals concerned. Moreover, the followers apply a kind of test in order to decide whether or not they will obey an order. This test consists of four conditions (Barnard, 1952: 181): (1) Is the order understood? (2) Is it consistent with the purpose of the organization? (3) Is it compatible with the worker's personal interest as a whole? (4) Is the worker mentally and physically able to comply? Barnard coined the term "zone of indifference" to explain why most orders go unchallenged despite this seemingly rigid test. Orders that fall within this zone are accepted by the followers without any conscious questioning of the leader's action, while orders falling outside of the zone are resisted because they conflict with one aspect or another of the worker's value system. Additionally, Barnard observed that the breadth of the zone of indifference depends on the degree to which the inducements offered by the organization—the material and nonmaterial rewards—exceed the burdens borne by the workers in making their contributions. This so-called inducement/contribution calculus determines the level of the worker's adhesion to the organization; the greater the difference between inducements and contributions, the broader the zone of indifference.

THE ETHICS QUESTION

Barnard's work on inducements and contributions anticipated the field's later preoccupation with professional ethics and its role in holding civil servants accountable to higher authority. Because of the significant power that public employees wield over the lives and property of citizens, one of government's chief obligations is to ensure that these employees do not betray the public's trust. This task is complicated by many factors, including the sheer size and scope of government activity, the insular and secretive nature of bureaucratic behavior, the accretion of expertise within public agencies, and the general lack of effective political control over employee decision making.

Power in our governmental system is highly fragmented, leaving civil servants exposed to many conflicting expectations and demands. In addition to being tempted by illegal opportunities to transform official positions into private gains, civil servants are buffeted by demands from politicians, interest groups, and different factions within their own organizations. And, as Herbert Simon first pointed out, technical expertise rarely provides succinct and authoritative guidance on the "correct" course of action. Decisions involving important matters require public administrators to make sense of the "seamless web" combining ethics and factual judgments (Simon, 1947). Each civil servant asks the same eternal question: "To what ends should my efforts be directed; whom do I serve"

Public employees searching for answers to these questions are usually pointed in two complementary directions. The first is often termed the "low road" to ethical conduct because it relies on formal codes and other legal strictures to compel appropriate behavior (Rohr, 1978). Although such measures certainly have a place in government's scheme to promote accountability, their inadequacy at controlling all but the most notoriously corrupt behavior is apparent.

For this reason, "public administration has moved away from formalism toward a greater interest in the human side of ethical behavior" (Gortner and Plant, 1990: 247). This human side encompasses a number of guideposts that are used to direct civil servants through the ethical quagmire of contemporary public management. Perhaps the most significant is the reliance on professionalism, and the use of professional codes of ethics, to provide public employees with ethical anchors. Most of these documents strive to delineate the core values that public managers should keep in mind as they exercise discretion. The American Society for Public Administration (ASPA), for example, encourages workers to commit themselves to such values as "professional development . . . the elimination of all forms of illegal discrimination . . . fairness and impartiality, efficiency and effectiveness . . . and the highest standards of personal integrity, truthfulness, honesty and fortitude in all public activities" (American Society for Public Administration, 1984).

Obviously, codes of ethics mean little if their provisions are not widely disseminated and clearly understood by their target audience. Training, therefore, has become a major focus of the ethics discussion within public administration. A broad consensus exists concerning the need to expose civil servants to specialized training in ethics. Although opinions vary over the appropriate content, there seems to be wide support for training programs that present trainees with simulations, hypothetical situations, and value-laden choices that compel them to confront their biases.

Another approach is to include instruction that focuses specifically on the employee's agency. For example, some experts contend that each agency ought to create its own code of ethics in light of the peculiar needs and demands of the work being performed. John Rohr believes that training in ethics should focus on: (1) careful consideration of the employee's oath of office; (2) instruction on the organization's statutory, administrative, and judicial history; and (3) a thorough analysis of the chief executive's political vision (1980: 206-212).

This discussion clearly reflects the fact that, in contrast to the beliefs of classical management thought, power and authority do not flow in an uninterrupted line from political leaders to citizens. The intermediaries—civil servants—must interpret the instructions of their political superiors and give them meaning. Likewise, even as we descend from the top of public bureaucracies into the lower levels, additional power and authority leaks into the hands of civil servants at every grade, level, and location. It is for this reason that questions of accountability and ethics will continue to hold the attention of the public management community.

TYPES AND USES OF POWER

Another important problem in the understanding of leadership is the identification and analysis of the sources of power. By far the most widely used categories of power are those first proposed in 1959 by French and Raven (1977). They posited five major bases of power:

1. *Reward power* is based on the leader's ability to provide material and nonmaterial inducements.
2. *Coercive power* is based on the leader's ability to threaten or punish, either by withholding desired rewards or by dispensing termination, reprimands, undesirable work assignments, and the like.
3. *Legitimate power*, which is related to Weber's conception of authority, is derived from the follower's view that the leader has the *right* to lead and that they have an obligation to accept his or her orders.
4. *Referent power* stems from the workers' admiration for, and desire to identify with, the leader as a person.
5. *Expert power* is based on the leader's job-related knowledge and expertise.

French and Raven did not assert that these categories are exhaustive of all types of power, nor did they imply that they are mutually exclusive. Indeed, they noted that the five sources of power are interrelated, in that the use of one form might have a positive or adverse affect on other forms (for example, the excessive use of coercive power would be likely to reduce both referent and legitimate power).

Two additional sources of power, both of which are almost implicit in the original typology, have been identified. One of them, arising out of research done by Raven and Kruglanski (1975), is *information power*. Since information is a valuable resource in any formal organization, anyone who has access to it, or who can control its flow, has power. However, as Harlan Cleveland (1985) notes, few executives know how to harness information, and even fewer organizations know how to teach leaders to do so. Specialization and the segmentation of information inhibit the development of "knowledge executives" (Cleveland, 1985; Porter, 1986).

The second newly identified source of power is *connection power* (Hersey and Blanchard, 1982). This is closely related to information power, in that it stems from a person's connections with important individuals both inside and outside of the organization. In a university setting, for example, a department head who is a close friend of the university president is likely to be more influential than department heads who do not enjoy such a relationship.

Once the various sources of power had been identified, researchers began to explore such issues as the types of power that are most suitable to different situations. Although the results of this research are far from definitive, they do hold considerable interest. For example, Student (1968) found, in a study of manufacturing employees, that legitimate power was most significant in explaining why workers complied with orders; it was followed by expert, reward, referent, and coercive power. However, expert and referent power were most important in determining *performance* among the employees. Other research, most notably that of Bachman, Bowers, and Marcus (1968), has found that expert power is strongly correlated with work satisfaction and performance among diverse employee populations. Legitimate power was found to be consistently related to compliance but not clearly related to performance. Finally, coercive power was the least significant reason for complying and tended to have a negative impact on performance.

On the basis of this and other research, it is possible to draw a few tentative conclusions. First, coercive power is almost always negatively correlated with employee satisfaction and effectiveness. Second, the nonformal power bases, expert and referent, tend to be most highly correlated with performance (Luthans, 1977: 462)—a conclusion that is ripe with implication concerning the means by which we select and empower our public administrators. Third, worker compliance with orders appears to be most responsive to expert and legitimate power and almost unrelated to coercive power (meaning, of course, that the application of sanctions is not likely to produce positive results). Finally, worker satisfaction tends to be positively influenced by expert and referent power. But because most of the research in this area finds a high degree of interrelatedness among the various types of power, too much confidence should not be placed in our knowledge about the effects of different kinds of power.

There still remains the question of how power is actually exercised—that is, how a leader brings power to bear on subordinates, co-workers, and superiors. A study by Kipnis, Schmidt, and Wilkinson (1980) attempts to provide at least a partial answer. These researchers asked 750 respondents to complete a questionnaire identifying specific incidents in which the exercise of influence resulted in an "effective outcome." In the analysis of results, eight major categories of "tactics" emerged; in order of frequency of use, they were:

Reason: Using data, facts, and logic; most commonly used with superiors

Friendliness: Relying on personal regard and good will; generally used with peers and subordinates

Making Coalitions: Getting others to join in and support a position; used with all groups

Bargaining: "Horse-trading" and negotiating; used primarily with peers and subordinates

Assertiveness: Employing a forceful and direct manner; used almost exclusively with subordinates

Upward Appeal: Asking higher levels of authority for support; used sparingly, usually with peers and subordinates (since to go over the heads of superiors would be a violation of organizational etiquette)

Sanctions: Rewarding and punishing the behavior of others; used almost exclusively with subordinates

Blocking: Failing to cooperate in order to subvert the actions of another employee; used almost exclusively with co-workers

Perhaps the most interesting aspect of these findings is that the most commonly used tactics are based on referent and expert power rather than on the formal powers (reward, coercive, and legitimate). Indeed, tactics that require positional authority appear to be fairly systematically avoided. These findings will take on greater significance in the next section, in which human motivation is analyzed.

EMPLOYEE MOTIVATION

In order to utilize their power and authority effectively, all managers need to be amateur psychologists. Anyone who has ever supervised even a single employee will probably admit that the behavior of workers is occasionally (if not regularly) unpredictable or even seemingly irrational. The most committed and apparently loyal employee may resign without notice or provocation; another worker may become sullen and irritable after being promoted or begin to withdraw and to expend little energy after years of conscientious service. In attempting to predict and explain the great variety of human responses to the work situation, theorists and researchers have generated a considerable body of literature that both aids in the understanding of why workers behave as they do and provides cues that can assist leaders in getting workers to behave in a desirable manner.

THEORIES OF MOTIVATION

When theorists attempt to elucidate a phenomenon as broad as human behavior, the resulting explanations resemble a giant jigsaw puzzle. Each piece of the puzzle helps us to see the picture more clearly, but no single piece provides a clear picture by itself. At least 20 major approaches to the study of motivation have been proposed, the following appear to have the greatest utility for practicing managers.

Need Theory. The question at the center of need theory is, "What do workers want? That is, what are their needs or motives?" By far the most widely read and quoted need theorist is Abraham Maslow (1954, 1962, 1965). He posits that human needs are arrayed in a hierarchy that ranges from basic "lower-order" drives to what has become the catchword for the ultimate in motivation, self-actualization:

1. *Physiological needs:* very basic, "instinctual" needs that are necessary to the individual's survival. They include the needs for food, water, shelter, and sex (procreation).
2. *Safety needs:* the individual's desire to be free from danger and from frustration of the basic physiological needs.
3. *Social needs:* a person's desire to belong to a group, to have friends, and to be accepted by others (often termed "affiliation needs").
4. *Esteem needs:* occur in two forms. The *ego* need is a desire for self-esteem, self-respect, and a feeling of internal worth. The need for

recognition from others is exemplified by an individual's desire for respect and admiration.

5. *Self-actualization:* the need to develop one's capabilities fully, to achieve what one is capable of achieving. This need is closely related to self-development, to the proper application of one's talents, and to creativity.

Maslow asserted that these five needs must be satisfied in the order shown, moving up the hierarchy from physiological needs to self-actualization. As each successive level of the hierarchy is achieved, the individual moves to the next higher level. However, a need does not have to be *completely* satisfied to allow the individual to pursue a higher-order need. As the level of satisfaction of need increases, the *prepotency* of the next-higher need increases. In other words, as a need is satisfied, it ceases to motivate behavior, and the next-higher need increases in motivational effect. For example, when hunger and thirst have been sufficiently satisfied to avoid death, the individual will be motivated to seek safety. Maslow also recognized that people's needs change with circumstances (their ages, career stage, personal problems) and that different levels of needs may be operative in the same person at the same time (a starving mountain climber caught in a snowstorm is probably driven by needs at two or even three levels).

Another major contribution to need theory was made by David McClelland (1953, 1961, 1962). Drawing on a list of needs developed by Henry Murray (1938), McClelland focused on the needs for achievement, power, and affiliation. Through the examination of cross-cultural differences in these needs, he concluded that both children and adults can *learn* the need for achievement (McClelland, 1965; McClelland and Winter, 1969). Additionally, he detected interesting differences in the need patterns of successful leaders in large organizations ("successful" leaders being those in charge of profitable or growing organizations and those whose colleagues believed the leaders were successful). The most successful leaders were found to have a stronger need for power than for achievement and a relatively low need for affiliation. His explanation for the success of such leaders was based on a comparison of their behaviors: leaders with very high levels of achievement motivation are so preoccupied with results that they often fail to delegate authority wisely, while leaders with a strong need for affiliation allow their desire to be liked to interfere with the making of difficult decisions. Finally, McClelland noted that successful leaders with high power needs use their power solely to help the organization; they are not inclined to use power for its own sake or merely to further their own interests.

Table 5-1 Effects of Organizational Characteristics on Motivation

Organizational Characteristic	Effect on Need for:		
	Achievement	Power	Affiliation
Structure	Reduced	Aroused	Reduced
Support	Aroused	Unchanged	Aroused
Conflict	Aroused	Aroused	Reduced
Standards	Aroused	Aroused	Reduced
Reward	Aroused	Unchanged	Aroused
Responsibility	Aroused	Aroused	Unchanged
Risk	Aroused	Reduced	Reduced

Source: Adapted from George Litwin and Robert Stringer, *Motivation and Organizational Climate* (Cambridge, Mass.: Harvard Business School, 1968), 72, 84, 90-91.

McClelland's theories served as the basis for a study by Litwin and Stringer (1968) of the relationship between the work environment and the strength of various needs. They concluded that certain characteristics of the work situation determine which needs will be aroused in individuals at any given time. They identified conflict, standards, reward, responsibility, structure, support, and risk as the most significant situational factors in predicting motive strength (Table 5-1). A work environment characterized by conflict was said to reduce affiliation needs and arouse the needs for achievement and power. Highly structured work situations (with clearly defined duties and large numbers of rules) were found to reduce the needs for achievement and affiliation and increase the need for power. The delegation of responsibility downward ("decentralization") tended to arouse the needs for achievement and power without exerting any effect on the affiliation motive.

Two-Factor Theory. The two-factor theory of motivation arose from the research of Frederick Herzberg and his colleagues (1959, 1968). They conducted extensive interviews with approximately 200 engineers and accountants, asking the respondents to recall situations and occurrences in their work histories that resulted in either very high or very low job satisfaction. On the basis of the information obtained, Herzberg concluded that certain factors contribute to job satisfaction ("motivators") but a *different* set of factors leads to job *dis*satisfaction ("hygiene factors"). The terms that he ultimately applied to these factors were motivators and hygiene factors, respectively. According to Herzberg, motivators arise from the content of the job itself and include such considerations as the nature of the work and the possibilities it affords for responsibility, recognition, and growth. Hygiene factors, on the other hand, are elements of the environment or context of the job and encompass such factors as salary, status level, interpersonal relations, organizational procedures, the degree of supervision, working conditions, and the employee's personal life.

In contrast to Maslow's conception of a hierarchy, Herzberg's theory holds that motivators and hygiene factors operate independently of one another. The absence of dissatisfiers will not motivate workers; motivation arises only in the presence of satisfiers. According to this formulation, then, leaders would need both to reduce dissatisfiers and to increase satisfiers in order to produce a motivated work force.

Although Herzberg's theory differs in important ways from Maslow's, both of them imply that workers are motivated more by intrinsic than by extrinsic factors. Intrinsic motivation is that which stems from Maslow's higher-order needs (esteem and self-actualization) or from Herzberg's motivators. Wexley and Yukl (1977: 89) define motivation as "effort that is expended in an employee's job to fulfill growth needs such as achievement, competence, and self-actualization." Extrinsic motivation is attributable to Maslow's lower-order needs and to Herzberg's job-context variables, or dissatisfiers. Herzberg's contention was that, since the survival (physiological and safety) needs of most modern workers are already met fairly effectively by the economic system (at least in the industrialized nations), higher-order needs are now required to stimulate motivation. The pursuit of promotions and pay will motivate workers up to a point but will not lead to long-term commitment and to feelings of self-worth and fulfillment. This conclusion prompted Herzberg to devise the job-enrichment concept, which was discussed in Chapter 4.

Expectancy Theory. Whereas the need and two-factor theories focus on *identifying* motives, expectancy theory is concerned with explaining how the *process* of motivation works. Victor Vroom (1964), the founder of expectancy theory, based the concept on a tendency of human beings to function as rationally calculating animals. Simply stated, the theory assumes that human behavior is a function of the value that one expects to receive as a result of the effort expended.

Three concepts are central to expectancy theory: valence, instrumentality, and expectancy (thus leading it also to be called "VIE theory"). If workers are to be willing to initiate goal-directed activity, they must first have a valued goal or objective in mind. "Valence" refers to the importance that any particular goal (power, a raise, a promotion) has for an individual. Next, the workers must believe that the desired goal will be available when it has been earned. If workers think, for example, that an increase in their productivity will bring them a raise, their "instrumentality" is said to be high. On the other hand, if past experience has shown them that high performance is not regularly rewarded with raises, their instrumentality will be low. Instrumentality is defined as "the subjective probability that a person will estimate that the achievement of an organizational goal will lead directly to a desired personal goal" (Hays and Reeves, 1984: 261). Finally, workers will not be motivated unless they believe that they are capable of accomplishing the goal or activity on which the reward is based. If management makes the granting of raises contingent on the achievement of levels of output so high that only a few (if any) workers can meet them, then the workers' "expectancy" will be low.

In effect, then, the theoretical underpinnings of this approach to motivation are nothing more than the common-sensical notions that govern almost any exchange relationship. Despite its apparent simplicity, the theory has attracted far more professional and scholarly attention than any other explanation of human motivation. Several refinements, as well as a good bit of controversy, have resulted.

One of the most highly regarded refinements is the expectancy model developed by L. Porter and Lawler (1968). Their model takes into account a number of variables that were not explicitly contained in Vroom's original conception (Figure 5-1). They suggest that employee effort is primarily determined by two factors: the value placed on a goal or outcome by the worker, and the degree to which the worker believes that the goal is attainable through a given level of effort. Other factors that influence the output of effort include the workers' abilities and traits and the clarity of their role perceptions (what they are supposed to be doing and how they are supposed to do it).

The workers' record of past performance is also an important consideration because it (1) facilitates goal achievement if the task has been performed previously and (2) provides the workers with an indication of both the amount of effort required to accomplish an objective and the probability of being rewarded. The satisfaction that the worker derives from performance is a function of both intrinsic and extrinsic rewards, as well as of the workers' assessment of the fairness (equity) of the reward received. And because motivation is conceived as a feedback loop, the level of performance attained and the ultimate satisfaction derived from the experience will be largely determinative of future effort.

In summary, expectancy theory provides managers with a checklist of variables that are potentially important in the exercise of leadership. In addition to providing important clues as to how to manage workers, these variables again reflect the interrelated nature of the management functions. To motivate workers, one must consider their level of ability

Figure 5-1 The Porter and Lawler Model of Expectancy Theory

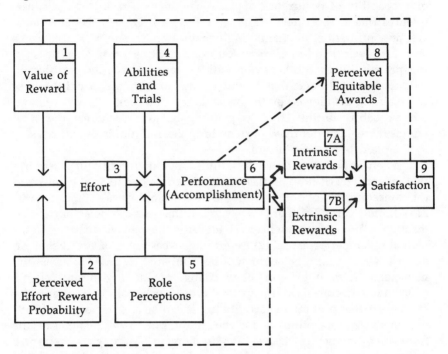

Source: Lyman Porter and Edward Lawler, *Managerial Attitudes and Performance* (Homewood, Ill.: Irwin, 1968), p. 17. Reproduced by permission.

(which relates to the selection, orientation, and training activities), their role perceptions (involving authority and responsibility relationships), their organization's reward systems, and a variety of other factors that derive from the organizing, staffing, and control functions. Moreover, expectancy theory points to the realization that leaders must be sensitive to the differences among their employees' goals, ambitions, and expectations. It is a huge task, yet one that every successful leader must confront and accomplish.

Other Approaches. Although the need, two-factor, and expectancy theories have attracted the lion's share of attention, they are by no means the only widely used motivational strategies. Others that deserve at least a passing comment are "organizational behavior modification" (O.B. Mod) and "goal-setting theory." O.B. Mod (also called "reinforcement theory") is based on the principles of operant conditioning, derived primarily from the work of B. F. Skinner (1953, 1969, 1971,

1974). Operant conditioning is "the process of changing the frequency or probability of occurrence of ... behaviors as a result of the consequences that follow them" (Pinder, 1984: 190). The consequences that are most influential in channeling behavior are *reinforcement* (Skinner's term for reward) and *punishment*. Reinforcement results in an increase in the probability that a behavior will be repeated, while punishment reduces the likelihood that it will recur. For example, a child whose complaining is followed by the presentation of a cookie (reinforcement) will probably continue the complaining behavior, whereas the child who is rebuked or deprived of something desired (punishment) is likely to complain less in the future.

When applied to the work setting, operant conditioning requires that leaders "learn how to diagnose and influence the antecedents and the consequences of the behavior of their employees" (Pinder, 1984: 219). Luthans and Kreitner (1975) suggest that this can be accomplished through a five-step sequence: (1) Identify the behavior that is detrimental to job performance. (2) Determine a "baseline" of such behavior, against which future behavior will be compared in order to assess the manager's success in bringing about change. (3) Identify the antecedents of behavior (factors leading up to the dysfunctional activity) and the reinforcers that prolong the activity (these can be as diverse as the profit generated by office pilferage and the laughter of co-workers that results from misbehavior). (4) Devise and implement a strategy to reinforce positive behavior and to punish the undesirable behavior and thereby extinguish it. (5) Evaluate the intervention in terms of the frequency with which positive behavior has replaced negative behavior. O.B. Mod is thus a more systematic and thoughtful way of correcting employee behavior than is usually practiced by managers. While most managers engage in activities of these kinds, they seldom do so with the degree of precision and purposiveness that is implicit in the O.B. Mod sequence.

Goal-setting theory is based on four broad assumptions (Aldis, 1961; Pinder, 1984: 160). First, human behavior occurs in response to goals and intentions, and these goals can take many forms (deadlines, levels of performance, and others). Second, because goals are responsible for effort, *"higher* and *harder* goals will result in higher levels of performance than easy goals"* (Pinder, 1984: 160). Third, clear and measurable goals result in higher levels of performance than ambiguous goals. Finally, neither extrinsic nor intrinsic incentives will have any effect on behavior unless they result in the setting of goals that are ambitious and specific.

Goal-setting theory leads to a few rules that, at least on an intuitive level, should make a leader more effective. It appears logical that workers will perform better, for example, when goals are specific rather than vague, and that hard goals will generate more heroic efforts than easy goals. There is a considerable body of empirical research that tends to substantiate these assumptions (Pinder, 1984: 160-163). Goal-setting theory is an implicit (if not explicit) component of many of the leadership styles that will be discussed later in this chapter.

Three lesser known explanations of employee motivation include "personal and material resource theory" (PMR), "group and norm theory," and "sociotechnical system theory." The focus of PMR is on exogenous factors that impede or promote worker motivation. PMR maintains that "constraints on workers' abilities or opportunities to attain their work goals are demotivating," while conditions that facilitate goal accomplishment are inducements to motivation (Katzell and Thompson, 1990: 144). These factors, both positive and negative, can arise from either personal (for example, skill levels) or material (supplies and equipment) sources. Inadequate equipment, for example, has been shown to have adverse effects on worker attitudes and on their perceived levels of extrinsic rewards (Katzell and Thompson, 1990). Obviously, the lesson for managers is to provide subordinates with the necessary training, equipment, and materials to perform their jobs efficiently.

Group and norm theory, in contrast, rests on the belief that the work group is an essential element in the motivational puzzle. Simply stated, group norms must support and reinforce goal attainment. Supportive, cohesive, and team-oriented work groups tend to foster and maintain high levels of motivation (Turban and Jones, 1988). Work groups that are selected on the basis of complementary interpersonal needs (such as friendship) and attitudes are likely to reflect such characteristics, as are groups that are headed by effective leaders using a team management philosophy.

The final theory of motivation combines elements from several of the other approaches. Sociotechnical systems theory holds that workers are motivated "when the work system is designed so that conditions for effective personal, social, and technological functioning are harmonized" (Katzell and Thompson, 1990: 145). Relevant conditions include challenging and diverse tasks, sufficient resources and equipment, and a work situation characterized by autonomy and effective superior-subordinate communications. Understandably, management interventions that follow the sociotechnical approach are system-wide in nature, and are often referred to as Quality of Work Life (QWL) improvements (Guzzo and Bondy, 1983).

Each of the theoretical approaches that has been described contains one or more "motivational imperatives" (Katzell and Thompson, 1990). These consist of hints to managers on how to motivate workers, along with insights into the interrelationships among the various theories. Table 5-2 presents an overview of these "imperatives," as well as corresponding programs that can be implemented to achieve the intended motivational objectives.

THE STATE OF KNOWLEDGE ABOUT MOTIVATION

With all the attention that has been devoted to the topic, one would think that by now we should have a fairly sophisticated understanding of the nature and process of employee motivation. The truth of the matter is that, while light has been shed on some of the most obscure aspects of the motivational process, few irrefutable answers have been found; some evidence supports each of the theories of motivation, but other evidence refutes them. After a review of both kinds of evidence, this section will conclude with a summary of what can be said about worker motivation at this point with more or less confidence. To anticipate, the safest assumption is that no one theory is adequate to explain a phenomenon as complex as employee motivation.

Despite the popularity of Maslow's needs hierarchy, there is very little support for the theory's basic tenets. Hall and Nougaim (1968), for example, found that people's needs change as they progress through their careers. Security and achievement needs tend to be paramount among younger workers, while in the later stages of a person's career the so-called higher-order needs take on primary importance. Several researchers have challenged the five levels of Maslow's hierarchy. Lawler and Suttle (1972), for example, suggest that a two-level hierarchy, with biological needs at one level and all other needs at the other level, is a better representation of reality. Alderfer (1972) found a three-level hierarchy to be most useful: existence needs (combining physiological and safety), relatedness needs (social interaction), and growth needs (self-esteem and self-actualization). Moreover, Alderfer posits that a "frustration-regression" phenomenon is present. This means that, if satisfaction of a particular need is blocked (frustrated), the individual will regress to a lower level of need (for example, if a person's desire for growth cannot be met, relatedness will become increasingly important). In short, perhaps the only conclusions that we can draw concerning the validity of Maslow's theory is that levels of needs probably do exist but that no single hierarchy applies to all individuals.

Whereas Maslow's theory has been amended by later thought and research, Herzberg's has been seriously undermined. For the most part criticisms of Herzberg's two-factor theory focus more on the methodology that he employed than on the theory itself. The controversy grows out of the fact that he asked his respondents to relate personal stories

Table 5-2 Approaches to Improving Work Motivation

Imperative and programs	Exogenous variables						
	1. Personal motives and values	2. Incentives and rewards	3. Reinforcement	4. Goal-setting techniques	5. Personal and material resources	6. Social and group factors	7. Sociotechnical systems
Motivational imperative	Workers' motives and values must be appropriate for their jobs	Make jobs attractive, interesting, and satisfying	Effective performance must be positively reinforced, but not ineffective performance	Work goals must be clear, challenging, attainable, attractive	Provide needed resources and eliminate constraints to performance	Interpersonal and group processes must support goal attainment	Personal, social, and technological parameters must be harmonious
Illustrative programs	Personnel selection, job previews, motive training, socialization	Financial compensation, promotion, participation, job security, career development, considerate supervision, job enrichment, benefits, flexible hours, recognition, "cafeteria" plans	Financial incentive plans, behavioral analysis, praise and criticism, self-management	Goal setting, management by objectives, modeling, quality circles, appraisal and feedback	Training and development, coaching and counseling, equipment, technology, supervision, methods improvement, problem solving groups	Division of labor, group composition, team development, sensitivity training, leadership, norm building	Quality of worklife programs, sociotechnical systems designs, organizational development, Scanlon plan

Source: Raymond Katzell and Donna Thompson, "Work Motivation: Theory and Practice," *American Psychologist* 45 (February 1990): 147.

concerning job satisfaction and dissatisfaction. When this method is repeated, similar results are obtained; but when a different methodology is utilized, Herzberg's conclusions are not supported. This has been explained by the tendency for individuals to attribute good things to themselves (the job-content factors) and bad things to others (the job-context factors). From this point of view, Herzberg's findings were merely an artifact of his methodology. This has led to a continuing and sometimes bitter debate within the academic community (see Bockman, 1971). Most theorists now believe that the distinction between *hygiene factors* and *motivators* is not as clear-cut as Herzberg suggested. Both content and context variables can act as either motivators or hygiene factors in different individuals. Additionally, achievement, responsibility, and recognition appear to be more important for job satisfaction *and* dissatisfaction than such variables as job security and working conditions (Korman, 1977: 142-143). In Herzberg's defense, the empirical record confirms that he was at least on the right track. Although insufficiently elegant, the theory does draw attention to the importance of higher order needs to job satisfaction and motivation. Herzberg's motivators do appear to promote high levels of job satisfaction among a variety of public employee groups (Park, Lovrich, and Soden, 1988). Likewise, extrinsic factors do not appear to be as highly correlated with job satisfaction as a general rule (Blackburn and Bruce, 1989; Staw, 1986). Obviously, this debate will continue for some time to come.

Perhaps because of its highly systematic conceptualization, expectancy theory has been a favorite target of researchers ever since it was set forth. The considerable body of literature that has resulted provides mixed, but generally positive, signals as to the theory's validity and predictive capability. In a review of 32 studies, Filley, House, and Kerr (1976) concluded that each of the VIE variables has been found to have significant predictive powers. The most consistently positive findings involve the expectancies that high performance will result in extrinsic rewards while intrinsic satisfaction will flow from the work itself. When these expectancies are high, they have been shown to be positively correlated with both effort and performance. Other researchers have discovered that the VIE and the Porter and Lawler models are useful in predicting employee responses to incentive programs. For example, Lawler (1968) concluded that expectancy is related to performance among individuals of high ability but not among those of lesser competence. The findings are promising but not conclusive; the correlations between variables are often of low or moderate magnitudes. Moreover, several published studies have concluded that the VIE theory's predictive powers are less potent than some researchers have claimed (Sobel, 1971; Arvey, 1972; Daley, 1986). For these reasons, care must be taken not to jump to conclusions about the generalized applicability of the theory.

Based on the evidence to date, what do we really know about motivation? Probably the most valuable lesson that we have learned is the most obvious: motivation is a very complex process that defies simple description or explanation. The most serious mistake made by both Maslow and Herzberg was to try to oversimplify it. Thus, expectancy theory's relatively good record of empirical substantiation may be largely attributable to the model's higher level of complexity. The inclusion of such variables as employee ability, role clarity, and the equity of the reward system is thought by most commentators to be an enormous contribution to our understanding of the motivation process (Steers, 1977a). At a minimum, they sensitize leaders to the fact that offhand or intuitive motivational schemes are not likely to be very effective. More positively, they provide leaders with some guidance in making managerial decisions. Studies of motivation have fairly convincingly shown that placing an inadequately trained or otherwise incapable worker in a job that is too big for the person is an open invitation to disaster. Likewise, employees who are uncertain about their responsibilities or their roles in the organization are very likely to become frustrated and unhappy with their jobs. Investigations of the goal-setting process (emerging out of both the VIE and the goal-setting theories) have also demonstrated that the establishment of goals that are specific and difficult to achieve is an effective motivational technique.

Another major finding of the motivational research is that both intrinsic and extrinsic factors influence worker effort. In contrast to management theory's past assumption that workers are motivated entirely by material rewards, contemporary theorists acknowledge the significant role that other types of incentives play in workers' behavior. This has pushed our understanding of such incentives as recognition, achievement, and responsibility to new heights. One theorist, for example, has suggested that while performance is related to intrinsic satisfaction, it is extrinsic considerations (salary, promotions) that *lead to* performance in the first place (Wanous, 1974). Findings such as this, in turn, have brought management theory to an appreciation for the effects that different leadership styles have on worker motivation. This will be examined more thoroughly in a later section.

One final aspect of our knowledge about motivation requires mention. For some time now, researchers have been very disturbed by their inability to uncover any clear proof that highly motivated employees work harder or produce more than less motivated employees. Indeed, an early examination of this topic concluded that there is "no consistent relationship between job satisfaction and productivity"

(Brayfield and Crockett, 1955). If this is true, one might ask whether it is worth spending so much time and energy worrying about motivation. Two answers seem appropriate. The first is very unscientific yet exceedingly compelling. Common sense insists that motivated workers must be better than unmotivated ones. Hence, the lack of definitive scientific evidence must be due to the inadequacy of our research methods, not to the absence of relationships between motivation and productivity. In other words, the linkages are there, but we just haven't proved them yet. Second, there is a substantial body of evidence that at least some positive job outcomes, if not increased productivity, can be attributed to the motivation or satisfaction of workers. After an exhaustive review of the literature, Vroom (1964) concluded that high job satisfaction results in lower turnover, fewer unexcused absences, and a slightly lower accident rate than does low job satisfaction. Additionally, high job satisfaction has been shown to lead to better *quality* of output and to a healthier work force, measured in terms of the frequency of sick days and stress-related illnesses. Other research has linked the level of job satisfaction to "lax and disregardful behavior" (Kolarska and Aldrich, 1980), "good citizenship" among employees (Bateman and Organ, 1983), and organizational "commitment" (Romzek, 1990). Thus, strong motivation appears to be a sufficiently desirable condition to prompt the continuing interest of theorists and practicing managers alike.

MOTIVATION IN THE PUBLIC SECTOR

As was noted in the discussion of the staffing function (Chapter 4), there are a number of structural constraints in public-personnel systems that inhibit managerial flexibility. Job-protection provisions, unwieldy procedural requirements, and other limits on administrative discretion tend to complicate the management process in many public jurisdictions. Another important consequence of these characteristics of merit systems is the adverse effect that they can have on employee motivation.

One of the most widely known truisms about public employment is that public workers enjoy a relatively high level of job security. By virtue of the numerous procedural protections provided to them, it is difficult to terminate or otherwise discipline employees of public agencies (aside from termination or furloughs compelled by budgetary shortfalls, which nullify most procedural protections).

Unusual levels of job security can be viewed in two contrasting ways. Conventional wisdom has held that workers in such a system are insulated from managerial authority and are, therefore, difficult to motivate. In the context of motivational theory, they can be viewed as

being fixed at low levels in the needs hierarchy, or, in terms of VIE
theory, they are characterized by low valences.

In contrast, more recently job security has begun to assume a more
positive cast in light of the Japanese system of management. Workers
who can count on their employer to stick by them during difficult times,
and who look at their organization as a life-long commitment, exhibit
levels of loyalty and motivation that are unusual in the American
setting. Thus, although job security is occasionally blamed for discourag-
ing motivation and performance among U.S. civil servants, it may be
having a more positive impact that simply has not been measured or
discussed widely in the relevant literature.

Another possible criticism is that public-personnel systems provide
fewer incentives to their employees than do private systems. Beyond
some obvious illustrations of this difference (there is no such thing as a
Christmas bonus or true profit sharing in public employment), it is most
apparent in the manner in which material rewards are allocated. The
government payroll is often the first place that elected officials look
when financial exigencies require budget reductions. Reduction or
elimination of annual pay increases is one common result, and layoffs
have been a more recent one. Many public compensation systems are
also plagued by inequities, cumbersome paperwork, and corresponding
declines in employee satisfaction (Silverman, 1982). These factors
amount to an apparent shortage of extrinsic incentives among public
workers.

On the positive side, government workers often enjoy benefits
packages that are far superior to those generally available in the private
sector. This is especially true in regard to health and retirement benefits,
the two most costly and consequential "fringes" within any compensation system. Logically, the public sector's emphasis on benefits probably
aids recruitment and retention of workers to a high degree. Whether or
not employees are motivated in their daily activities on the basis of a
benefits package can be debated.

An additional consideration in assessing the motivational setting of
public employment is the availability of *intrinsic* satisfiers. Here again
the picture is mixed. On the negative side is the high level of public
irritation that has been directed at civil servants for many years. Anger
over high taxes and cynicism about politics have made them a target for
the public's frustration with government.

If seething public resentment were the *only* side of the story,
government workers would have few intrinsic satisfactions indeed.
Fortunately, the situation is more balanced. Most of the public's anger is
unfocused, so it does not directly affect many civil servants. Moreover,
the jobs being performed by many public workers are *inherently* satisfy-

ing, rewarding, and challenging. Managers in the public sector generally achieve a higher level of responsibility at an earlier age than do their counterparts in business and industry. Most deal with interesting and meaningful problems with great regularity, and their actions can often be seen to truly make a difference in the lives of citizens. Workers who find such conditions appealing are probably attracted to government jobs through a process of self-selection, thereby assuring a given level of intrinsic satisfaction.

In summary, the motivational status of public employment gives cause for both optimism and pessimism. To what extent does the available empirical evidence shed light on the situation? Is there any evidence that public workers are less motivated than their private sector counterparts? The answer is probably yes, although much of the evidence is anecdotal, or is contradicted by studies that conclude that the situation is not as bleak as is often suggested. On the negative side are the conclusions of such groups as the Volcker Commission (see Chapter 4), which point to a "quiet crisis" in public employment. This position is bolstered by a good bit of empirical evidence, most of which focuses on high-level federal workers (Ingraham and Barrilleaux, 1983). Literature of this genre emphasizes a "brain drain" of civil servants, demoralized by political manipulation (Ban and Redd, 1990), low pay, unreliable performance appraisals, and a general lack of both intrinsic and extrinsic motivators.

Surprisingly, perhaps, some of the current research on public employee attitudes paints a much more optimistic picture. One of the most broad-based studies, for example, concludes that "public sector employees manifest significantly *higher* levels of job satisfaction than their private sector counterparts" (Steel and Warner, 1990: 4). The authors offer no explanation for this phenomenon, but note that newly hired civil servants are, on average, more highly educated and have higher work aspirations than comparable private employees. Research focusing on both large and small cadres of civil servants reinforces the iconoclastic conclusion that public sector job satisfaction is equal to, or higher than, that in private industry (Lewis, 1991; Soden, 1990). Obviously, it is impossible to say with any precision that either of the two perspectives is accurate. The noteworthy point is that, after many years of doom and gloom, for some inexplicable reason the sun might be peeking through the clouds.

One possible explanation for the apparently improving outlook of civil servants is the attention that is now being paid to such concerns as productivity and quality. Government has recently "discovered" these output-oriented considerations, and has adjusted its incentive system accordingly. Jurisdictions throughout the nation have implemented incentive award strategies that are intended to promote excellence and to encourage performance.

In addition to pay for performance (see Chapter 4), the following types of incentives have gained in popularity:

1. *Attendance Incentives.* The use of monetary and nonmonetary inducements to reduce sick leave and tardiness.
2. *Scheduling Innovations.* The use of flextime, the four-day work week, and other preferential schedules to reward deserving workers and/or to improve morale throughout the organization.
3. *Shared Savings.* A portion of the cost savings attributable to a department's specific efforts is distributed among the workers.
4. *Suggestion Awards.* Workers who make suggestions that result in reduced costs and/or improved operations share in the savings or receive nonmonetary recognition.

A significant trend in the design of incentive systems is the utilization of highly targeted programs to enhance performance or service delivery. Within the federal government, for instance, departments regularly establish specific productivity improvement targets and structure their incentive systems accordingly. Organizations that purchase large quantities of supplies and spare parts often give workers monetary rewards for negotiating lower prices. Employees who are credited with reducing equipment downtime are rewarded with 30 percent of the savings in another popular incentive program. Of a more general nature, some agencies empower their managers to write on-the-spot bonus checks (usually for about $100) for workers who have performed extra duties or otherwise improved office performance. The following examples give an indication of the amount of energy and creativity that are being devoted to motivating today's civil servants (U.S. Office of Personnel Management, 1990).

1. The General Services Administration "Fast Track Awards Program" provides $50 to $250 cash bonuses to recognize efforts by employees who go beyond the normal response to satisfy a client agency's needs. The award is presented within 48 hours of the service being rewarded.
2. Several agencies give cash awards of from $200 to $1000 to employees who help recruit workers in high-need specialties, such as engineers and nurses.
3. Effective supervisors are identified and rewarded with bonuses through a nomination process controlled by their subordinates. Supervisors receiving acclaim from their own work groups are

granted cash awards, preferential parking, and other forms of recognition.

4. Hospital workers in some installations are nominated and rewarded for acts that are especially sensitive, compassionate, and skillful in patient care. The "Hands and Heart" award, for instance, is granted to workers who provide the most emotional support, help, and guidance to patients at each Veteran's Administration facility.

5. A variety of recognition programs encourage physical fitness by granting monetary awards (up to $1000) for workers who meet explicit health standards (for example, non-smokers who earn a given number of points each week for aerobic exercise).

6. Other programs reward employees for such diverse activities as projecting a positive image for their agencies; being extremely active in community activities; creating an invention that wins a patent that benefits the public ($35,000 awards are available in such instances); accurately forecasting floods and other natural disasters; and publishing scholarly articles.

LEADERSHIP STYLES AND STRATEGIES

In a popular book on leadership, Blanchard and Johnson (1982: 97) offer the proposition that "goals begin behaviors, consequences maintain behaviors." This aphorism contains an important lesson for students of leadership. The primary tasks of leaders are to stimulate workers to goal-directed activity and to ensure that, once started, the activity is nurtured. If achievable goals are not provided, or if the worker's efforts are not properly recognized and rewarded, the leader will likely fail.

EVOLUTION OF CONCEPTS OF STYLE

For about three decades after 1920 the most widely used approach to the study of leadership was to concentrate on the traits of leaders. This approach was premised on the belief that leaders possess different qualities than followers. Both historical and contemporary observations tended to show that certain great people emerged as more or less natural leaders. Figures as diverse as Napoleon, Churchill, Hitler, and Henry Ford seemed to have a certain something that catapulted them into positions of great power. By identifying the special traits of such people and then basing the selection of leaders on the possession of those traits, it was thought that effective leadership would be achieved. Hence, researchers devoted great effort to the investigation of such traits as physical size, intelligence, moodiness, extroversion, fairness, sense of humor, and enthusiasm. For a short while, a consensus formed around the less-than-startling idea that leaders are generally larger and slightly more intelligent than their followers.

The trait-based theory of leadership was greatly weakened by an analysis of over 120 trait studies that was made by Stogdill (1948). He concluded that there was no real pattern in the research, that no characteristic or trait consistently distinguished leaders from nonleaders. As a partial explanation, Stogdill noted that leadership *situations* vary significantly, thereby placing widely differing demands on leaders. This led him to suggest that future theories should encompass both the personal and the situational characteristics of leadership.

The demise of trait-based leadership theory dovetailed with the wave of behaviorism that was sweeping the social sciences in the 1950s. The focus of research shifted to the analysis of the actual behavior of leaders. One of the first to provide valuable new insights into the effects of leader behavior was Kurt Lewin, the father of group dynamics (Lewin, 1948). Earlier in his career, Lewin had supervised the work of two collaborators in a study of the effect of different leadership styles on members of boys' clubs (Lewin, Lippitt, and White, 1939). Each club was subjected to three distinct kinds of leadership: authoritarian, democratic, and laissez-faire. Authoritarian leadership was characterized by tight control of group activities; club members were excluded from any participation in decision making. Democratic leaders, conversely, operated through a process of group participation and majority rule, while laissez-faire leaders essentially did nothing but instead gave complete freedom to group members to behave as they wished. The researchers found that authoritarian leaders obtained more output from their groups than did the other two kinds of leaders, but that boys working under democratic leaders displayed greater originality and higher levels of motivation. The boys overwhelmingly (19 out of 20) preferred the democratic leadership style. This project, coupled with the findings of later research, led Lewin (1948) to conclude that motivation (and hence effective leadership) depends on both situational elements in the work environment and the attitudes and feelings of the workers.

Lewin's work prompted a considerable amount of further study of authoritarian and democratic styles of leadership. Unfortunately, the results were anything but conclusive. Some studies seemed to confirm the implication that democratic leadership was best (see, for example,

Katz, Maccoby, and Morse, 1950), while others produced neutral or even conflicting results (Morse and Reimer, 1956). Several researchers concluded that, at least in the short run, authoritarian leadership (close supervision) results in higher productivity than a more participative style. But for the most part, confusion reigned in the assessment of the utility of differing leadership styles.

The Michigan Studies. Beginning in 1947, the University of Michigan Survey Research Center conducted a series of studies that eventually added to the general confusion concerning the optimal leadership style (Likert, 1961). The purpose of this project was to develop quantitative measures of the variables that influence both group output and satisfaction. The methodology consisted of making carefully controlled comparisons between high- and low-producing work units performing identical tasks. High-producing units were found to have leaders who were *employee-oriented* (as opposed to *production-oriented*) and who used a general (as opposed to a close) supervisory style. Additionally, effective leaders tended to spend more time supervising than did their less effective colleagues, and they seemed to be more comfortable with the responsibilities that were assigned to them.

Although these conclusions appeared to support the superiority of democratic leadership, later studies at the University of Michigan (Kahn, 1956) and elsewhere challenged them. The most enduring legacy of the Michigan studies is the perception that leader behavior is explainable in terms of a continuum ranging from employee-centered to production-centered.

The Ohio State Studies. Instead of focusing on the nature of good and bad leadership, the series of studies at Ohio State University were intended to identify and describe its various dimensions (Stogdill and Coons, 1957). Toward this end, researchers designed a survey instrument called the Leader Behavior Description Questionnaire (LBDQ). This instrument, which was administered to entire work teams (including a supervisor's subordinates, superiors, and peers), provided a relatively comprehensive portrait of how leaders actually behave. Through repeated administrations of the LBDQ, an initial list of 14 leadership dimensions was compiled. These dimensions were subjected to factor analysis, out of which two dimensions emerged strongly and consistently. They were given the names of "consideration structure" and "initiating structure."

Consideration structure is defined as a leader's tendency to engage in warm, supportive, and respectful behavior toward subordinates. Leaders with strong orientations in this direction can be expected to foster two-way communications between themselves and their employees and to demonstrate a sincere concern for the welfare of others. Other terms that have since come to be used interchangeably with consideration structure are *relationship-oriented, people-oriented,* and *concern for people.* On the other hand, *initiating structure* is the tendency of leaders to carefully define the duties and roles that govern superior-subordinate relationships. The establishment and maintenance of work routines and formal channels of communication also characterize initiating-structure behavior. Other terms that are applied to this concept include *task-oriented* and *concern for production.*

The most important conclusion of the Ohio State studies concerned the relationship between the two dimensions of leadership behavior. While most earlier studies concluded that such dimensions were arranged along a continuum and were therefore mutually exclusive, the OSU researchers contended that the leadership factors were independent of one another. Each dimension was a separate and distinct type of behavior that was not tied in any direct way to the other. Thus a high level of initiating structure did not preclude the leader from exhibiting a high degree of consideration behavior, and vice versa. This finding forced a reconsideration of the debate between advocates of the authoritarian and democratic approaches to management. By pointing out that leader behavior is a function of *both* types of activity, the OSU studies fostered a less polarized view of leadership. This, in turn, provided researchers with a basis for generating increasingly complex and sophisticated explanations of leadership behavior.

The Managerial Grid ®. One of the first systematic applications of the OSU studies was the creation of the Managerial Grid ® (Blake and Mouton, 1964). [This figure was republished in 1991 as the Leadership Grid and is found in *Leadership Dilemmas—Grid Solutions* (Robert Blake and Anne A. McCanse, Gulf Publishing Company, 1991).] It consists of a vertical axis for "concern for other people" and a horizontal axis for "concern for production." Each axis is divided into a nine-point scale reflecting degrees of concern for the two factors (see Figure 5-2).

Five broad leadership styles can be located on the grid. Style 1,1, which Blake and Mouton called "impoverished" or "default" leadership, is characterized by very low activity levels; the leader goes through the motions without any apparent commitment or involvement. Style 9,9, in contrast, features a high concern for both people and the tasks of production; it is called "eye-to-eye" or "team" leadership. Leaders with a 9,1 style ("task" or "authority-compliance" leaders) emphasize production at the expense of the human element of task accomplishment. Style

Figure 5-2 The Leadership Grid ® Figure

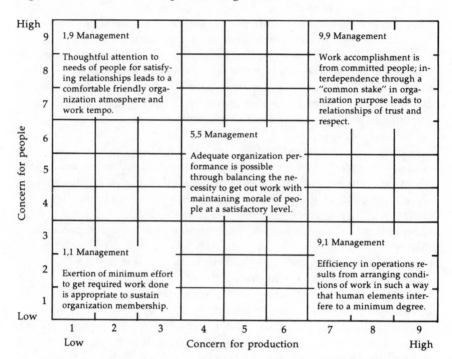

Source: Robert R. Blake and Anne Adams McCanse, *The Leadership Grid ® Figure* from *Leadership Dilemmas—Grid Solutions*. Houston: Gulf Publishing Company, Copyright © 1991 by Scientific Methods, Inc., p. 29. Reproduced by permission.

1,9 ("good-neighbor" or "country-club" leadership) is characterized by strong concern for people but little emphasis on goal achievement, task structure, or authority relationships. Finally, in the 5,5 style, called "middle-of-the-road" leadership, leaders attempt to walk a tightrope between goal accomplishment and worker satisfaction. Middle-of-the-road leaders would probably be regarded as wishy-washy or compromisers by their subordinates.

Because Blake and Mouton believe that the 9,9 leadership is always preferable, the names and descriptions of several of the other leadership types are clearly pejorative. Who, for example, would welcome being tagged a default or country-club leader? This, as well as Blake and Mouton's own use of the grid in training programs that were intended to maximize the scores of participants on both axes, indicates a clear preference for the 9,9 or team style. Indeed, it is now generally accepted that the grid implies a bias toward the team style of leadership. Overemphasis on the task orientation (9,1), for example, is perceived as being too stern and uncaring, resulting in worker alienation. Country-club leaders (1,9), on the other hand, are seen as being too soft, which would invite workers to take advantage of the situation. Thus, the Managerial Grid ® turned out to be another step in the search for the one best way to lead.

Effects of Leadership Styles. The curiosity of researchers was next directed at the effects that each style of leadership had on workers. The findings gave mixed and even conflicting signals. In a study of over 1,000 managers (including many in public agencies), Stogdill (1965) found that the subordinates of considerate leaders had higher levels of job satisfaction than did employees with task-oriented supervisors. Other researchers concluded that (1) leader consideration resulted in lower employee turnover rates, at least in the short run; and (2) initiating structure was positively correlated with employee grievance rates (Fleishman and Harris, 1962). Further, where leaders demonstrated high levels on both dimensions (9,9), both employee turnover and grievance rates tended to be lower. Another research project showed that leaders with high levels of initiating structure were rated higher by their superiors than were leaders with lower initiating orientations (Filley and House, 1969). These findings have led to the conclusions that, in general, the subordinates of considerate leaders have greater job satisfaction, yet most superiors would prefer their lower-level supervisors to be task-oriented.

However, the seeming clarity of these findings has been clouded by further research. While several studies have shown that initiating structure is resented by certain types of workers, especially the unskilled and semiskilled, employees in *large groups* tend either to prefer initiating activity or to object to it less strenuously than their colleagues in small work groups (Vroom and Mann, 1960). Group conflict seems to be reduced by initiating structure (Oaklander and Fleishman, 1964), and high-level workers tend to be more satisfied in work environments where leaders engage in initiating activity (House, Filley, and Kerr, 1971). And, despite repeated efforts to do so, no one has been able to establish with any degree of certainty that work groups headed by any particular type of leader are more productive than groups supervised by other types of leaders. Likert (1961) found that employee-oriented leadership was most highly correlated with output, yet he also discovered numerous task-oriented leaders in charge of high-performing work groups. Conclusions such as these prompted later researchers to devote increased attention to other organizational variables that might be influential in determining the impact of different leadership styles.

CONTINGENCY THEORIES

By the mid-1960s, management theorists were beginning to develop a new approach to the study of organizations that started from the premise that there is no one best way to do anything in the management field. In other words, the search for eternal truths and basic prescriptions concerning the best ways to organize and lead is bound to fail. Proponents of the new school of thought, called *contingency theory*, declared that the proper way to perform any management function must be discovered through an examination of the whole range of organizational variables. Thus, an appropriate organizational structure can be designed only after one assesses such variables as the agency's environmental complexity, the nature of the tasks it performs, its size, and a number of related factors (see Chapter 3). An entire body of literature has grown up around various contingency approaches to organizational structure, and a host of contingency explanations of leadership have been put forth. Three of the best known of these, and certain derivative leadership approaches, will be discussed.

Situational Leadership Theory. The first real attempt to devise a model of leadership effectiveness was made by Fiedler (1967). Over the course of nearly two decades, Fiedler had been measuring leadership styles with the use of a questionnaire that asked leaders to think of all the people with whom they had ever worked and to focus on the single person with whom they had "the most difficult time in getting a job done"—that is, their "least preferred coworker" (LPC). Once the respondents had an LPC in mind, they described this person according to a series of descriptive adjectives; using an eight-point continuum, the leaders rated their LPC as "smart/stupid," "energetic/lazy," "good/bad," and so on. The leaders whose attitudes toward their LPC were relatively positive were assumed to be more lenient (and hence more "human-relations-oriented") than the respondents with negative LPC feelings (who were thus viewed as being more task-oriented). This seemingly roundabout methodology was prompted by Fiedler's original intention to determine if there were any differences in the productivity levels of work groups under lenient as opposed to highly demanding leaders.

As the research progressed, Fiedler became increasingly puzzled by inconsistent findings concerning work-group productivity. His initial research on Air Force bomber crews led him to the conclusion that the most effective leaders (those whose crews hit their targets most frequently) were those with negative LPC scores (task-oriented), but later research with different groups and in different situations contradicted this finding. Fiedler therefore began a search for other factors that might explain variations in leader effectiveness. This search culminated in the development of a Contingency Model of Leadership Effectiveness.

This model combines Fiedler's typology of leadership styles (considerate versus task-oriented, or positive versus negative LPC) with three situational variables that he considers to be the most important. These are:

Leader-member relations: The extent to which relationships are friendly and supportive, and the extent to which the workers trust and are loyal to the leader

Task structure: The degree to which the group's task is routine and predictable

Position power: The source and clarity of the leader's authority; the leader's ability to get followers to comply with commands

Where leader-member relations are mutually supportive, the group's task is highly structured, and the leader enjoys strong position power, Fiedler characterizes the situation as "favorable"; where the opposite conditions prevail, he describes it as "unfavorable." He then postulates that when the situation is either clearly favorable or clearly unfavorable, a task-oriented approach will be more effective; when it is neither clearly favorable nor clearly unfavorable, a considerate style will be more effective. He argues that, in a favorable situation, "the group is ready to be directed ... and expects to be told what to do," and he uses the example of an airplane crew: "consider the captain of an airliner in its final landing approach. ... We would hardly want him to turn to his crew for a discussion on how to land" (Fiedler, 1967: 147). In an unfavorable situation, a task-oriented approach is again more effective, because "the group will fall apart without the leader's active intervention and control." As Korman (1977: 444) has observed, "the leader who makes a wrong decision in a highly unfavorable type of situation is probably better off than the leader who makes no decision at all." On the other hand, a considerate style is held to be more effective in the in-between situations because it is more conducive to a "nonthreatening, permissive environment ... in which members feel free to make suggestions and to contribute to discussions" (Fiedler, 1967: 147).

Fiedler's contingency model has generated a considerable amount of debate. One of its most controversial components is the LPC score. Fiedler equates it with the consideration and initiating structures of the OSU studies, but this equation has not withstood empirical analysis. For example, studies in which respondents' LPC scores are compared with their LBDQ results (based on the OSU questionnaire) have shown that the two are not the same (Chemers and Rice, 1974). Leaders who have high initiating or consideration structure scores on the LBDQ do not necessarily have corresponding LPC scores.

Another controversy centers on Fiedler's apparent presumption that leaders should alter their situations instead of altering their leadership style. Whereas many theorists place the onus on leaders to change their style to fit the situation, Fiedler has developed a leader-training program designed to help managers improve their effectiveness by manipulating the situational variables. The leader's basic style is taken more or less as a given, and participants are instructed in ways of altering their power positions, task structures, and intergroup relations according to the prescriptions of the model. This "Leader Match" program leads logically to the proposition that leaders should seek out job assignments that best fit their style. Interestingly, studies by Fiedler, Chemers, and Mahar (1976) conclude that it *is* possible to train leaders to recognize disadvantageous situational variables and to engineer changes. Improvements in the job performance of Leader Match participants have been reported with some degree of regularity (Fiedler and Mahar, 1979). Other researchers, however, contend that Fiedler's positive findings are attributable to the "Hawthorne effect": participants perform better merely because someone is paying attention to them, even if in the context of a scientific experiment (Csoka and Bons, 1978).

Path-Goal Theory. A number of theories link leader behavior to employee motivation. One of these is *path-goal theory*, which views the role of the leader as that of an expediter whose major responsibility is to remove obstacles that stand in the way of workers' pursuit of personal and organizational goals. According to its chief proponent, Robert House,

> the motivational functions of the leader consist of increasing personal pay-offs to subordinates for work-goal attainment, and making the path to these pay-offs easier to travel by clarifying it, reducing road blocks, and increasing the opportunities for personal satisfaction en route. (House, 1971: 324).

Drawing their inspiration from expectancy theory, advocates of the path-goal approach attempt to specify ways in which leaders can enhance worker performance by manipulating expectancy, valence, and instrumentality. The leader's primary task is to increase employee motivation by ensuring that workers believe that their efforts will result in task accomplishment and that desired rewards will be forthcoming. Strategies that might be utilized include clarification of subordinates' incentives, introduction of feasible goals where none exist, and elimination of structural and interpersonal impediments to goal attainment. In the process, leaders may select from among four leadership styles (House and Mitchell, 1974):

Directive: As in the task-oriented or initiating structure style, the leader directs subordinates without providing them with opportunities to participate; leader tasks include making work assignments, sequencing and structuring work, and enforcing performance standards.

Supportive: The leader's behavior is characterized by friendliness and respect for subordinates; workers are treated as equals, and the leader tries to make the work environment more pleasant.

Participative: The leader confers with subordinates before making decisions and talks over problem situations and plans with them.

Achievement-oriented: The leader sets challenging goals for subordinates while exhibiting confidence in their ability to perform adequately.

In contrast to Fiedler's contingency model, path-goal theory assumes that managers can alter their leadership style as needed, leading its proponents to offer prescriptions for the optimal style for varying situations. For example, ambiguous or uncertain work situations should be handled in a directive manner, because workers are uncomfortable and anxious in uncertain situations, and thus will regard the use of initiating structure as both legitimate and desirable. Conversely, where the work situation is routine, the imposition of a task-oriented style is unnecessarily stifling and will result in employee dissatisfaction. Consequently, dull and repetitive jobs call for a supportive or participative leadership style. If the task is "frustrating and stress inducing, consideration will result in increased social support" and higher job satisfaction (House, 1971: 325).

Due to its relatively recent appearance, path-goal theory has not been thoroughly tested by researchers. The studies that were conducted immediately before and after it was first introduced (see House, 1971) seem to support its basic contention concerning the relationship between leader directiveness and task ambiguity. As always, however, contrary evidence is available. A study by Schriesheim and Schriesheim (1980) indicates that employee reactions to leader directiveness are affected by factors that the theory does not take into account. For instance, directive leaders who were also considerate (9,9 leaders) produced employee responses different from those produced by "cold" leaders who imposed structure (9,1 leaders). Moreover, varying employee feelings about ambiguity—some don't seem to mind it as much as others—also appear to weaken the relationships that path-goal theorists predict. Such evidence indicates that path-goal theory does not capture the immense complexity of leadership and motivation, but, as we have already pointed out, *no* theory is ever likely to do so.

Path-goal theory has nevertheless made several notable contributions to the understanding of leadership. The most significant of these stems from its exploration of the connections between leader behavior and employee motivation. By building a conceptual bridge between these important concepts (and, parenthetically, the two related bodies of literature), path-goal theory begins to address questions that are of pressing concern to practicing managers. It provides guidance in determining how employees will react to certain situations and offers corresponding suggestions as to how leaders should behave. This implies that leaders have more responsibility to followers than many previous theories have suggested. In asserting that leaders can and should alter their styles to fit the work situation, path-goal theorists are in effect demanding that managers diagnose situations and change their own behaviors accordingly. This realization has already resulted in a number of worthwhile suggestions, not the least of which is that there are some situations in which leaders are well-advised to "avoid leading." Kerr and Jermier (1978) have observed that this is a reasonable and appropriate response to situations characterized by intrinsically satisfying work, unambiguous tasks, experienced and well-trained workers, and an adequate reward system. Both task and consideration structures would seem to be unnecessary in such an agreeable work environment.

Follower-Based Theory. The version of situational leadership theory that is most popular among management consultants and trainers is the *follower-based theory* formulated by Hersey and Blanchard (1982). It shares many similarities with the path-goal approach, including the notion that different leadership styles are needed under different circumstances and that leaders can and should alter their behavior to fit changing situations. But whereas path-goal theory emphasizes the degree of ambiguity in the work situation, Hersey and Blanchard believe that *task maturity* is the most important situational variable. They define this concept as "the ability and willingness of people to take responsibility for directing their own behavior" (Hersey and Blanchard, 1982: 151). Task maturity rests on such considerations as past job experience, relevant job knowledge, understanding of job requirements, general willingness to take responsibility, organizational commitment, and achievement motivation. Workers with high levels of these attributes are deemed to be mature, and those who lack such traits are immature. Because task maturity relates only to the job being performed at the time, a worker may be mature with regard to one task and immature with regard to another (for example, an experienced file clerk who is given a new and unfamiliar responsibility).

The underlying premise of the model growing out of Hersey and Blanchard's theory is that managers should alter their leadership style in accordance with the task-maturity level of the employees they are supervising at the time. Thus, a manager might be called on to demonstrate several leadership styles in a single work group and on a single day. The styles that are appropriate to varying maturity levels are termed *telling, selling, participating,* and *delegating* (see Table 5-3). At low levels of follower maturity, managers would engage in telling behavior: defining subordinates' roles, explaining how to accomplish tasks, and monitoring performance. This is roughly analogous to task orientation or concern for production. As follower maturity increases, leaders would use less task-oriented behavior and more relationship (consideration) behavior. When subordinates are at the highest level of maturity, the leader's style should be low in both task and relationship behavior— reminiscent of the argument by Kerr and Jermier (1978) that both initiating and consideration structures are irrelevant to workers who are both internally motivated and competent.

Since these leadership styles are similar to those used in the Managerial Grid ®, Hersey and Blanchard make use of a form of the grid to help managers understand the implications of matching leadership style to follower maturity (see Figure 5-3). The mix of style characteristics follows a parabolic course across the grid, suggesting the shifting combinations of task-oriented and relationship-oriented behavior that are called for at different levels of maturity.

The chief attraction of the Hersey and Blanchard model is its use of task maturity as a virtual proxy for several other situational variables that are not as easily observed or evaluated. In essence, Hersey and Blanchard assume that such factors as task ambiguity and leader-member relations will be manifested in followers' reactions to the work situation. Thus, leaders need to focus on only one variable in selecting a leadership style. This, of course, requires that leaders be both (1) very perceptive in assessing their subordinates' characteristics, attitudes, and abilities and (2) familiar with their subordinates' past job assignments, special talents, and so on. These might be considered stiff demands.

Ongoing developments in workplace demographics are clearly complicating the leaders' tasks even further. The celebrated Hudson Institute's *Workforce 2000* report, for example, forecasts a labor pool that has *diversity* as its most distinguishing characteristic. The trends that are

Table 5-3 Implications of Follower-Based Theory for Leadership Style

Maturity Level	Description	Leadership Style	Description
Low	Workers are *unable* and *unwilling* to perform; insecure	Telling	Leader defines roles, explains how to accomplish tasks, closely monitors compliance and performance
Low to moderate	Workers are *unable* to perform but are *willing* and/or confident	Selling	Leader combines directive and supportive behavior to reinforce workers' willingness and enthusiasm; engages in two-way communication and explanation of tasks
Moderate to high	Workers are *able* to perform but *lack willingness* or confidence	Participating	Leader is supportive but nondirective; decision making is shared; primary role is to facilitate the work process through reinforcement and communication
High	Workers are *able* and *willing* to perform; they are confident and competent	Delegating	Leader adopts a "low profile"; may still identify goals and problems but leaves task accomplishment to the workers

Source: Adapted from Paul Hersey and Kenneth Blanchard, *Management of Organizational Behavior*, 2d ed. (Englewood Cliffs, N.J.: Prentice-Hall, 1982), 153-154.

Figure 5-3 Grid for the Follower-Based Model of Leadership Style

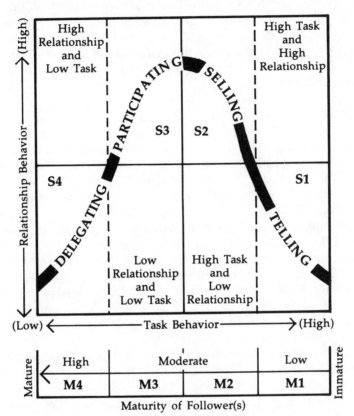

Source: Paul Hersey and Kenneth Blanchard, *Management of Organizational Behavior: Utilizing Human Resources,* © 1982, pp. 153, 154, 248. Reprinted by permission of Prentice-Hall, Englewood Cliffs, New Jersey.

highlighted include: (1) the number of young workers is declining, and the average age is increasing; (2) women are becoming a dominant influence, accounting for almost two-thirds of the new entrants by the year 2000; (3) blacks and Hispanics will comprise greater and greater fractions of the labor force; and (4) immigrants will represent the largest share of the increase in population and in the work force since World War I (1988: 17-19).

The diverse backgrounds of this new work force will also reflect a comparable variation in cultural expectations concerning work, motivation, and the role of the individual within complex organizations. Leadership will not mean simply figuring out what style is appropriate to a given subordinate; it may well mean learning more about their cultural norms and consequent behavior patterns. Also, it will undoubtedly require workplace adjustments ranging from the provision of childcare facilities to the wholesale alteration of benefits packages and incentive systems. In summary, the rising tide of diversity will require levels of leader flexibility and sensitivity that are probably unprecedented in history.

LESSONS FROM JAPAN: THEORY Z AND TOTAL QUALITY MANAGEMENT

In 1960, Douglas McGregor described two different kinds of managerial leadership based on contrasting views of human nature that he called "Theory X" and "Theory Y." Theory X assumes that most workers lack ambition, have little capacity for creativity, are motivated only by lower-level needs, and have an inherent distaste for work. Theory X leaders, therefore, rule in an autocratic style, emphasizing control and coercion. Theory Y assumes that workers are inner-directed, want to be creative and to contribute to their organizations, are motivated by higher-order needs, and view work as a natural and potentially enjoyable activity. Thus, Theory Y leaders emphasize supportive and facilitating behaviors that are intended to allow workers a maximum of on-the-job freedom (McGregor, 1960). "Theory X" and "Theory Y" soon became popular terms in the management field.

Later, another letter was added to the management alphabet. "Theory Z" was derived by William Ouchi (1981) from the management practices that are commonly used in Japan, and which have presumably contributed to that nation's remarkable industrial achievements. The basic assumption of Theory Z is that workers are the key to high productivity. Management's role is thus to structure the work situation in such a way that employees can *work together* more effectively. In order to accomplish this goal, Ouchi contends that the work climate must contain certain attributes that are often lacking in American organizations. These are:

Long-term employment: Employees should expect to work in a single organization for all or most of their careers and to accept a variety of responsibilities.

Trust: Employees should believe that their contributions over a lifetime will ultimately be rewarded in an equitable and just manner.

Discernment: Employees should develop norms of behavior that emphasize the utility of working together with other employees to improve productivity.

Intimacy: Employees should develop close personal relationships that reflect such values as care, unselfishness, and
sacrifice for others.

Specific management strategies that can promote these attributes include
close and frequent personal contact between supervisors and subordinates, relatively flat organizational structures consisting of only a few
hierarchical levels, and group involvement through such devices as
"quality circles" (work groups that jointly attempt to devise more
productive and effective ways of performing their tasks) (Denhardt,
Pyle, and Bluedorn, 1987). Additionally, Japanese firms tend to utilize a
"family" approach to management, which is somewhat paternalistic in
its attitude toward subordinates. This participative approach tends to
foster a sense of belonging and group-centered enthusiasm among the
workers, who in turn view management with a deep feeling of trust.
The leadership practices are supplemented with selection, training,
compensation, promotion, and appraisal strategies that serve to reinforce
the communal and familial values of the organization (Bowman, 1984).

Some commentators have suggested that, because Theory Z management stems from values and attitudes endemic to Japanese society, it
is unreasonable to expect it to be generally applicable in the United
States. American culture may be an inhospitable environment for a
familial type of management, for its value system stresses individualism
and fosters tensions between labor and management. Nevertheless,
Japanese firms operating in the United States have had success with the
Theory Z approach. Moreover, many indigenous organizations have
successfully experimented with quality circles and other Japanese management methods (Denhardt, Pyle, and Bluedorn, 1987).

Another management concept that some view as a Japanese import
is Total Quality Management (TQM). Actually, this popular strategy is
traced directly to the works of W. Edwards Deming, an American
statistician who is credited by many as most responsible for Japan's post-
war "economic miracle." Deming's philosophy of management is based
on an interesting blend of participatory leadership, statistical control
systems, and an abiding concentration on quality improvement
(Deming, 1986).

Deming offers a blistering critique of American management practices, and identifies such failings as a "lack of constancy of purpose,"
emphasis on short-term goals, annual performance ratings, excessive
management mobility, and the over-reliance on quantitative rather than
qualitative control data systems. His proposed remedy is heavily imbued
with a human resources focus. Included within his 14 point program for
quality improvement are such steps as:

1. Create constancy of purpose for improvement of product and service (in other words, make quality and productivity the major goals);
2. institute training for workers on the management system, and teach them how to identify and correct weaknesses in the system;
3. drive fear from the workplace (no blame-finding);
4. break down barriers between specialties and line and staff;
5. remove barriers to pride of craft;
6. encourage education and self-improvement; and
7. end the practice of awarding business on price tag alone.

After preaching more-or-less in the wilderness for 50 years, Deming's message began to catch on in the late 1980s (Ebel, 1991; Dobyns and Crawford-Mason, 1991). In its current form, TQM is viewed as a bottom-up process in which quality awareness becomes a personal concern of all employees. To achieve this goal, various authors call for such initiatives as the establishment of quality councils and teams (Juran, 1988), the creation of systematic communication channels, focusing on productivity enhancement (Crosby, 1986), and various means of recognizing and rewarding group (*not* individual) accomplishment. Thus, TQM embodies many of the more progressive facets of contemporary management thought, and welds them to a new, long-awaited emphasis on doing it right the *first* time. As such, TQM may well be more long-lived than the management strategies that preceded it.

CONCLUSION

There are a few conclusions that can, with caution, legitimately be drawn from the research in leadership up to this point. The first conclusion is the most obvious and yet perhaps the most important: there are no easy solutions. There have been a number of fads in the management field, but no enduring tricks. All one needs to do to develop a healthy sense of skepticism is reread the early reports acclaiming such innovations as Scientific Management, Management by Objectives, and T-Group Training. TQM may be an exception, but it is much too early to tell.

This is not to say that there has been no progress in our understanding of the linkages between leadership and motivation. One of the most valuable contributions has come from contingency theory. In addition to definitively establishing that there *is* a connection between leadership and motivation, contingency theory has provided us with several guideposts along the road to effective leadership. These consist of the various job elements that must be considered in devising appropriate leadership behavior. The nature of the task structure, the leader's level of power and authority, the quality of leader-follower relations, and the subordinate's willingness and ability to perform are all significant considerations that have been proven to exert a direct effect on leader effectiveness. These conclusions, coupled with the findings on organizational structure that were discussed in Chapter 3 (relating organizational structure to such variables as environmental complexity, task complexity, time constraints, and size), permit a degree of descriptive and explanatory precision that is substantially greater than what was possible only a few years ago. Moreover, by identifying and describing major leadership styles, the necessary raw material has been provided with which any leader can begin the iterative process of matching his or her own styles and talents to the work situation. Although we are not at the point at which any absolutes can be offered, a sufficient number of relationships have been identified to give us a material advantage over our predecessors.

REFERENCES

Alderfer, Clayton P. 1972. *Existence, Relatedness, and Growth.* New York: Free Press.

Aldis, Owen. 1961. "Of Pigeons and Men." *Harvard Business Review* 39 (July/August): 59-63.

American Society for Public Administration. 1984. *Code of Ethics of the American Society for Public Administration.* Washington, D.C.: American Society for Public Administration.

Arvey, Richard. 1972. "Task Performance As a Function of Perceived Effort: Performance and Performance-Based Contingencies." *Organizational Behavior and Human Performance* 8 (December): 423-433.

Bachman, Jerald, David Bowers, and Phillip Marcus. 1968. "Bases of Supervisory Power: A Comparative Study in Five Organizational Settings." In *Control in Organizations,* ed. Arnold Tannenbaum, 229-238. New York: McGraw-Hill.

Ban, Carolyn, and Harry C. Redd. 1990. "The Status of the Merit System: Perceptions of Abuse in the Federal Civil Service." *Review of Public Personnel Administration* 10 (Summer): 55-72.

Barnard, Chester. 1938. *The Functions of the Executive.* Cambridge, Mass.: Harvard University Press.

_____.1952. "A Definition of Authority." In *Reader in Bureaucracy,* ed. Robert K. Merton, Ailsa P. Gray, Barbara Hockey, and Hanan C. Selvin, 180-185. New York: Free Press.

Bateman, Thomas, and Dennis Organ. 1983. "Job Satisfaction and the Good Soldier: The Relationship between Affect and Employee 'Citizenship.'" *Academy of Management Journal* 26 (December): 587-595.

Bierstedt, Robert. 1950. "An Analysis of Social Power." *American Sociological Review* 15 (December): 730-736.

Blackburn, J. Walter, and William M. Bruce. 1989. "Rethinking Concepts of Job Satisfaction." *Review of Public Personnel Administration* 10 (Fall): 11-28.

Blake, Robert, and Jane Srygley Mouton. 1964. *The Managerial Grid.* Houston: Gulf.

Blanchard, Kenneth, and Spencer Johnson. 1982. *The One Minute Manager.* New York: Morrow.

Bockman, Valerie. 1971. "The Herzberg Controversy." *Personnel Psychology* 24 (Summer): 155-189.

Bowman, James. 1984. "Japanese Management: Personnel Policies in the Public Service." *Public Personnel Management Journal* 13 (Fall): 197-219.

Brayfield, Arthur, and Walter Crockett. 1955. "Employee Attitudes and Employee Performance." *Psychology Bulletin* 52 (November): 396-424.

Chemers, Martin, and Robert Rice. 1974. "A Theoretical and Empirical Examination of Fiedler's Contingency Model of Leadership Effectiveness." In *Contingency Approaches to Leadership,* ed. J. G. Hun and L. Larson, 91-123. Carbondale: Southern Illinois University Press.

Cleveland, Harlan. 1985. *The Knowledge Executive: Leadership in an Information Society.* New York: E. P. Dutton.

Crosby, Philip B. 1986. *Running Things: The Art of Making Things Happen.* New York: McGraw-Hill.

Csoka, Lewis, and Paul Bons. 1978. "Manipulating the Situation to Fit the Leader's Style: Two Validation Studies of LEADER MATCH." *Journal of Applied Psychology* 63 (June): 295-300.

Dahl, Robert. 1957. "The Concept of Power." *Behavioral Science* 2 (April): 201-215.

Daley, Dennis. 1986. "Humanistic Management and Organizational Success: The Effect of Job and Work Environment Characteristics on Organizational Effectiveness, Responsiveness, and Job Satisfaction." *Public Personnel Management* 15 (Summer): 131-142.

Deming, W. Edwards. 1986. *Out of the Crisis.* Cambridge, Mass.: MIT Press.

Denhardt, Robert, James Pyle, and Allen Bluedorn. 1987. "Implementing Quality Circles in State Government." *Public Administration Review* 47 (July/August): 304-309.

Dobyns, Lloyd, and Clare Crawford-Mason. 1991. *Quality or Else: The Revolution in World Business.* Boston: Houghton Mifflin.

Ebel, Kenneth. 1991. *Achieving Excellence in Business: A Practical Guide to the Total Quality Transformation Process.* New York: Dekker.

Elazar, Daniel. 1972. *American Federalism: A View from the States.* New York: Crowell.

Etzioni, Amitai. 1964. *Modern Organizations.* Englewood Cliffs, N.J.: Prentice-Hall.

Farquhar, Katherine. 1991. "Leadership in Limbo: Organization Dynamics During Interim Administrations." *Public Administration Review* 51 (May/June): 202-210.

Fiedler, Fred. 1967. *A Theory of Leader Effectiveness.* New York: McGraw-Hill.

Fiedler, Fred, Martin Chemers, and Linda Mahar. 1976. *Improving Leadership Effectiveness.* New York: Wiley.

Fiedler, Fred, and Linda Mahar. 1979. "The Effectiveness of Contingency Model Training: A Review of the Validation of Leader Match." *Personnel Psychology* 32 (Spring): 45-62.

Filley, Allan, and Robert House. 1969. *Managerial Process and Organizational Behavior.* Glenview, Ill.: Scott, Foresman.

Filley, Allan, Robert House, and Steven Kerr. 1976. *Managerial Process and Organizational Behavior.* Glenview, Ill.: Scott, Foresman.

Fleishman, Edwin, and Edwin Harris. 1962. "Patterns of Leadership Behavior Related to Employee Grievances and Turnover." *Personnel Psychology* 15 (Spring): 43-56.

French, John, and Bertram Raven. 1977. "The Bases of Social Power." In *Organizational Behavior and Management,* ed. Henry Tosi and W. C. Hammer, 442-456. Chicago: St. Clair. (First Printed in *Studies in Social Power,* ed. D. Cartwright, 1959.)

Gortner, Harold, and Jeremy F. Plant. 1990. "Ethics and Public Personnel Administration." In *Public Personnel Administration: Problems and Prospects,* ed. Steven W. Hays and Richard C. Kearney, 243-260. Englewood Cliffs, N. J.: Prentice-Hall.

Gouldner, Alvin. 1954. "The Problems of Succession in Bureaucracy." In *Reader in Bureaucracy,* ed. Robert K. Merton, Ailsa P. Gray, Barbara Hockey, and Hanan Selvin, 339-351. New York: Free Press.

Guzzo, R. A., and J. S. Bondy. 1983. *A Guide to Worker Productivity Experiments in the United States, 1976-1981.* New York: Pergamon.

Hall, Douglas, and Khalil Nougaim. 1968. "An Examination of Maslow's Need Hierarchy in an Organizational Setting." *Organizational Behavior and Human Performance* 3 (February): 12-35.

Hambleton, R., and R. Gumpert. 1982. "The Validity of Hersey and Blanchard's Theory of Leader Effectiveness." *Group and Organizational Studies* (June): 225-242.

Hays, Steven W., and T. Zane Reeves. 1984. *Personnel Management in the Public Sector.* Boston: Allyn and Bacon.

Hersey, Paul, and Kenneth Blanchard. 1982. *Management of Organizational Behavior.* 2d ed. Englewood Cliffs, N.J.: Prentice-Hall.

Herzberg, Frederick. 1968. "One More Time: How Do You Motivate Employees?" *Harvard Business Review* 46 (January/February): 53-62.

———, Bernard Maysner, and Barbara Synderman. 1959. *The Motivation to Work.* New York: Wiley.

Hirschman, Albert. 1970. *Exit, Voice, and Loyalty.* Cambridge, Mass.: Harvard University Press.

House, Robert. 1971. "A Path-Goal Theory of Leader Effectiveness." *Administrative Science Quarterly* 16 (September): 321-338.

House, Robert, Allan Filley, and Steven Kerr. 1971. "Relation of Leader Consideration and Initiating Structure to R and D Subordinates' Satisfaction." *Administrative Science Quarterly* 16 (March): 19-30.

House, Robert, and Terrence Mitchell. 1974. "Path-Goal Theory of Leadership." *Journal of Contemporary Business* 3 (Autumn): 81-97.

Hudson Institute. 1988. *Civil Service 2000*. Washington, D.C.: U.S. Office of Personnel Management.

Hunt, Sonja. 1984. "The Role of Leadership in the Construction of Reality." In *Leadership: Multidisciplinary Perspectives*, ed. Barbara Kellerman, 157-178. Englewood Cliffs, N.J.: Prentice-Hall.

Ingraham, Patricia W., and Charles Barrilleaux. 1983. "Motivating Government Managers for Retrenchment: Some Possible Lessons from the SES." *Public Administration Review* 43 (September/October): 393-402.

Jamieson, David, and Kenneth Thomas. 1974. "Power and Conflict in the Student-Teacher Relationship." *Journal of Applied Behavioral Science* 10 (September): 321-336.

Juran, J. M. 1988. *Juran on Planning for Quality*. New York: Free Press.

Kahn, Robert L. 1956. "The Prediction of Productivity." *Journal of Social Issues* 12 (December): 41-49.

Katz, Daniel, Nathan Maccoby, and Nancy Morse. 1950. *Productivity, Supervision, and Morale in an Office Situation*. Ann Arbor: Institute for Social Research, University of Michigan.

Katzell, Raymond, and Donna Thompson. 1990. "Work Motivation: Theory and Practice." *American Psychologist* 45 (February): 144-153.

Kerr, Steven, and John Jermier. 1978. "Substitutes for Leadership: Their Meaning and Measurement." *Organizational Behavior and Human Performance* 22 (December): 375-403.

Kipnis, David, Stuart Schmidt, and Ian Wilkinson. 1980. "Intraorganizational Influence Tactics: Explorations in Getting One's Way." *Journal of Applied Psychology* 65 (August): 440-452.

Kolarska, L., and H. Aldrich. 1980. "Exit, Voice, and Silence: Consumers' and Managers' Responses to Organizational Decline." *Organizational Studies* (March): 41-58.

Korman, Abraham. 1977. *Organizational Behavior*. Englewood Cliffs, N.J.: Prentice-Hall.

Lawler, Edward. 1968. "Equity Theory as a Predictor of Productivity and Work Quality." *Psychological Bulletin* 70 (December): 596-610.

———, and Lloyd J. Suttle. 1972. "A Causal Correlation Test of the Needs-Hierarchy Concept." *Organizational Behavior and Human Performance* 7 (April): 265-287.

Lewin, Kurt. 1948. *Resolving Social Conflict*. New York: Harper and Row.

———, Ronald Lippitt, and Ralph White. 1939. "Patterns of Aggressive Behavior in Experimentally Created Social Climates." *Journal of Social Psychology* 10 (May): 271-301.

Lewis, Gregory B. 1991. "Pay and Job Satisfaction in the Federal Civil Service." *Review of Public Personnel Administration* 11 (Summer): 17-31.

Likert, Rensis. 1961. *New Patterns of Management*. New York: McGraw-Hill.

Litwin, George, and Robert Stringer. 1968. *Motivation and Organizational Climate*. Cambridge, Mass.: Harvard Business School.

Luthans, Fred. 1977. *Organizational Behavior*. New York: McGraw-Hill.
_____, and Robert Kreitner. 1975. "The Management of Behavioral Contingencies." *Personnel* 51 (July/August): 7-16.
McClelland, David. 1953. *The Achievement Motive*. New York: Appleton-Century-Crofts.
_____. 1961. *The Achieving Society*. Princeton, N.J.: Van Nostrand.
_____. 1962. "Business Drive and National Achievement." *Harvard Business Review* 40 (March/April): 99-112.
_____. 1965. "Achievement Motive Can Be Developed." *Harvard Business Review* 43 (January/February): 6-24.
_____. 1975. *Power: The Inner Experience*. New York: Irvington.
McClelland, David, and D. H. Burnham. 1976. "Power Is the Great Motivator." *Harvard Business Review* 54 (March/April): 110.
McClelland, David, and David Winter. 1969. *Motivating Economic Achievement*. New York: Free Press.
McGregor, Douglas. 1960. *The Human Side of Enterprise*. New York: McGraw-Hill.
Maslow, Abraham. 1954. *Motivation and Personality*. New York: Harper and Row.
_____. 1962. *Toward a Psychology of Being*. New York: Van Nostrand.
_____. 1965. *Eupsychian Management: A Journal*. Homewood, Ill.: Irwin.
Mintzberg, Henry. 1983. *Power in and around Organizations*. Englewood Cliffs, N.J.: Prentice-Hall.
Morse, Nancy, and E. Reimer. 1956. "Experimental Change for Major Organization Variables." *Journal of Abnormal Social Psychology* 52 (January): 120-129.
Murray, Henry. 1938. *Explorations in Personality*. New York: Oxford University Press.
National Commission on Productivity and the Quality of Working Life. 1975. *Employee Incentives to Improve State and Local Government Productivity*. Washington, D.C.: Government Printing Office.
Nigro, Lloyd. 1982. "CSRA Performance Appraisals and Merit Pay: Growing Uncertainty in the Federal Work Force." *Public Administration Review* 42 (July/August): 371-375.
Oaklander, Harold, and Edwin Fleishman. 1964. "Patterns of Leadership Related to Organizational Stress in Hospital Settings." *Administrative Science Quarterly* 8 (March): 520-532.
Ouchi, William. 1981. *Theory Z: How American Business Can Meet the Japanese Challenge*. Reading, Mass.: Addison-Wesley.
Park, Chunoh, Nicholas P. Lovrich, and Dennis L. Soden. 1988. "Testing Herzberg's Motivation Theory in a Comparative Study of U.S. and Korean Public Employees." *Review of Public Personnel Administration* 8 (Summer): 40-60.
Pinder, Craig. 1984. *Work Motivation*. Glenview, Ill.: Scott, Foresman.
Porter, Elsa. 1986. "Harlan Cleveland: The Knowledge Executive." *Public Administration Review* 46 (November/December): 673-674.
Porter, Lyman, and Edward Lawler. 1968. *Managerial Attitudes and Performance*. Homewood, Ill.: Irwin.
Raven, Bertram, and William Kruglanski. 1975. "Conflict and Power." In *The*

Structure of Conflict, ed. P. G. Swingle, 177-219. New York: Academic Press.

Rodgers, Robert, and John Hunter. 1992. "A Foundation of Good Management Practice in Government: MBO." *Public Administration Review* 52 (January/February): 27-39.

Rohr, John. 1978. *Ethics for Bureaucrats: An Essay on Law and Values.* New York: Dekker.

———. 1980. "Ethics for the SES." *Administration and Society* 12 (August): 203-216.

Romzek, Barbara. 1985. "The Effects of Public Service Recognition, Job Security, and Staff Reductions on Organizational Involvement." *Public Administration Review* 45 (March/April): 282-291.

———. 1990. "Employee Involvement and Commitment: The Ties that Bind." *Public Administration Review* 50 (May/June): 374-382.

Rosow, Jerome. 1976. "Public Sector Pay and Benefits." *Public Administration Review* 36 (September/October): 538-543.

Schriesheim, Janet, and Chester Schriesheim. 1980. "A Test of the Path-Goal Theory of Leadership in a Health-Care Facility." *Personnel Psychology* 33 (Summer): 349-370.

Silverman, Buddy R. 1982. "The Merit Pay System: Prognosis." *Review of Public Personnel Administration* 2 (Summer): 29-34.

Simmel, George. 1950. *The Sociology of George Simmel,* ed. and trans. Kurt Wolff. Glencoe, Ill.: Free Press.

Simon, Herbert A. 1947. *Administrative Behavior.* New York: Macmillan.

Skinner, B. F. 1953. *Science and Human Behavior.* New York: Macmillan.

———. 1969. *Contingencies of Reinforcement: A Theoretical Analysis.* New York: Appleton-Century-Crofts.

———. 1971. *Beyond Freedom and Dignity.* New York: Knopf.

———. 1974. *About Behaviorism.* New York: Knopf.

Sobel, Robert. 1971. "Tests of Preperformance and Postperformance Models of Satisfaction with Outcomes." *Journal of Personality and Social Psychology* 19 (August): 213-221.

Soden, Dennis L. 1990. "Esprit de Corps among Army Corps of Engineers Executives." *Review of Public Personnel Administration* 10 (Summer): 41-54.

Staw, B. M. 1986. "Organizational Psychology and the Pursuit of the Happy/Productive Worker." *California Management Review* 28 (Summer): 40-53.

Steel, Brent, and Rebecca L. Warner. 1990. "Job Satisfaction among Early Labor Force Participants: Unexpected Outcomes in Public and Private Sector Comparisons." *Review of Public Personnel Administration* 10 (Summer): 4-22.

Steers, Richard. 1977a. *Organizational Effectiveness.* Santa Monica, Calif.: Goodyear.

———. 1977b. "Antecedents and Outcomes of Organizational Commitment." *Administrative Science Quarterly* 22 (March): 46-56.

Stogdill, Ralph. 1948. "Personal Factors Associated with Leadership: A Survey of the Literature." *Journal of Psychology* 25 (January): 35-71.

———. 1965. *Managers, Employees, Organizations.* Columbus: Bureau of Business Research, Ohio State University.

Stogdill, Ralph, and Alvin Coons, ed. 1957. *Leader Behavior: Its Descriptive Measurement*. Columbus: Bureau of Business Research, Ohio State University.

Student, Kurt. 1968. "Supervisory Influence and Work Group Performance." *Journal of Applied Psychology* 52 (June): 188-194.

Turban, D. B. and A. P. Jones. 1988. "Superior-Subordinate Similarity: Types, Effects, and Mechanisms." *Journal of Applied Psychology* 73: 228-234.

U.S. Office of Personnel Management. 1990. *Promoting Government Excellence*. Washington, D.C.: Office of Personnel Management.

Vroom, Victor. 1964. *Work and Motivation*. New York: Wiley.

_____, and Floyd Mann. 1960. "Leader Authoritarianism and Employee Attitudes." *Personnel Psychology* 13 (Summer): 125-139.

Wanous, John. 1974. "A Causal-Correlational Analysis of the Job-Satisfaction and Performance Relationship." *Journal of Applied Psychology* 59 (April): 139-144.

Weber, Max. 1947. *The Theory of Social and Economic Organization*. Glencoe, Ill.: Free Press.

Wexley, Kenneth, and Gary Yukl. 1977. *Organizational Behavior and Personnel Psychology*. Homewood, Ill.: Irwin.

6

Reporting and Budgeting

The reporting element in POSDCORB refers to the way the manager keeps informed as well as the way the manager keeps "subordinates informed through records, research and inspection" (Gulick and Urwick, 1937: 13). As Fayol (1937: 105) has pointed out, "the report on operations carried out is the complement of the plan of operations." The plan of operations is expressed through the budget; for the manager, budgeting means fiscal planning, accounting for the dollars spent, and monitoring expenditures to make sure the money is spent for purposes intended by the legislature or council. Reporting is the means by which managers learn about implementation of the plan of operations.

Reporting and budgeting are processes by which managers exercise control over the organization and its actions. More than 50 years ago, Follett (1937: 161) observed that in the "best-managed industries," control was "coming more and more to mean fact-control rather than man-control" and "the correlation of many controls rather than a superimposed control." The effectiveness of organizational controls based solely on facts rather than on facts and people has been challenged by recognition of the importance of behavior and human relations in organizations (see Simon, 1947), but Follett anticipated the impact of many types of controls on the centralized executive.

Managerial control through reports and budgets reflects the continuing effort to obtain information about and to evaluate organizational performance. This effort is particularly important in public organizations, since there is no price system to guide managers and since the political environment sends many, often contradictory signals to them. In Chapter 7 we will take up the problem of evaluation. In this one we will concentrate on the informational function of reporting and budgeting.

Organizational control through report and budget information available to outsiders is important to a democratic society because it is the way public organizations can be held more accountable to legislatures and executives and to the general public. Reports and budgets reveal what is going on in large bureaucracies and help inform the population concerning political and bureaucratic issues. Thus, reports and budgets are instruments by which citizens and political actors gain the information they need to exercise control over public organizations.

The success and effectiveness of managerial controls depend on the information with which the manager works. Generally speaking, there are three types of reports that link information with major managerial functions. There are *planning* reports, which managers use to anticipate future program developments and their consequences for the agency's services and budgets; *information* reports, which help managers analyze the impact of program activity and evaluate successes and failures; and *budget* reports, which measure fiscal performance and compare the costs of operations with available revenues. For public managers, controlling through reports and budgets helps establish credibility and support for an agency's operations and expenditures. The exercise of responsibility through effective internal controls makes bureaucratic action consistent with principles of democracy.

THE CONTROL PROCESS

In the chapter on planning, it was pointed out that organizations devise goals as general purposes for their operations and that these general purposes are restated more specifically as objectives or standards toward which the organization moves in the short term. Officially, goals for public organizations are set by public bodies such as legislatures. However, agencies and their managers play an important and sometimes a dominant role in what legislatures do. Government agencies typically have many specialists on their staffs who become quite expert by dealing with one set of problems over a long period of time. Legislators, on the other hand, have to deal with many different problems; furthermore, most local government legislators or council members are private citizens who serve only part-time. They are not likely to be as well informed about an agency's work as its managers are. As a result of all these factors, managers often have a major influence in the setting of goals.

In addition to strategic goals, the control process is concerned with assessing the achievement of objectives. Whereas goals are related to *external* or political considerations, the focus of objectives is primarily *internal*, the exercise of managerial discretion in government operations—that is, the making of decisions about the "selection, design, operation, control, and updating" of an agency's procedures (Rosenthal, 1982: 16).

The general purpose of control, then, is to evaluate and correct the organization's operation within a framework of external and internal standards. Successful control "eliminates chaos and provides consistency in an organization in order for goals to be attained" (Luthans, 1976: 143). Controls may be either direct or indirect. *Direct* controls refer to internal discipline and the rules for actions to deal with external threats. *Indirect* controls relate to the external environment and the reserves needed to deal with the unexpected (Katz and Kahn, 1978: 131). Control may also be exercised through *democratic* (multi-centered, decentralization) approaches or *hierarchical* (unified, centralized) approaches (Katz and Kahn, 1978: 327-330). Which of these are more effective depends on the situation; the evidence is that no one type is uniformly better than another (see Selznick, 1984; Sherman, 1966).

INTERNAL CONTROLS AND INFORMATION

The process of internal control has been defined as the "measurement and correction of performance in order to make sure that enterprise objectives and the plans devised to attain them are being accomplished" (Koontz, O'Donnell, and Weihrich, 1982: 463). Thus, the steps in the process may be thought of as (1) developing and stating a standard or set of standards for collective or individual performance; (2) measuring performance relative to the standard; and (3) taking steps to correct disparities between standard and performance. Correction occurs in one of two basic ways: through modification of the objectives or the plan (changing the standard) or through alteration of the organization's structure or its staff's composition, skills, or attitudes (changing the performance) (Koontz, O'Donnell, and Weihrich, 1982: 464-465). A *feed forward* system of control, which tries to anticipate the corrective actions that will be needed and to take them before a crisis occurs, is likely to be more effective than a *static* system, which merely reacts, often defensively, after problems have occurred (Koontz, O'Donnell, and Weihrich, 1982: 468-473).

Effective direction and coordination of the work of a unit require the manager to obtain continuous information about the outcomes of the organization's efforts to achieve its objectives. Such information is called *feedback*, and it is the basis for a systematic approach to control (Reeser and Loper, 1978: 427-434). Various reporting devices or budgeting systems are put into place to generate the needed information. These devices range from oral and written reports, visual inspections, and inventory reports to the comprehensive monitoring of operations. A feedback system enables an organization to better plan for and control the quantity and quality of work and the use of its resources—its personnel, its money, its materials and equipment, and its time (Higgins, 1976: 17-54).

Both reports and budgets and the information they contain follow several general rules to be of use. First, they must fit the work actually being done in the organization. Often, objectives change, and reports and budgets must be changed to keep them current. Controls must remain flexible and be designed to adjust to changes in plans. Second, the controls must be understandable; that is, they must indicate the corrective actions required as specifically as possible. This is the "feed-forward" aspect of controls. Controls must not only indicate that something is wrong (static controls); they must also show *what* is wrong (corrective controls), so that the manager can understand or interpret the information being provided. Interpretation of a control also assists employees in knowing what to look for and what to report (Hodgetts, 1982: 166-167).

Third, controls must give accurate and timely information about deviations from objectives. Information is often needed within *real-time* constraints. Real time means that the information and the action are on the same clock—the data are processed when received and used immediately (Krauss, 1970: 112-119). Batch-processing schedules, in contrast, accumulate data and then process a large amount at once; this may be acceptable (and economical) when the use of information lags behind its availability. The timing of information for controls must be reviewed periodically to ensure that the information is relevant, that the reports are used, and that costs of gathering and processing the information are not too high in proportion to the work being controlled.

Anticipation allows more flexibility in choosing corrective actions. Corrective action requires that the people of the organization and their manager learn what is going on around them. Feedback facilitates learning through repeated analysis of a situation (Wiener, 1954: 60, 83-85, 156-158). *Sequential analysis* is the statistical evaluation of an operation in "a continuous process going along with the production" (Wiener, 1954: 158). Although, as was noted earlier (see Chapter 2), regression analysis as a predictive tool can be treacherous, continuous analysis makes possible the constant improvement of corrective actions, and therefore better control, by those managers who are good learners.

MEASUREMENT OF PERFORMANCE

Public managers implement public policies through decisions that are consistent with the policies' general goals. Public managers monitor program implementation through a variety of techniques, to enable them to have at least some control over outcomes. "Rising costs, public dissatisfaction, and unsuccessful implementation efforts" all point toward the need for better control by public managers (Altman, 1979: 31). Altman calls the continuous interplay between information and management action a *performance monitoring* system (1979: 32). A critical element of a performance monitoring system is the development of performance measures. Finding adequate data sources and methods of measuring performance are constant problems. One way is through accounting concepts and budgetary definitions of organizational activity. Cost per action or number of occurrences per program, for example, are convenient and precise measures. Personnel records are sources of measures, too—for example, turnover and absence rates. Computerization of these records makes them especially easy to use for such purposes.

Measurements of performance are often most useful when they can be placed on a scale that indicates their relative magnitudes. A scale may be an ordinal or an interval one. An *ordinal* scale merely ranks observations as first, second, third, and so on, or as high, medium, low. An interval scale goes beyond that and defines the exact distance between the points on the scale (Kleijnen, 1985).

Rigorous interval scales are rarely possible in the measurement of human behavior. However, an analogy with temperature may be useful to the practicing manager. If a manager measures the performance of subordinates on a seven-point scale, for example, ranging from −3 to +3, with 0 in the middle, then the region from 0 to +2 might be considered a zone of acceptable performance—a kind of comfort zone. Performance measured at below 0 might be a sign that actions are needed to warm things up, and measures above +2 might call for special attention, too, since such a level may be too hot to sustain over time and the manager may have to cool things down in the organization in order to achieve continuous and stable performance.

Performance measures, however they are used, can be no better than the information on which they are based. It is to the techniques and problems of collecting reliable information that we turn next.

PUBLIC MANAGEMENT INFORMATION SYSTEMS

Today, a public sector manager who enters into a new job will usually find a computerized management information system in place. The use of computers of all types and sizes has steadily expanded since the 1950s (Kraemer and King, 1986). Only the smallest operations or the most remote jurisdictions will use the traditional pencil-and-paper approach. Expected payoffs from computerization, including more power for technical experts and greater efficiency and availability of information, have come slowly, if at all (Northrop, et al., 1990). Therefore, evaluation, redesign, and maintenance of the existing management information system (MIS) is most likely one of the major concerns of today's public manager.

Bozeman and Bretschneider (1986) provide a theoretical framework for conceptualizing an MIS in a public organization setting. A public management information system (PMIS) must recognize the importance of organizational context as indicated by "size, structure, time frame, organizational resources, and organizational maturity" (1986: 477-478). The characteristics of internal actors are also important for a PMIS. These characteristics are suggested by each individual's "cognitive style, level of satisfaction with the MIS and other such personal and demographic attributes" (1986: 478). But, a PMIS is more inclusive since it relates information needs to the external environment.

External environments are important to the public organization because they represent requests for data. The broader external environment emphasizes economic concerns, such as efficiency and allocation of resources, as well as political concerns, such as comprehensive but politically sensitive policy making (Bozeman and Bretschneider, 1986: 482-485). More narrow external environments relate the public organization to its work context through better information about purchasing decisions and to its personnel system through better information about its labor supply (Bozeman and Bretschneider, 1986: 484-485). Significantly, extensive empirical research confirms that a PMIS has a more interdependent, constrained environment than a private sector MIS, and that standard MIS practices are not automatically adopted and may be changed as they are implemented in a PMIS situation (Bretschneider, 1990).

PUTTING A PMIS IN PLACE

Ideally, a PMIS is specifically designed for the unique needs of an organization. The design development typically starts with an in-depth analysis of the organization's operations, much like the objective-setting elements of planning (see Chapter 2 and Rubin, 1986). The analysis determines the limits (parameters) and framework (structure) of the PMIS and the organization (Ein-Dor and Seger, 1978: 23-42). Costs and benefits of a proposed system are then assessed. There is sometimes a tendency to plan for more information-processing capacity than is needed. It is true that information-processing requirements may expand to use up excess capacity, but it is inefficient to commit to system machinery that will stand idle. On the other hand, it is also inefficient to install only what is currently needed and thus force the organization to use older and often slower technology when needs increase. Cost considerations include acquisition and maintenance of the machinery or hardware of the system, the computer programmers, and other personnel, and the software—the technical manuals and prepackaged programs.

If the in-depth analysis leads to a go-ahead, a preliminary design is drawn up to describe the skeleton of the PMIS (McCosh, Rahman, and Earl, 1981: 97-127). A major concern at this juncture is the standardization of information and its flow. Organizational units and operations need to be given standard identification codes. The orderly classification of organizational inputs, outputs, and the information needed about them is called a *taxonomy*. Many new terms are generated by the classification scheme and these are incorporated in the PMIS dictionary or *glossary*. Systems charts, field designs and layouts, inputs and outputs, data formats, and various mathematical formulae also are part of the preliminary design. Collectively, these tools define the operations that the PMIS will cover and show how the information system will work for managers.

Once the skeleton is defined, it is given muscle, with the purchase and installation of the computer, and brains, as the computer programs are tested and debugged. The data fed to the programs generate reports for managers to use in their decision making. Manuals of operations and procedures describe the techniques and languages that are needed to operate the system, interpret the results it produces, correct errors, and deal with emergencies. The documentation of computer programs, procedures, and equipment helps make sure that the system can be kept running even when the original employees have left. The manuals are also the basis for training programs that introduce new employees to the PMIS.

After all of the programs and equipment are tested and found to be working up to standards, the PMIS is put into operation. A system typically is brought up to speed gradually, as the previous one is phased out. Dealing with occasional system failures, maintaining the system's flexibility, and increasing its efficiency through redesign or new hardware or software will continue to occupy the manager's time and interest.

RUNNING A PMIS

Managers once had to be encyclopaedic. They gathered information through direct participation and observation, stored it in their heads, and applied it to the problems they encountered. Often they worked by intuition or by the seat of their pants, combining experience with some guesswork. Their techniques were not communicable to others, or if they were, they took the form of contradictory management proverbs (Simon, 1946).

Some organizations developed a collective or organizational memory, the joint product and possession of secretaries, clerks, colleagues, workers, and customers (Dery, 1981: 200-212). The proper *evocation agent*, or the person in the know about a particular problem, could be found through reading records or reports or by asking around. In an agency with much mobility and a high rate of technical change, it might simply be the person who had been there the longest. But the recollections were often partial and distorted by overgeneralization or limited purview.

Rapid change, the gravity of economic and political issues, and the sheer mass of information forced organizations to cease operating with this collective memory and to replace it with a computer's bank. The new evocation agent is a computer programmer—a member of a new, highly paid, and respected profession (Mosher, 1982: 110-142).

Computer technicians and program analysts represent a significant new level in management. They enter from a perspective of specialized control, which enables them to tell a generalist manager what can or cannot be done. Indeed, the generalist is in danger of losing control to the programmers, who may withhold information or influence its availability with a declaration that "there is no way the computer will do that." The general manager's best protection against this threat is to become computer literate, so as to be able to interact intelligently with programmers as well as with vendors of computer equipment, supplies, and services (Meindl, 1989).

Coordination and control of the reporting activity are traditional functions of general managers (Meltzger, 1981: 76-90). This does not change when the reporting is computerized. Selection and assignment of the computer programming staff, organization of the computer base, planning development and operations, coordination of job descriptions with performance standards, and *budgeting* for operations are major managerial concerns (Burch, Strater, and Grudnitski, 1979: 40-61). Managers must also determine priorities for mainframe computer use as well as alternative applications of computing capacity. Priorities and applications are critically important because of the explosive growth of microcomputers or personal computers (PCs) since the 1980s. PCs have dispersed computing throughout the organization with varying impacts on reporting (Sacco and Ostrowski, 1991: 9-14).

Computerized information systems can store and analyze large quantities of data with far greater accuracy and speed than earlier manual systems. The results are timely and informative reports, leading to improved decisions, more sensitive controls, and more productive analysis, in public- as well as private-sector organizations.

Nevertheless, "there is nothing magic about computers that can turn loose supervision into tight control" (Dery, 1981: 251). The central questions of the reporting function have not changed. What is the purpose of the report? How much data will it require? When and how will the report be produced? Who gets the information? What do they do with the information once they get it?

BUDGETS

Like reports, budgets are an important organizational control tool for managers. Budgets express expected organizational resources and outcomes in terms of specified revenues and expenditures. Budgets connect planning, staffing, organizing, and reporting decisions with the authority exercised at various levels within the organization. They reflect the length of the chain of command as well as its specific links. In sum, budgets are a way of correlating planning and operational decisions with the specific authority delegated through the hierarchy (Koontz, O'Donnell, and Weihrich, 1982: 484-486).

In private-sector organizations, the market price furnishes some guidance as to whether or not a service should be produced. Pricing systems are based on the logic that the costs of a good are allocable (consumers are willing to pay for them) and that the benefits are exhaustible (the person who pays uses up or exhausts the benefits of the good). Governmental goods and services, however, are not easily controlled by a market-price system. Most governmental revenues are in the form of either taxes or *user fees,* charges levied directly on the specific recipient of a governmental service. The fees may or may not cover all the costs; governments *subsidize* some services—that is, charge less for them than they cost to provide. State and local governments have a special problem of *tax avoidance:* some of the people who use their services do not live in their jurisdiction and therefore do not pay taxes there (such people are often called "free riders"). User fees offset the free-rider problem somewhat, but since people who live in the jurisdiction also have to pay the fees, they sometimes feel that they are bearing more than their fair share of the costs. The national government has a similar problem in choosing between taxes and user fees for such services as health care for veterans and the poor and aids to air and sea travel such as air traffic control, weather services, or electronic navigation systems.

Setting a price for governmental services is also difficult because use by one person often does not prevent use by another—that is, the benefits are nonexhaustible. If the government provides national security, clean water, and safe streets, everyone enjoys it, whether or not they have paid for it. Thus, the market offers no guidance. The decisions are ultimately political rather than economic, arrived at by a constant process of comparing the cost of a budget item with the general preferences and values of citizens and legislators as they vote and voice their opinions to support or oppose governmental decisions.

Budgets are a good example of the famous summary by Harold Lasswell (1958) of the core questions of politics: "Who gets what, when, where, and how?" Without much exaggeration, it may be said that the budget is the single most important policy statement of a government. As Mikesell (1978: 513) has put it, budgeting is partly the control of spending based on a "planning process to select desirable public allocations of resources" and partly the control of revenue generation based on "a planning process to choose reasonable distributions of the total burden among economic units in society." The budgetary process provides the mechanisms by which governmental programs are reviewed, program costs are related to financial resources, and choices are made among alternative programs and costs. Budgeting is the process by which the financial future of a government is decided. Budgeting translates politics and management into an agreed-upon work plan and puts the controls into place to implement it.

THE BUDGET CYCLE

There are four basic phases or stages in the budget cycle: (1) *preparation*, including planning and analysis; (2) *adoption*, or policy formulation; (3) *execution*, or policy implementation; and (4) *audit*, or evaluation. Thus, there are always three budgets at once, as shown in Table 6-1. This overlapping of budgets creates many problems for the manager. As audits are beginning to reveal what happened to last

Table 6-1 Overlapping Budget Cycles

			Fiscal Year 1	Fiscal Year 2	Fiscal Year 3	Fiscal Year 4
Budget for fiscal year 1	Prepara-tion	Adoption	Execution	Audit		
Budget for fiscal year 2		Prepara-tion	Adoption	Execution	Audit	
Budget for fiscal year 3			Prepara-tion	Adoption	Execution	Audit

year's budget, start-up problems are emerging in this year's budget, and planners and legislators are asking questions about next year's budget.

A budget's implementation phase typically lasts for one 12-month period, called a *fiscal year*. This is often not concurrent with the *calendar year*; in many jurisdictions, the fiscal year runs from July 1 through June 30. The fiscal year for the United States government currently runs from October 1 through September 30. In some places, budgets are passed for two years at a time. A budget *schedule* or calendar, established by law (perhaps supplemented by management directives), lays down the steps for budget preparation and adoption and connects them to a deadline for completion, describing the sequence of events necessary for legal adoption of a budget before the beginning of the fiscal year. A hypothetical budget calendar for a small unit of government is presented in Table 6-2. The lead time of six months shown in the table is typical for small governmental units, but at federal levels, estimates of revenues and expenditures are made several years in advance, and the preparation phase begins about 18 months before the start of the fiscal year (LeLoup, 1977: 96). Although there are many more twists and turns in large jurisdictions and the problems are of broader scope, the basic steps outlined in Table 6-2 are followed by all levels of government.

Stage 1: Preparation. The basic tasks of the preparation phase are to assess the expenditures and programs of the current year and to project what will be needed in the next fiscal year. In some cases, the governing body takes the first steps; these are called *legislative* budgets.

Table 6-2 Hypothetical Budget Calendar for a Fiscal Year Beginning
January 1

Date	Activity
July 1	Instructions and forms are sent from the manager's office to department heads for proposed capital improvements. An overall schedule for all events affecting department heads in the preparation and approval phases is also provided.
July 31	Deadline for submission of capital improvements proposed by departments. Preparation of the proposed capital improvements program is begun by the planning department or a planning consultant, within the context of the overall capital improvement plan.
August 7	Operating budget request forms and instructions are sent from the manager to each department, with detailed salary listings of current operating budget filled in. Instructions also include rate of salary increase proposed by the manager and a description of any other policies that may affect departmental budgets.
August 14	The manager or planning commission begins study of the capital improvements program.
September 10	Manager completes the preliminary revenue estimates, based on eight months' experience in the current fiscal year. Any surplus from last fiscal year is also considered in the estimate.
September 10	Deadline for all departmental budget requests to be submitted to the manager.
September 14	Budget conferences begin with department heads.
September 21	Budget conferences between manager and department heads are completed.
October 10	Final revenue estimates are made, based on nine months' experience.
October 14	Preliminary operating budget with manager's recommendations is completed; final typing and printing authorized.
November 7	Budget submitted to council.
November 21	First reading of budget ordinance and resolution. Budget is made available to press and public.
December 7	Public hearing on budget ordinance and resolution; beginning of preparation of final budget.
December 14	Council votes on budget ordinance and resolution.
December 21	Final budget is sent to departments.
January 1	Fiscal year begins.

If the mayor, manager, or an administrator takes the lead in budget preparation, it is called an *executive* budget. There are strengths and weaknesses in each approach. Legislative budgets are felt by some to be more sensitive to citizen needs, since legislators are theoretically more in touch with the public. Realistically, however, legislators may be most concerned with the specific interests or area they represent and not really representative of a broader community interest, a condition that may lead to budgetary "logrolling," in which legislators swap support for the proposals of others in return for support of their own proposals. In the process, the general interest of the community as a whole may be neglected (McConnell, 1966: 166-195).

Executive budgets were thought at one time to be a remedy for logrolling. Fiscal responsibility would be placed in the hands of a competent, visible executive. This person—a president, governor, or strong mayor—would be an elected official and thus responsible to the electorate. In cities with machine politics, at-large rather than ward elections would help ensure that the council would represent community-wide interests rather than narrow territorial ones. Budgets would be the subject of public, printed documents, not the result of handshakes behind closed doors. Generally, the trend toward executive budgets has been identified with the good government movement (Harrigan, 1989: 93-98). It began in the cities of the northeast and was picked up by states and the federal government. At the national level, the Taft Commission report in 1912 gave impetus to an executive-dominated approach in budget-making.

But the executive budget has its problems, too. Some say it tends to overlook important concerns of citizens, that it is marked by "too much process, too little participation." Another criticism is that executives depend too much on expert advice, resulting in the separation of budgetary discussion from political considerations, fragmentation of the budget among the competing needs advanced by experts, and a loss of executive control. Finally, instead of being prevented from logrolling, council members or legislators may merely roll the logs of their special projects on top of the executive proposals.

Once basic fiscal policy has been settled, preparation of the budget begins, with the instructions and forms that come from the manager. There is often a problem right at the outset: next year's budget may be a prisoner of this year's budget. The budget calendar makes it difficult to propose any but minor adjustments for the next year. This is called budgeting *on the margin*. In other words, budget preparation may have a conservative bias, which discourages innovation and suppresses funding for major changes. Sharkansky (1968) found that the spending patterns of the American states changed very little from 1900 through

1965. The other side of this coin is that governmental spending is made more predictable.

Expenditures and revenue projections are actually elements of planning and are typically called forecasts or estimates (see Chapter 2). Forecasting may be done simply by taking last year's expenditures and increasing them by some growth factor. If the inflation rate is used as the growth factor, the projection in effect calls for no change in the level of services, since any additional revenue would be absorbed by the increased costs of operations.

Population, salary, and service variables are important influences on municipal revenue and expenditure levels. Population variables refer to changes in the number or composition of people living in a jurisdiction; a plant opening or closing may sharply change tax collections or service demands through its effects on employment. Salary changes reflect swings in the standard of living generally and in the relationship between public-sector and private-sector salaries. The service variable refers to changes in the levels and types of services provided by the municipality (Scott, 1972: 4-5). The rates and even the directions of change in these variables may be widely different. If they are projected erroneously, the fiscal year may end with an operating deficit—that is, with more expenditures than revenues. Operating deficits are generally illegal in state and local governments, so if one is expected, managers will usually initiate a cutback or austerity program.

Occasionally, an unexpected change occurs in local government revenue because of changes in funding or requirements by other levels of government. States allocate some of their revenues to local governments, but in a given year a state may fail to make the payment of its share that was anticipated. Thus, a local government's revenue may be reduced and its budget unbalanced accordingly. Also, many states require or mandate local jurisdictions to make certain expenditures—for example, payment of a specified percentage of a state program that is administered locally; street lighting, highway maintenance, and social services are often funded this way. The state legislature may make changes on short notice that increase municipal outlays. There may be administrative requirements for federal grant-in-aid or block-grant programs that affect local expenditure patterns. Federal revenue-sharing is another area for which local governments have to make provisions. Beginning in 1972, the national government made annual grants of money to state and local governments for general purposes. A specific amount for each jurisdiction was calculated by a formula. By 1987, however, federal general revenue-sharing was discontinued by Congress for states as well as local governments.

In sum, a manager's budget amounts to a set of recommendations that the legislative body will consider when the budget process moves into its next stage.

Stage 2: Adoption. A city manager presents the proposed budget together with a budget message that discusses the major assumptions and forecasts behind the specific recommendations. At state and federal levels, the governor or president typically uses the occasion to make a formal address to the legislature.

The proposed budget is also accompanied by much detailed information. Based on the request forms circulated to department heads in the preparation phase, each line item or program has a description explaining the recommended changes. The proposed expenditures are compared with the previous year's actual expenditures and the expenditures estimated for the current year. The manager's recommendations provide a structure for legislative debate. Since a balanced budget is usually a legal requirement for local and state governments, the manager generally recommends a budget that is balanced. If legislators want to increase expenditures in one category, they are faced with the problem of decreasing spending in another category or finding new revenue to fund them all. Both are potentially unpopular political decisions. It is not easy to redesign the revenue package during an approval phase of six weeks or so. Anticipating the demands on revenue, the manager may recommend a tax increase and the uses to which it should be put.

The adoption process may be quite protracted, partly because it is handled by many different committees (Fenno, 1973). This is especially true of the federal budget, but some states have similar problems. Legislators tend to favor an important role for committees because it gives them prominence in the adoption process and allows them to focus on specific budget items. In most medium-sized municipal governments, this fragmentation by committee is not a primary characteristic (Lee and Johnson, 1983: 55-56). The budget is typically reviewed by the local governing body as a whole, except perhaps for a preliminary review by a finance committee. Furthermore, the governing body does not vote on the budget program by program, but rather deals with the revenue and spending package in its entirety.

The adoption process is the occasion for an interchange between executive and legislative branches (Lee and Johnson, 1983: 198-219). At the national level, more coordination for congressional budget adoption was outlined in the Congressional Budget and Impoundment Control Act of 1974. This act gives Congress a fairly tight timetable for passing its authorizations and appropriations. An *authorization*, normally passed before an appropriation, establishes or continues the legal basis for a program's operation or gives legal permission for specific program obligations or expenditures. Authorizations may be indefinite or for limited periods. An appropriation is the most visible means by which Congress provides agencies with money that they may obligate or spend. An obligation is a transaction, such as the placement of an order, for which the agency promises to make a future payment. Agencies also may incur obligations by borrowing and entering into contracts for services.

Before enacting any appropriations bills, both houses of Congress are now required to adopt a concurrent resolution that sets target amounts for budget authorizations along with outlays or net disbursements to be made during the fiscal year, the expected volume of federal receipts, and the size of the federal debt. These targets become standards by which Congress, in its adoption considerations, evaluates new appropriation requests from the agencies and the revenue measures that may be necessary to fund them. The 1974 act also created a new coordinating budget committee in each house to oversee the concurrent resolutions and to report on how well the authorization targets are being met.

In addition, the 1974 act allows Congress to manage authorizations and appropriations through a *reconciliation* process. Reconciliation occurs in a second budget resolution or bill, in which targets for spending, taxing, and borrowing become binding. Laws, bills, or resolutions may have to be changed to comply with the totals for the budget thus established. Reconciliation allows Congress to compare its taxing and spending decisions on an annual basis. One result of the comparison is the calculation of the expected annual federal deficit, when the amount of expected federal revenue is subtracted from the approved spending levels.

The ability of Congress to influence the budget was also advanced in the 1974 act through the creation of the Congressional Budget Office (CBO). The CBO is the legislative balance to the Office of Management and Budget (OMB) in the executive branch. The CBO's function is to gain extensive information from executive-branch agencies in order to conduct policy studies. CBO also makes five-year budget projections, with which Congress evaluates the president's plans. OMB still puts together the budget proposals, but the CBO presents its view of the proposals to give Congress an additional perspective. The budget proposals coming from the executive branch often clash with the desires of individual legislators who tend to express the values of their constituents and may advocate different expenditures or object to proposed reductions. For example, OMB may recommend a cut in Amtrak funds or in cost-of-living increases in Social Security payments;

for a member of Congress from a state or district where rail passenger service is important or which has a large number of elderly people among its voters, these recommendations may be unacceptable.

Whether in national, state, or local governments, the budget policy debates and the adoption process as a whole may be characterized according to whether decisions are made on the basis of comprehensive criteria or marginal ones. A *comprehensive* approach follows an idealized model of planning, in which expenditures are derived from a rational survey of alternatives. A *marginal* approach begins with the present year's expenditures and makes incremental adjustments for the upcoming year. Incremental budgeting is a way to control political power but, paradoxically, it may also become a way to heighten the rationality of budgetary decision making by raising the level and improving the types of information necessary to make politically acceptable decisions. Lindblom (1959, 1979) has called this the "science of muddling through."

Stage 3: Execution. When formal approval of the budget is complete, each agency receives its operating budget in the form of an appropriation. An agency has to revise its original budget if the legislature has made changes in it. This is not usually a problem at local levels, since the budget is adopted *before* the start of the fiscal year. However, before passage of the Congressional Budget and Impoundment Control Act of 1974, Congress had a habit of passing appropriations piecemeal *after* the start of the fiscal year, and that required extensive adjustment by federal agencies. The 1974 act also dealt with two other budget execution problems in the national government: rescission and deferral or impoundment. The authority of an agency to incur obligations may build up if it is not all used in a specific fiscal year, and so the act allowed the president to propose *rescission* legislation that would cancel unneeded budget authorizations. If Congress does not approve the proposed rescissions within 45 days, the budget authority must again be made available by the president for obligation. *Impoundment* refers to the action of an official who prevents the making of an obligation or expenditure of money that has been appropriated by Congress. The act requires the president to report an intended impoundment to Congress, which can then vote to override the decision. If Congress does not act before the end of the fiscal year, the impoundment must be withdrawn and the president has to make a new report for impoundments in the next fiscal year. (For a more detailed discussion of impoundment and related terms describing the federal budget-making process, see General Accounting Office, 1981: 31-83.)

Some observers have argued that the real issue in federal budgeting is how to control spending. Both Congress and the executive branch have important roles in the budget outcomes. Congress often passes entitlement legislation, which requires payment to eligible persons or state and local governments, and the intended recipients then have legal grounds for forcing payment if it is not made. Social Security benefits are one example of an entitlement. But it is the executive branch that determines allowances for unanticipated expenses or contingencies relating to entitlements and which supervises the agencies that exercise contract authority. Current appropriations are not required for many of these decisions; spending is based on permanent appropriations, or other commitments that Congress must honor. These conditions avoid annual reviews by the appropriations committees and are called uncontrollable or "backdoor" spending. According to one estimate, uncontrollable expenditures amount to as much as 75 percent of the total federal budget (Shuman, 1984: 44-45).

These control and implementation problems are not usually found at state and local levels. Many states have a constitutional requirement for a balanced budget. Some states maintain reserve funds to draw on should their spending unexpectedly exceed revenue. Deficit financing, the use of borrowed money, is permitted only for capital development projects. Of course, state and local governments do occasionally run an operating deficit; if the reserve fund is not adequate, services will be reduced or revenue increased.

Local governments are usually also required to balance their budgets by the laws of the state in which they are chartered or incorporated. Authorizations and appropriations are generally passed simultaneously as part of the jurisdiction's budget ordinance. The property tax is typically treated by the city or county as a balancing tax: the rate is set during the approval phase to close any gap between projected expenses and the projected level of all other local revenues. Local governments depend heavily on the property tax, while sales taxes are an important revenue source for states; the national government dominates the corporate and personal income tax source (although states also make use of the income tax). This pattern is known as *tax specialization* (Mikesell, 1982: 149-151).

After the budget bill is passed, the manager devises an allotment schedule for each department. In the federal government, there is an intermediate step of apportionment, which limits the overall obligations that may be made by an agency or program. Both have the effect of controlling the rate of spending and preventing cash overruns. Allotments spread spending out at a planned rate on either a monthly or quarterly basis. One result is to allow better cash management by the jurisdiction; idle cash, which is not to be immediately used, may be invested to earn interest. By regulating the flow of cash, interest income can be increased by investing larger amounts for longer periods.

During the execution phase, financial management is reviewed through a system of budget reports based on accounting information. In these reports, each department is listed in a *chart of accounts*, which includes balance-sheet and operating accounts for each fund in the local government, utilizing standardized classifications.

Municipal governments also use a system of *fund accounting*. A fund is a sum of money set aside for carrying on a specific set of activities. A municipality will have a general fund, which provides for the administrative operations of the government. It may also have an *enterprise fund*, under which it furnishes services in return for charges to users. Cities often operate legal monopolies to provide water, sewers, or electricity. Funds are also set up for other needs, such as working capital (the work that one department, such as a central garage, does for other departments), debt service, or capital projects.

Each fund has a separate chart of accounts. Expenditures may be recorded when they are actually spent or when they are obligated or *encumbered*. Revenues may be treated similarly—recorded when collected or when billed or due. If the accounts show actual expenditures and collections, the fund is said to be on a cash basis; if entries are made when the expenditure or revenue is obligated, the fund is said to be on an *accrual* basis. The accrual rule is the more common one, for two reasons. First, if expenditures are recorded at the time they are obligated, transfers of money between fiscal years are prevented. If a large obligation were incurred in, say, the 1991 fiscal year but not reported until the 1992 fiscal year, it would disrupt the 1992 budget. All of the encumbrances for a given year must come out of appropriations for that year, even if they are not actually paid until the next year. When all commitments for a fiscal year have been paid, no more transactions on that year's budget are allowed, and the books are closed in preparation for the final audit. Second, recording taxes when they are billed or collectible establishes the revenue base for a specific fiscal year.

Even though it is the legislative body that has the power of the purse, there is enough flexibility in budget implementation to support the assertion that it is actually the executive who has the real power to decide how appropriated funds will be spent and for what purposes. This power may even result in altering the legislative intent for specific programs and in reordering the priorities established by the legislative body. The control of budget implementation by managers is called *centralization* or *central clearance*. Legislatures sometimes move against the executive branch in an attempt to exercise more influence and control over budgets, but this is difficult to achieve because managers are so intimately involved in all phases of the budget cycle. The battles often spill over into the audit phase.

Stage 4: Audit. Among the many types of audits are fiscal, operational, program, performance, and management audits (Mikesell, 1982: 34-36). The *fiscal* or financial audit is an examination of the accounting records made during budget execution. It verifies that the financial transactions during the fiscal year have been handled as required by law and that the records and financial reports produced from them are accurate (Municipal Finance Officers Association, 1968: 127-147). Auditors may be hired by the state and dispatched to local governments, or the local jurisdiction may be required by state law to contract with a private firm of certified public accountants. An audit does not necessarily look at every transaction; a statistical sample may be used to audit a category of transactions, such as the payment of property taxes.

Operational, performance, and management audits are closely related but have different applications. A *performance* audit may be more properly included among program evaluation tools, but auditors are also interested in performance measures. *Operational* and *management* audits refer to reviews of management policies and the administration of the jurisdiction. A management audit assesses the activity and performance of managers; an operational audit focuses on specific tasks or programs and the way they are accomplished or conducted. Thus, although the concerns are similar, the objectives differ (Enke, 1975: 297-298).

Management audits may contain recommendations for changes in overall policies, usually transmitted in the form of a *management letter.* The manager and the council often discuss the recommendations and have a plan of action ready before the management letter is made public, in order to ward off critical attacks. The timing of the disclosure of the management letter can be an ethical problem, because protection of the credibility of the government competes with the public's right to know. Managers may also seek confidentiality to mask a reluctance to make needed changes.

In 1921, Congress created the General Accounting Office (GAO) as its auditing arm. The GAO's functions have expanded over the years to include studies of efficiency as well as of program performance. These studies aid congressional oversight of executive and administrative agencies, although the performance of Congress itself in this function "has been neither systematic nor comprehensive" (Ippolito, 1978: 132; see, for a general discussion of congressional performance, 1978: 120-134). Several states have established legislative audit councils or an equivalent, which parallel the work of the GAO.

Audits not only make sure that funds have been spent legally, appropriately, and effectively, but they may also include studies of a specific program and make recommendations that play a part in the preparation of new budgets.

FORMS OF BUDGETS

The quality of budget information and the availability and use of information at various budget stages are not constant. Budget reformers have advocated ways of making the budget process more effective and have developed various forms of budgets to improve budgetary decision making and to enhance managerial control. The most general formats are line-item budgets and program budgets. Performance budgets are an adaptation of program budgets. Refinements such as the Planning-Programming-Budgeting System and Zero-Base Budgeting have attempted to recombine elements of the general formats into new packages. An overview of budget formats is presented in Table 6-3, and the formats are described more completely in the discussion that follows. (For a historical account of budgeting techniques, see Schick, 1966.)

Line-Item Budgets. The rationale for budgeting in government was based initially on the need to control expenditures. Before regular budgetary processes were devised, agencies simply came to the legislature whenever they needed money. The legislature made an appropriation or searched for a revenue source in order to meet the agency's request. This custom led to a jumble of commitments, remembered or forgotten, and to charges of special-interest influence, mismanagement, waste, or overspending. To bring order and control into this process, centralized personnel systems and uniform accounting and auditing methods were instituted, along with centralized budget authorities using line-item budgets. The line-item budget gets its name from the fact that it expresses each kind and quantity of expenditure and revenue as a single item on one line of the budget. This highlighting of specific objects of expenditure and accompanying appropriations is intended to facilitate control over transactions (Bubunakis, 1976; Swann, 1983). An illustration of part of a line-item budget is given in Table 6-4.

The line-item budget specifies each expenditure exactly by department, by object, and by dollar amount. If the line item shows $19,000 for a crew supervisor in street maintenance, no more than that amount can be spent, and it can be spent only to pay the salary of that type of employee in that department. This format has been criticized for being too rigid and mechanical; it poses difficulties in adapting to changing conditions that may develop during the fiscal year. It may contribute to

Table 6-3 Summary of Characteristics of Major Budget Formats

Format	Major Objective	Prominent Actors	Control Measures	Complexity
Line-item budget	Fiscal control Identification of administrative responsibility Focus on operational resources	Fiscal officers Budget officers Accountants	Objects of expenditures Details	Fairly simple; detailed listing of expenditure items
Program and performance budgets	Better analysis aggregates (programs) Promotion of efficiency in performance	Managers Efficiency analysts	Work-load data	More complicated than line-item; use of quantitative methods, based on direct measures or observations
Planning-programming-budgeting system	More planning Focus on products of government action	Planners Economists Systems analysts	Cost of alternatives Cost-benefit analysis Systems analysis	Highly interrelated and complex; long- and short-term concerns
Budgeting by objectives	Clarify objectives New role for managers Better measures of performance or accountability	Managers with business experience Specialized analysts Strong central executive	Impact analysis Results measures Feedback	Complexity and long-term concerns narrowed to specialized areas; reduced general paperwork
Zero-base budgeting	Contain or reduce the size of government	Generalists Agency directors Political leaders	Efficiency or unit costs Ranked decision packages Cutback strategies	Somewhat complex; time-consuming and much paperwork

Table 6-4 Illustrations of Line-Item and Performance Budgets

(a) Line-Item Budget, 1992 and 1993

Account Number	Item	1992	1993
Department Account Code: Street Maintenance—5000 Personnel Services—200			
5202	Salary, director	$24,000	$25,000
5203	Salary, clerk	15,000	16,000
5204	Salary, crew supervisor	18,000	19,000
5205	Salary, crew supervisor	18,000	19,000
5206	Salary, worker	12,000	12,500
5207	Salary, worker	12,000	12,500
5230	Overtime	1,000	1,000
5250	Social Security (FICA)	9,500	10,500
5260	Health insurance	6,000	6,500
	Supply Series—300		
5302	Disposable office supplies	500	575
5303	Hand tools	300	350
	Total	$116,300	$122,925

(b) Performance Budget, 1993

Program Code:	Street Maintenance			
Function:	01	Surface repair		
Performance:	011	Resurfacing	y cubic feet	
	012	Repainting surfaces	y linear feet	
Function:	02	Surface cleaning		
	021	Sweeping	y miles	
	022	Cleaning drains	y number	
Expenditure Objects:	2001	Personnel		$100,000
	3001	Supplies		10,000
	4001	Operating expenses		12,925
		Total appropriation		$122,925

the escalation of overall expenditures, since each unit requests funds individually. Budget requests may be padded by asking for duplication of items, so that if the legislature reduces an agency's request there will still be enough money to allow it to perform as it wanted to. Longer-range questions of effectiveness are not asked, and concerns of resource utilization relative to program goals are not addressed. This type of budget lends itself to budgeting on the margin, merely making small increments in each item from one year to the next.

Program and Performance Budgets. After line-item budgets had been in use for some time, the need for more flexible management of public spending came to be recognized. Unanticipated events such as a natural disaster or a plant closing would affect both revenues and expenditures, and it was impossible to wait for next year's budget to deal with the resulting problems. Managers had to be given more flexibility and discretion. Increasing dependence on managerial decision making became a major trend in the operations of government, as well as of business (Burnham, 1941).

Managers could obtain the needed flexibility if line items were to be collected into activities or programs. Furthermore, the attainment of program objectives, which is to say the manager's performance, could be more easily measured and assessed in this format. Hence, there arose program or performance budgeting (Burkhead, 1956: 139; Koontz, O'Donnell, and Weihrich, 1982: 72-73). This type of budget was given particular impetus by the recommendation of the 1949 Hoover Commission that the federal government use it exclusively (Nigro and Nigro, 1977: 383).

Performance budgets start with financial descriptions of major programs and then connect these descriptions to work-load requirements (see the illustration in Table 6-4). Instead of specifying expenditures in great detail, a program is allocated a certain amount of money and the manager is given discretion in determining how the money will be spent (though some limits may be imposed, such as total number of personnel or maximum salary costs). Thus, the efficiency with which organizational resources are being converted into organizational outputs can be calculated, and the result is a measure of organizational performance, a powerful tool for managerial control. Measures of organizational performance allow comparisons to be made both between agencies and of the activities of a single agency over time. Unit cost—the cost of a single operation in terms of the performance unit specified in the budget, such as case or cubic foot—can be made the guide for the manager's behavior. This focus on unit cost rather than total cost may encourage exploitation of economies of scale. Managers are thus encouraged to be creative as well as scientific.

Legislators criticize performance budgets because they give too much power to managers to make decisions. Performance budgets may sometimes fail if suitable measures of performance are not found. For example, cost per cubic foot may be an excess of detail and not the best way to measure efficiency in the repair of potholes. In addition, the measures assume that the quality of an activity and its content are the same each time, a characteristic that economists call *homogeneity of product*. This assumption may not be valid; potholes, for example, vary by the type of roadbed. Some can be filled quickly with asphalt-patching material, while others require excavation and have to be filled with concrete. Crews in the same department may then display quite different performance measures, depending on where they have been assigned.

Performance analysis does indicate the relative costs of governmental activities and may assist managers and legislators in deciding how to go about the business of governing. One might even say that performance analysis makes government more like a business. But some critics argue that budgeting should have an impact beyond specific departmental or fiscal-year performance. Others have sought to arrest the rising costs of government by demanding that programs already in place be required to continually justify themselves. Other budget formats were devised to achieve these ends.

The Planning-Programming-Budgeting System. In the planning-programming-budgeting system (PPBS), the emphasis is on systematization of the budget-making process. According to Smithies (as cited in Marvin and Rouse, 1969: 802), PPBS moves through the following series of steps:

1. Appraisals and comparisons of various government activities in terms of their contribution to objectives
2. Determination of how given objectives can be obtained with minimum expenditure of resources
3. Projection of government activities over an adequate time horizon
4. Comparison of the relative contribution of private and public activities to national objectives
5. Revision of objectives, programs, and budgets in the light of experience and changing circumstances

PPBS was expected to liberate managers from the routines of fiscal-year budgets and allow them to raise questions about the future as well as about the immediate costs and benefits of alternative courses of action. In many instances, it brought about the first statement of agency objectives.

The approach had notable success in evaluating alternatives for purchasing military hardware in the Defense Department (Grafton and Permaloff, 1983: 100), and in August 1965, President Lyndon Johnson issued a memorandum applying PPBS to all federal agencies. There was little follow-up by the president, but agencies felt they had to respond nevertheless. A two-track system developed as a result. Agencies continued their traditional approach to budgeting and painted a PPBS veneer over it. Practices varied widely among agencies. Training systems analysts proved to be difficult, and staffing was a major problem. Furthermore, the bureaucratic reluctance to change was complemented by congressional indifference to the new budgeting format.

PPBS turned out to be expensive and time consuming. All the analysis, even if done enthusiastically, appeared to have little effect on reducing the uncertainties involved in decision making. Many managers held negative views about PPBS because of its complexity and the possibility that it would give control to a new kind of governmental executive, one who was more interested in planning to please the current administration than in running an agency in a regular, dependable manner. Managers also feared the threat of a centralizing tendency, with more power accruing to noncareer political executives around the president. They could not see a need for abandoning the tried and true techniques of program and performance budgeting in favor of the new approach (Schick, 1973). PPBS did not fare well in states and cities, either (Mosher, 1969; Mushkin, 1969).

One early critic of PPBS, Aaron Wildavsky (1969), questioned the relevance and wisdom of basing policy more on numbers than on political and managerial judgment and proposed that policy analysis be "rescued" from the system. In Wildavsky's view, PPBS was not being done well, and so the policy choices it was supposed to be studying were not being made.

PPBS was eliminated as an official federal budget format by the Nixon administration. The massive amounts of federal aid in Great Society programs have influenced state and local governments to follow the budgeting approaches used by the national government, so the elimination of PPBS at the national level hastened its decline at the lower levels.

Budgeting by Objectives. The redesignation of the Bureau of the Budget as the Office of Management and Budget (OMB) in 1970, during President Nixon's first term, signaled a shift toward increased control of government and governmental costs through better management. The OMB endorsed a new approach to budgeting called "budgeting by objectives," which is related to MBO ("management by objective") (see Chapter 2). Essentially, budgeting by objectives links the objectives outlined in the budget to an MBO plan. For budgeting by objectives to work well, the goals of the budget system and the goals of the MBO system must be related or similarly focused. The process depends on communications from within the organization rather than the imposition of planning goals from outside. Managers are expected to coordinate their agency's objectives with larger policy goals.

When MBO and budgeting by objectives were tried in the old Department of Health, Education, and Welfare (since split into the Department of Health and Human Services and the Department of Education), a number of problems emerged (Brady, 1982). These included difficulties in writing clear definitions of objectives in the public sector, uncertainties about the role of the chief executive, and a tendency for communication and coordination to degenerate into staff politics. However, there were benefits, too: the clarification of agency objectives, the measurement of achievements through defined milestones (objectives expressed in terms of time), and cost savings.

Both are concerned with making organizational objectives as explicit as possible and with generating and using corrective feedback for future decisions. MBO may be less cumbersome, because it encourages participation by managers in decision making. On the other hand, MBO's weaknesses are its vagueness about planning and a tendency for objectives to become so tailored to agency needs that problems of interagency coordination and exchange of information arise (De Woolfson, 1975).

In any case, OMB soon lost interest in budgeting by objectives, in part because the internal development of objectives by the agencies left little for OMB to do. To regain political initiative, OMB rediscovered the traditional budget techniques—programs, performance indicators, negotiations between executive and legislature—and merged MBO among them (Rose, 1977). MBO activities are inevitable in agency operations, but they may be given different names from time to time so that their importance and use are acceptable to managers and to political executives.

Zero-Base Budgets. Like MBO, the zero-base budget (ZBB) started out as a business practice. It had been applied extensively at the Texas Instruments company and was proposed for use in government (Pyhrr, 1977). Jimmy Carter had had experience with it while he was governor of Georgia, and when he became president in 1977 he instructed OMB to adopt ZBB as the official federal budgeting practice (Herbert, 1977; Carter, 1977).

ZBB operates on the premise that existing programs as well as new budget proposals should compete for resources each fiscal year. In previous practice, existing programs were often carried over from previous years as a base that was not closely examined or evaluated. By contrast, ZBB encourages systematic and comprehensive evaluation of all programs and proposals according to the jurisdiction's priorities. Resources may then be reallocated if existing programs are not contributing effectively.

The first step in ZBB is for managers to draw up their *decision packages:* this includes documents that describe "the information necessary for managers to make judgments on program direction and resource requirements" (Sarant, 1978: 66). The decision packages are reviewed and ranked by the managers who prepare and submit the budget. Thus, the approach tended to be management-dominated. It was also attractive to managers because it did not change the basic practice of budget preparation by increments (Schick, 1978) and because it gave them a chance to clarify agency operations internally · and to explore the consequences of an increase or decrease in revenue before making recommendations.

Pyhrr has contended that ZBB was a practical, flexible approach that was really based on evaluation (1977: 7). Managers did not have to return to a zero level of appropriations and rebuild an entire budget every year. Scrapping a program resulted only when poor program performance or attractive alternatives merited reformulation. And reformulation could occur by degrees as program components were identified, ranked, and evaluated.

However, critics said that ZBB activities simply recreated the paperwork of PPBS. Indeed, if every element of an existing or new program had been ranked, the work would have been enormous. The approach also had a limited perspective; many influences outside an organization alter the internal ranking of priorities (Mikesell, 1982: 91). The Reagan administration discontinued ZBB as official policy in 1981.

Some local governments also applied ZBB (McCaffery, 1981). In these cases, the process was often simplified by preparing decision packages that would reduce operations only by some decrement. Also, if only part of a program was involved, ranking did not have to be done (Wholey, 1978). While ZBB may well have improved budget making in local governments, shifting social priorities or changes in executive or legislative policies may frustrate managerial attempts to review and evaluate decision packages consistently.

Recent Developments. Allen Schick is responsible for two landmark books on congressional budgeting. The first, *Congress and Money: Budgeting, Spending, and Taxing* (1980) was written in the aftermath of the Congressional Budget and Impoundment Control Act of 1974. The book held out the hope that the act's changes to the budget process would produce better budgets. Schick's newer book, *The Capacity to Budget*

(1990), is more pessimistic. National budget decisions are now more uncertain and confused, more limited and weaker. For example, the Balanced Budget and Emergency Deficit Control Act of 1985 (generally known as the Gramm-Rudman-Hollings Act or G-R-H) did not work. G-R-H set progressively lower ceilings on new federal deficits with the target of reducing any additions to the existing deficit to zero by 1991. G-R-H did not work because of a general political standstill when it came to making cuts and because part of its mechanism for estimating reduction targets was invalidated by the United States Supreme Court (*Bowsher v. Synar*, 478 U.S. 714, 1986).

According to Schick, today the federal budget is a composite of budget policies and the budget process. It does not take an expert to recognize that the federal budget is in crises. Established budgeting methods have collapsed and the president and the Congress are at odds. The expected roles of major legislative and executive participants in budget decisions are unstable and the budget is largely created by methods made up to fit the situation. The process appeared to break down altogether in 1990, but was resolved by a budget "summit" in which the Bush administration and Congressional leaders agreed to basic taxing and spending rules to prevent additional deficits. Now, there are caps on discretionary, or appropriated spending. If Congress exceeds specific caps for defense, domestic, and international spending, then there must be an automatic spending cut in that category. There cannot be any shifting of funds among categories. Also, there are *pay-as-you-go restrictions* on mandatory spending for entitlement programs, such as for many social services programs, and for taxes. Pay-as-you-go means that if some benefits are raised, taxes must be raised also, or spending for other benefits must be cut. Some entitlement spending is exempt, for example, payments to the recently unemployed. However, spending caps and pay-as-you-go restrictions do not apply to fiscal problems that Congress does not directly cause. Contrary to popular opinion, the current federal deficit continues to rise because of the 1991 Gulf War and bailout requirements for the banking system (Hager, 1991).

In spring 1992, public pressure prompted some members of Congress to revive proposals for an amendment to the U.S. Constitution to require an annual balanced federal budget. Their resolution fell nine votes short of passing the U.S. House of Representatives and it was not voted on in the Senate.

CAPITAL BUDGETS

The foregoing discussion has emphasized operating budgets, or the annual, recurring expenditures of government. But governments also spend money from time to time for major assets that are expected to provide benefits for several years into the future. Such an expenditure is called a *capital* expenditure. These spending decisions are reflected in separate *capital budgets,* which use the same formats as operating budgets and raise equally significant problems. (The federal government does not have separate operating and capital budgets.)

Capital items are large, one-time projects that are so expensive they cannot be paid for when they are built. Smaller capital items, such as patrol cars or personal computers, are typically included in the operating budget. They may be more expensive than other items in the operating budget, but they are likely to be recurring items because they wear out or are replaced by technologically superior models. Capital expenditures provide for large and durable facilities such as a water-supply system or a parking garage. The money for them is borrowed and the facility is then paid for (the loan is paid back) as it is used. Raising money in this way is called *debt financing.* While long-term borrowing for operational expenses at state and local levels is virtually always prohibited, it is the rule for capital projects.

The money for capital projects is usually raised by selling bonds. These bonds are of two major varieties: general-obligation and revenue. *General-obligation bonds* pledge the full faith and credit of the jurisdiction as security. This means that a general tax may be levied to pay for them. The total amount of general-obligation bonds that a government may have outstanding at one time is often limited to a percentage of the total assessed value of property in the local government, or the amount of interest that can be paid on bonds in any one year may be limited to a percentage of state revenue. Even below these limits, issuance of general-obligation bonds may require approval in a referendum.

Revenue bonds are usually issued by authority of the governing body to build a facility for which a user charge is collected. A city parking garage where a parking fee is charged is a common example. The city may have to build it, since the rate of return on the investment or the amount of capital required for construction may discourage private investors. The revenue bonds for a jurisdiction are given a credit rating by private services; this helps inform potential buyers about the reliability of the bonds and influences their price and interest rate. Bond buyers are typically large investment houses, which resell their purchases to individuals or institutions. Both general-obligation and revenue bonds have been made attractive by exempting the interest payments not only from state income taxes but also from federal income taxes.

A special form of revenue bond is the *industrial development bond,* which is used by state and local governments to construct facilities that will be used by industry or business—for example, an industrial park. Income is derived from leasing or renting the site. Extensive use of industrial development bonds has led to criticism on the ground that they amount to subsidies for private enterprise, and Congress has limited the amount state and local governments may issue taxfree.

Capital budgets are formulated in the context of a *master plan*, which estimates needs for capital projects ten or even twenty years ahead, and of a *capital plan*, which covers the next five years. Each time the capital budget is made, the capital plan is redone to keep it abreast of implementation, and about once a decade the master plan is reworked. Capital projects not included in these plans are occasionally built, but only after they have been very carefully scrutinized and discussed.

When a facility has been built, the jurisdiction must add the costs of operating it to its annual budget. These new costs may be covered by user charges, but in the case of facilities like schools or prisons, the operating costs must be paid for out of general tax revenues. This is one of the reasons why the issuance of general-obligation bonds must be approved in a referendum.

A capital project is held to be economically justified if the present value of its future benefits equals or exceeds its costs. Benefits take the form of the stream of income expected each year of the defined life of the facility, but each year's return must be discounted to obtain its present value, since future dollars are worth less than present ones (the difference being indicated by the interest rate). The methods of calculating present value vary in detail (Aronson and Schwartz, 1975: 303-310), but the criterion that it should equal or exceed costs holds for all of them.

Research on the policy implications of capital budgeting is not extensive (White, 1978), but it is ongoing (Pagano and Moore, 1985). One particular problem is the development of facilities, such as those for waste-water treatment, that are required by federal legislation; local jurisdictions are often unprepared for these projects and have to make hasty decisions about borrowing and spending large sums of money. Another problem is the need to refurbish the nation's infrastructure—its roads, bridges, and other standing public facilities. Many of these were financed out of bond issues that have not yet been paid off. Some states and cities have exceeded their fiscal capacity to issue bonds.

CONCLUSION

Reporting and budgeting are processes through which public-sector managers relate to policy-making bodies in planning, organizing, and directing the resources, programs, and activities of government. These processes, together with the complementary ones of compiling information and analyzing the feasibility of alternative taxing and spending decisions, have become all the more important as legislators and voters have raised objections both to tax burdens they believe are too great and to cutbacks in government activities.

REFERENCES

Altman, Stan. 1979. "Performance Monitoring Systems for Public Managers." *Public Administration Review* 39 (January/February): 31-35.

Aronson, J. Michael, and Eli Schwartz. 1975. "Capital Budgeting." In *Management Policies in Local Government Finance*, ed. J. Michael Aronson and Eli Schwartz, 303-327. Washington, D.C.: International City Management Association.

Bozeman, Barry, and Stuart Bretschneider. 1986. "Public Management Information Systems: Theory and Prescription." *Public Administration Review* 46, Special Issue (November): 475-487.

Brady, R. H. 1982. "MBO Goes to Work in the Public Sector." In *Public Budgeting: Program Planning and Implementation*. 4th ed., ed. F. J. Lyden and E. C. Miller, 169-183. Englewood Cliffs, N.J.: Prentice-Hall.

Bretschneider, Stuart. 1990. "Management Information Systems in Public and Private Organizations: An Empirical Test." *Public Administration Review* 50 (September/October): 536-545.

Bubunakis, Michel. 1976. *Budgets: An Analytical and Procedural Handbook for Government and Non-Profit Organizations*. Westport, Conn.: Greenwood.

Burch, J. G., Jr., F. R. Strater, and G. Grudnitski. 1979. *Information Systems: Theory and Practice*. 2d ed. New York: Wiley.

Burkhead, Jesse. 1956. *Government Budgeting*. New York: Wiley.

Burnham, James. 1941. *The Managerial Revolution*. New York: Day.

Carter, Jimmy. 1977. "Planning a Budget from Zero." In *Federal Reorganization: The Executive Branch*, ed. T. G. Fain, 398-404. New York: Bowker.

Dery, David. 1981. *Computers in Welfare: The Mis-Match*. Beverly Hills, Calif.: Sage.

De Woolfson, B. H., Jr. 1975. "Public Sector MBO and PPB: Cross Fertilization in Management Systems." *Public Administration Review* 35 (July/August): 387-395.

Ein-Dor, Phillip, and Eli Seger. 1978. *Managing Management Information Systems*. Lexington, Mass.: Heath.

Enke, Ernest. 1975. "Municipal Accounting." In *Management Policies in Local Government Finance*, ed. J. Michael Aronson and Eli Schwartz, 283-302. Washington, D.C.: International City Management Association.

Fayol, Henri. 1937. "The Administrative Theory in the State." In *Papers on the Science of Administration*, ed. Luther Gulick and L. Urwick, 99-114. New York:

Institute of Public Administration.

Fenno, Richard F., Jr. 1973. *Congressmen in Committees*. Boston: Little, Brown.

Follett, Mary P. 1937. "The Process of Control." *Papers on the Science of Administration*, ed. Luther H. Gulick and Lyndall Urwick, 159-169. New York: Institute of Public Administration.

General Accounting Office. 1981. *A Glossary of Terms Used in the Federal Budget Process*. 3d ed. Washington, D.C.: GAO.

Grafton, Carl, and Ann Permaloff. 1983. "Budgeting Reforms in Perspective." In *Handbook on Public Budgeting and Financial Management*, ed. Jack Rabin and T. D. Lynch, 89-124. New York: Dekker.

Gulick, Luther H., and Lyndall Urwick, ed. 1937. *Papers on the Science of Administration*. New York: Institute of Public Administration.

Hager, George. 1991. "New Rules on Taxes, Spending May Mean Budget Standoff." *Congressional Quarterly Weekly Report* 49 (January 26): 232-237.

Harrigan, John J. 1989. *Political Change in the Metropolis*. 4th ed. Boston: Little, Brown.

Herbert, F. Ted. 1977. "Zero-Base Budgeting in Historical and Political Context: Institutionalizing an Old Proposal." *Midwest Review of Public Administration* 11 (September): 163-181.

Higgins, J. C. 1976. *Information Systems for Planning and Control*. London: Arnold.

Hodgetts, R. M. 1982. *Management: Theory, Process, and Practice*. Chicago: Dryden.

Ippolito, D. S. 1978. *The Budget and National Politics*. San Francisco: Freeman.

Katz, Daniel, and Robert L. Kahn. 1978. *The Social Psychology of Organizations*. 2d ed. New York: Wiley.

Kleijnen, Jack P. C. 1985. "On the Interpretation of Variables." *Simulation* 44 (May): 237-241.

Koontz, Harold, Cyril O'Donnell, and Heinz Weihrich. 1982. *Essentials of Management*. 3d ed. New York: McGraw-Hill.

Kraemer, K. L., and J. L. King. 1986 "Computing and Public Organizations." *Public Administration Review* 46, Special Issue (November): 488-496.

Krauss, L. I. 1970. *Computer-Based Management Information Systems*. New York: American Management Association.

Lasswell, H. D. 1958. *Politics: Who Gets What, When, Where, How?* Cleveland: World.

Lee, R. D., Jr., and R. W. Johnson. 1983. *Public Budgeting Systems*. 3d ed. Baltimore: University Park.

LeLoup, Lance T. 1977. *Budgeting Politics: Dollars, Deficits, Decisions*. Brunswick, Ohio: King's Court.

Lindblom, Charles E. 1959. "The Science of 'Muddling Through.'" *Public Administration Review* 19 (Spring): 79-88.

———. 1979. "Still Muddling, Not Yet Through." *Public Administration Review* 39 (November/December): 517-526.

Luthans, Fred. 1976. *Introduction to Management: A Contemporary Approach*. New York: McGraw-Hill.

McCaffery, Jerry. 1981. "Revenue Budgeting: Dade County Tries a Decremental Approach." *Public Administration Review* 41 (January/February): 179-189.

McConnell, Grant. 1966. *Private Power and Public Democracy.* New York: Knopf.

McCosh, Andrew W., Mawdudur Rahman, and M. J. Earl. 1981. *Developing Managerial Information Systems.* London: Macmillan.

Marvin, K. E., and A. M. Rouse. 1969. "The Status of PPB in Federal Agencies: A Comparative Perspective." In U.S. Congress, Joint Economic Committee, *The Analysis and Evaluation of Public Expenditures: The PPB System,* 801-814. 91st Cong., 1st sess., vol. 3.

Meindl, J. D., ed. 1989. *Brief Lessons in High Technology.* Stanford, Calif.: Stanford Alumni Association.

Meltzger, Morton F. 1981. *Information: The Ultimate Management Resource.* New York: American Management Association.

Mikesell, John L. 1978. "Government Decisions in Budgeting and Taxing: The Economic Logic." *Public Administration Review* 38 (November/December): 511-513.

_____. 1982. *Fiscal Administration: Analysis and Applications for the Public Sector.* Homewood, Ill.: Dorsey.

Mosher, F. C. 1969. "Limitations and Problems of PPBS in States." *Public Administration Review* 29 (March/April): 160-167.

_____. 1982. *Democracy and the Public Service.* 2d ed. New York: Oxford University Press.

Municipal Finance Officers Association. 1968. *Governmental Accounting, Auditing, and Financial Reporting.* Chicago: MFOA.

Mushkin, S. J. 1969. "PPB in Cities." *Public Administration Review* 29 (March/April): 167-178.

Nigro, F. A., and L. G. Nigro. 1977. *Modern Public Administration.* 4th ed. New York: Harper and Row.

Northrop, Alana, K. L. Kraemer, Debora Dunkle, and J. L. King. 1990. "Payoffs from Computerization: Lessons over Time." *Public Administration Review* 50 (September/October): 505-514.

Pagano, Michael A., and Richard J. T. Moore. 1985. *Cities and Fiscal Choice: A New Model of Urban Public Investment.* Durham, N.C.: Duke University Press.

Pfiffner, John, and Frank Sherwood. 1960. *Administrative Organization.* Englewood Cliffs, N.J.: Prentice-Hall.

Pyhrr, P. A. 1977. "The Zero-Base Approach to Government Budgeting." *Public Administration Review* 37 (January/February): 1-8.

Reeser, Clayton, and Marvin Loper. 1978. *Management: The Key to Organizational Effectiveness.* Glenview, Ill.: Scott, Foresman.

Rose, Richard. 1977. "Implementation and Evaporation: The Record of MBO." *Public Administration Review* 37 (January/February): 64-71.

Rosenthal, S. R. 1982. *Managing Government Operations.* Glenview, Ill.: Scott, Foresman.

Rubin, B. M. 1986. "Information Systems for Public Management: Design and Implementation." *Public Administration Review* 46, Special Issue (November): 540-552.

Sacco, J. F., and J. W. Ostrowski. 1991. *Microcomputers and Government Management.* Pacific Grove, Calif.: Brooks/Cole.

Sarant, P. C. 1978. *Zero-Base Budgeting in the Public Sector.* Reading, Mass.: Addison-Wesley.

Schick, Allen. 1966. "The Road to PPB: The Stages of Budget Reform." *Public Administration Review* 26 (December): 243-258.

———. 1973. "A Death in the Bureaucracy: The Demise of Federal PPB." *Public Administration Review* 33 (March/April): 146-150.

———. 1978. "The Road from ZBB." *Public Administration Review* 38 (March/April): 177-179.

———. 1980. *Congress and Money: Budgeting, Spending, and Taxing.* Washington, D.C.: Urban Institute.

———. 1990. *The Capacity to Budget.* Washington, D.C.: Urban Institute.

Scott, Claudia Devita. 1972. *Forecasting Local Government Spending.* Washington, D.C.: Urban Institute.

Selznick, Philip. 1984. *Leadership in Administration: A Sociological Interpretation.* Berkeley: University of California Press.

Sharkansky, Ira. 1968. *Spending in the American States.* Chicago: Rand-McNally.

Sherman, Harvey. 1966. *It All Spends: A Pragmatic Approach to Organization.* University: University of Alabama Press.

Shuman, Howard E. 1984. *Politics and the Budget.* Englewood Cliffs, N.J.: Prentice-Hall.

Simon, Herbert A. 1946. "The Proverbs of Administration." *Public Administration Review* 6 (Winter): 53-67.

———. 1947. *Administrative Behavior.* New York: Macmillan.

Swann, W. K. 1983. "Theoretical Debates Applicable to Budgeting." In *Handbook on Public Budgeting and Financial Management,* ed. Jack Rabin and T. D. Lynch, 3-59. New York: Dekker.

Wanat, John. 1978. *Introduction to Budgeting.* North Scituate, Mass.: Duxbury.

Welch, Susan, and J. I. Comer. 1983. *Quantitative Methods for Public Administration.* Homewood, Ill.: Dorsey.

White, Michael J. 1978. "Capital Budgeting." In *Essays in Public Finance and Financial Management,* ed. J. E. Petersen and C. L. Spain, 42-52. Chatham, N.J.: Chatham House.

Wholey, Joseph S. 1978. *Zero-Base Budgeting and Program Evaluation.* Lexington, Mass.: Heath.

Wiener, Norbert. 1954. *The Human Use of Human Beings.* 2d ed. New York: Doubleday.

Wildavsky, Aaron. 1969. "Rescuing Policy Analysis from PPBS." *Public Administration Review* 29 (March/April): 189-202.

7

Evaluation

There is probably no one who has not asked, from the back seat of a car, "How long before we get there?" Americans, perhaps even more than other people, have an intense need to *know*. Monthly, we total up our purchasing power, our cost of living, and our economic growth. Some calculations we make daily, hourly, or even minute-by-minute, as with stocks or the prices of commodities. We turn out quarterly reports and yearly assessments, complete with bar charts or colored pie diagrams comparing then with now. Students are concerned about their midterm and semester grades and watch with anxiety as their grade-point average is determined. These measures, indices, reports, and comparisons are all forms of evaluation.

Managers, too, need evaluation in order to learn where they have been and where they are going. Evaluation is integrally related to planning; each is a technique by which organizations define their meaning and purpose. It is through concepts and practices of planning that evaluation is connected to POSDCORB. Evaluation is an important source of information for planning, and it is thus a pivotal activity, which ends one round of decisions ("how did we do?") and becomes the start of another round ("what will we do differently next time?"). Evaluation transforms the elements of POSDCORB from a static to a dynamic process.

What this suggests is that POSDCORB can be recast in the form of a *policy cycle* (see Figure 7-1). Evaluation procedures generate the information necessary for making decisions in successive and repeated phases (sometimes called "iterations") as the programs are implemented. On the basis of the evaluation findings of one cycle, a new set of program decisions is made and the next cycle begins—unless the evaluation led to a decision to discontinue the program. The variation of decisions in

Figure 7-1   The Managerial Process

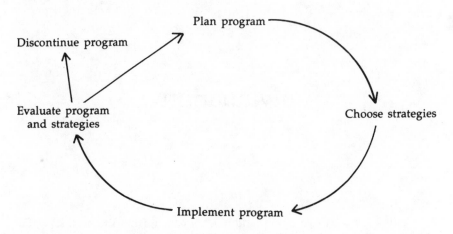

these cycles also indicates that the functions of management are applied in constantly changing ways.

Public managers are ultimately political actors whose choices are evaluated from many perspectives. Successful managers are not overwhelmed by exposure to evaluation. They try to adapt to external or political changes rather than fighting them unnecessarily. At the same time, social and technical changes occur inside the organization also, and evaluation techniques must be applied to them as well. The same kinds of evaluation techniques can be used for both these types of problems.

PURPOSES AND CONCEPTS

Evaluation concerns are connected to politics in at least three ways: (1) The programs being evaluated are "creatures of political decision" and therefore represent the interests of their political sponsors. (2) Evaluation reports compete with other forms of information for the attention of political leaders. (3) Evaluation studies make "implicit political statements" (Weiss, 1973: 37). Implementation decisions are rarely based solely on technical, internal considerations or events over which a manager has complete control, nor do the general criteria of effectiveness or efficiency always play a decisive role, if only because they are often difficult to define in a suitable way.

Managers share evaluation responsibilities with outside actors such as elected officials and program beneficiaries or clients, who have an interest in program outcomes. These political evaluations may bring about improved accountability for public management, although it is sometimes argued that they advance the relatively narrow interests of the particular evaluator and not those of the general public.

Evaluation also has internal dimensions. Technical program evaluations conducted by the organization document achievements as well as lead to recommendations for program improvements. These studies may also be used to build an organizational base from which to launch a campaign for political support for new programs. In this light, evaluation may be seen as an instrument of short-term managerial planning.

Both political accountability and internal flexibility underscore the importance of program evaluation. The following are the questions basic to evaluation for both of these purposes (adapted from Bernstein and O'Hara, 1979: 434-441):

1. How well is the program being managed?
2. Is the program doing what it is intended to do?
3. How well is the program achieving its objectives?
4. How was it able to accomplish all it was meant to do, or why were planned objectives not accomplished?
5. What difference did the program make, or what were its effects?

Implicit in all these questions is the assumption that the manager is both (1) a politician who uses the *art* of management as a negotiator and advocate and (2) a technician who employs the *science* of management in order to achieve public purposes.

Organizations undertake evaluation activities so that they can be more effective. An executive action is said to be *effective* when it accomplishes a specific aim or objective or when it gives direction and purpose to the organization's personnel (Barnard, 1938: 215-234; Stillman, 1984: 290-301). In the same way, the effectiveness of an *organization* may be conceptualized as the degree to which organizational activity leads to specific, measurable objectives that are among the organization's goals. Of course, organizations may have single to multiple goals and a single goal may be divided into many objectives.

Another approach to organizational effectiveness is to describe it in systems terms (Fesler, 1980: 30-34; Katz and Kahn, 1978: 18-34). The organization must fulfill its aims, but it must not use up all its resources or overstrain its main program elements in doing so. A system is a means of converting organizational resources, such as people, equipment, or skills, into the outputs necessary for goal achievement. Resource conversion affects the external social, political, and physical environment and influences the ability of the organization to obtain future resources. The systems model stresses the importance of change in the organization's environments and the importance of trade-offs in organizational maintenance and development.

In sum, evaluation is the management activity primarily concerned with the definition and determination of effectiveness. The developmental background of evaluation research includes many specific examples of program research findings (Caro, 1977: 30-38), for program information and program judgments are key elements of evaluation. Evaluators generate the information; managers use it to make judgments about the organization and its operation.

VARIATIONS IN APPROACH

Evaluation is a complex activity, involving both subjective and empirical concepts and methods of analysis. Initially, subjective elements predominate, until the empirical elements of evaluation are defined. Empirical elements are what the evaluator can measure objectively, though it remains vital for the manager to keep in mind the context within which the evaluation is conducted. Sometimes, managers are able to sense influences and interactions that cannot be discovered in planned, systematic evaluation studies. On the other hand, intuitive evaluation may be unreliable and short-sighted.

The work of evaluation is done through study of an organization's programs, associating the outcomes of program activity with the goals and objectives that the program was meant to accomplish. However, since program characteristics vary, it is logical that evaluation approaches may also have to vary. Among the characteristics that contribute to the distinctiveness of a program are scope, size, duration, clarity of goals, complexity of operations, and degree of innovativeness (Weiss, 1972: 5).

Scope, size, and duration may be measured by territorial extent or by numbers of people or amounts of time. Scope may range from a small program of a local government to a nationwide program conducted by the federal government. Some programs are national in scope but are delivered by state or local governments. A national program is likely to be accompanied by more intense evaluation research. Recent national policy has encouraged programs of statewide scope and administration, and states will have to increase their capacity for evaluation correspondingly.

The size of a program tends to vary directly with its scope; the larger the scope, the greater the number of people involved. A program's duration is either limited or continuous. A continuous program is one with no stated end date; indeed, it may never be clearly over. The importance of duration as an aspect of program evaluation arises out of the "maturation effect" on the evaluation measures (Campbell and Stanley, 1963: 59-61), by which is meant that the longer the program is in effect, the greater is the chance that extraneous, unplanned, unexpected, and even unknown factors will have an influence on program outcomes.

Clarity and complexity are more elusive program aspects and thus are harder to measure. Programs with unclear goals are more difficult both to implement and to evaluate. One beneficial effect of a planned program evaluation may be the clarification of goals that it impels. The complexity of a program refers to the number of its goals and objectives, the degree of their refinement, and the number of alternative ways of accomplishing them (including those outside the program as well as those within it). Complexity may be related to duration, since the achievement of more complex program goals may be possible only with a greater amount of time. Finally, the more innovative a program, the less certainty there is about the number and nature of its outcomes, and therefore the harder it is to evaluate.

Like its internal features, the external aspects of a program come in a wide variety of categories, dimensions, and levels, and evaluation approaches vary accordingly. One way to describe them is in terms of the way a program relates to individuals in everyday interactions (Lewis, 1981). A second way is in terms of the ways organizations adapt to changes in conditions around them (Bennis, 1981). Other approaches include a program's relation to larger schemes or systems of programs and the organization's receptiveness to public comments.

Program evaluation is most difficult for programs that are intended to produce behavioral changes in individuals, usually organizational clients. It is difficult to associate behavioral changes in individuals with the activities of a program, such as one in education or corrections. Evaluators often have to rely on expert judgments about behavioral changes, rather than measuring those changes directly. Several expert judges may be used to correct for their possible biases. Tests, interviews, and questionnaires may also be used to measure changes in attitudes, values, knowledge, or skills, but they do not eliminate the problem of distinguishing between outcomes due to program activities and those attributable to external circumstances. For example, a job-training program might be given credit for an increase in job satisfaction, when employees actually are happier because of a change in work schedules that happened to take place at the same time (perhaps in connection with implementation of the program). Another source of controversy is the use of an evaluation standard that is different—often for political reasons—from that used by program managers. Programs that are the object of keen public interest may have competing evaluation studies made of them, and many times the most negative evaluation comes from an evaluation group that is outside the organization.

In order to put the evaluation of single programs into a larger context, managers sometimes are led to evaluate the overall effectiveness of the organization itself, especially its ability to adapt to internal and external changes. Variations in employee performance or in the amount of the budget devoted to certain functions are examples of evaluation data for measuring and analyzing organizational adaptability. If performance is declining, then the internal environment is suggested as a target for more focused evaluation studies; if budgets are shrinking, success in adaptation to changing political or economic winds would be brought into question.

Programs that are part of larger programs or systems of programs are usually studied in that larger or *macro* context; examples are programs aimed at housing rehabilitation, transit improvement, and crime prevention (Poister, McDavid, and Hoagland, 1979). The purpose of macro evaluation may be to improve an entire delivery system by bringing about better cooperation among many units of government. The data for evaluation may include surveys, budgets, interviews, statistics on the status and actions of clients, and program documents. Large-scale programs may take steps to increase the consistency of the studies of the component programs so that the data can be aggregated.

A variety of decision-making options may emerge from the analysis of the evaluation data. Among them are the choices to continue or discontinue a program, to initiate or abandon particular strategies or techniques, and to add, extend, or delete program elements (Starling, 1986: 392; Van Maanen, 1973: 1-6). In addition, evaluation studies provide evidence for political support or criticism for existing and new programs. Evaluation studies may also contribute to decisions about new programs before they are launched, by providing data about the consequences of similar or related programs in the past. The mobilization and analysis of evaluation data for these purposes has come to be known as the *policy sciences*.

STEPS IN SYSTEMATIC EVALUATION

The first step in systematic evaluation for management purposes is to specify the conditions that need investigation or the decisions that have to be made. The manager usually recommends to the policy-making body (legislature or council) an explicit framework for analysis, so that the political overseers can play a general and guiding role in the evaluation effort. Evaluation is more than a private investigation; it is a public process, and one that places a heavy burden on the manager's judiciousness. During evaluation, the manager must be a politically neutral but technically competent mediator among the many interests affected by study of a program.

The second step in systematic evaluation is to designate the questions that are to be answered. The manager must be able to give the evaluator a clear idea of what information is needed.

A third step is the selection of the evaluator. In-house staff may be used; an outside, private consultant may be called in; or the manager may turn to one of the technical assistance groups that some states and federal agencies have on their staffs. These groups provide the objectivity of an outsider, usually at lower cost than a private consultant. Evaluations conducted by people within the organization consume large amounts of its personnel's skills and time and sometimes entail deflection from an organizational mission. Insiders have the advantage of starting out with some familiarity with the program, but they may find it difficult to be objective about a program in which they are involved. Outsiders are typically in the opposite position—though their objectivity, too, may be compromised by an effort to reflect the views of higher national or state officials who may want to see a particular program succeed (or fail) or by the prospect of additional contracts.

An effective evaluation is one that answers the questions that have been put to it, is based on sound and comprehensive data, and is developed with the confidence and support of policy makers and employees. Above all, managers must guard against producing interesting but unusable evaluations and against exceeding the resources of the agency allocated for evaluation (Havens, 1981).

USES OF EVALUATION

The most general uses of evaluation are in deciding whether to continue or terminate a program and in deciding how to improve a program. Evaluation conducted for the first of these purposes is called *summative evaluation* or program monitoring; that conducted for the latter purpose is *formative evaluation* or program development.

One aspect of summative evaluation is *impact analysis,* which compares the overall effects of a service or program "with what would have happened had the program not been implemented" (Mohr, 1988: 2-3), in other words, with what was predicted to happen with the present program. The basic question is whether individuals are better off because of the governmental activity, but impact analysis also deals with questions of unintended consequences. For example, did increased police patrols result in overcrowding of the local jail? Impact analysis may lead to the designation of services for reduction or termination, with due consideration given to the dislocations that may result should services be altered. In addition, summative evaluation is concerned with *productivity* or *performance evaluation*—that is, with how well a service is being performed and how efficiently an organization's resources are being used. Summative evaluation is conducted on the basis of a model derived from research design (Fitz-Gibbon and Morris, 1978: 9-14). Measurements of performance are built into the program at the planning stage, through such devices as objective performance standards, or at the implementation stage, by means of budgetary and accounting controls.

The use of short-term summative evaluation to abolish a program is increasingly being questioned (Palumbo and Nachmias, 1984). The decision to terminate is most frequently based on quantitative models using goal-directed research. However, qualitative case studies of individual programs may be just as useful in summative evaluation. Longer-term, incremental adjustments and program modifications will more likely result if credible evaluative case studies can be produced. *Case studies* deal with a specific set of circumstances and do not seek to develop statistical generalization.

Discontinuing a program is perhaps more difficult than adjusting or redesigning it. Resistance is likely to rise from several groups. Clientele, employees of the program, legislators, and others may rally behind an ongoing program. Gradual termination, by narrowing the program's boundaries or phasing out its services one by one rather than shutting it down abruptly, may be a preferable course of action. Programs may also be discontinued after they have been replaced by other programs.

A need for program modification may come from inadequate procedures or practices or the desire to reconsider standards of service or productivity. New circumstances may arise that were not anticipated when the program was designed and that make its priorities inappropriate, outdated, or unattainable. In other situations, the simple pressure of time may be enough to thwart the attainment of an objective. These are the conditions that give rise to a need for formative evaluation.

One problem with formative evaluation is that it is often conducted without clear guideposts (Fitz-Gibbon and Morris, 1978: 14). However, this can also be an advantage, for it allows for a variety of research designs, including alternatives assessment and pilot programs, and it permits the unexpected to be discovered. A necessary concomitant of formative evaluation is that the program be flexible, so that it can be modified in response to the findings.

CONDUCTING AN EVALUATION

Struening and Guttentag (1975, 1: 3) have divided the conduct of an evaluation into these steps: "(1) conceptualizing the problem; (2) reviewing relevant literature; (3) developing a research strategy; (4) determining a research design; (5) selecting and maintaining a sample; (6) choosing measures and assessing their ... properties; (7) selecting appropriate personnel to conduct the study; and (8) communicating the results" (see also Starling, 1986: 264-271). Each of these steps involves a number of technical problems (Sylvia, Meier, and Gunn, 1985). There is extensive literature on the variety of approaches to and findings in evaluation studies (see, for example, Glass, 1976; Wholey, Abramson, and Bellavita, 1986). What is important is that the evaluation carry *credibility,* which means that it reflects sufficient political considerations to be relevant and useful but also shows enough scientific rigor in its methods to be seen as independent of specific political influences (Stufflebeam and Webster, 1981).

EVALUABILITY ASSESSMENT

Even before an evaluation begins, it is often helpful to undertake an *evaluability assessment,* in which the program is scrutinized closely to make sure that it is important enough to warrant evaluation and that the standards for evaluation quality can be met—namely, that the program objectives are well defined, the program's activities are plausibly related to achievement of the objectives, and the questions the evaluation is to answer are clearly stated (Wholey, 1979: 17).

The steps in an evaluability assessment are these (adapted from Rutman, 1980: 89-161):

1. Prepare a "program documents model," which shows what the components and goals of the program are and how they are interconnected.
2. Interview program personnel to verify the program documents model, explain the evaluability assessment process, and clarify the intended uses of the proposed evaluation.
3. Develop an "evaluable program model," which shows what will actually be considered in the evaluation.
4. Analyze the feasibility of achieving the purposes of the evaluation by identifying the chances for implementation, the potential users, and the methodological and informational requirements, critiquing the research design, and assessing potential difficulties in data collection and analysis.

While the original purpose of conducting an evaluability assessment was to increase the likelihood that the results would actually be used, the process has evolved into a separate management tool. Sometimes enough information is developed at this early stage to allow managers to take appropriate actions without entering into a full-scale study.

RELIABILITY AND VALIDITY

If the data of an evaluation are to meet the criteria of scientific rigor, they must be shown to be *reliable* and *valid*. Reliability refers to the consistency of the data—that is, whether a measure generates the same results when it is used repeatedly in the same way in the same situation. In a word, reliability means *reproducibility*. A highly specific measure is more likely to be reliable.

Valid data result when the measures chosen actually describe what they were intended to describe. Data may be reproducible without being valid if, for example, the measure yields consistent results but the results are irrelevant to the evaluation question at hand. Where an evaluation study is directed at elusive concepts, such as program quality, validity can be enhanced with the use of multiple indicators.

A distinction has been made between internal and external validity. *Internal validity* deals with the question, "Did the experimental treatments in fact make a difference in this specific experimental instance?" *External validity* deals with the generalizability to other settings of the relationships among the measures (Campbell and Stanley, 1963: 5). Among the threats to internal validity are the impact of events that occur between observations, internal changes within or the mortality of the respondents, selection bias, or misleading results from the measures, or incorrectly scaling the measures. Threats to external validity include reactive effects, such as different responses to a pre- and post-test, and the interference of other influences or treatments (Campbell and Stanley, 1963: 5-6).

In the model proposed by McGrath and Brinberg (1984), internal validity stems from the correspondence of models and methods in the study. External validity is the confirmation of the findings by their rediscovery in subsequent studies.

In practice, reliability and validity are always limited by the costs of research. Sometimes the data collection itself may interfere with program operation or even create negative program effects. Program clients or agency personnel may be able to construct data favorable to their particular views.

One way of avoiding some of the obstacles to validity is the use of *unobtrusive measures*, which are the products of routine activities rather than of specially constructed research efforts (Webb et al., 1965). An example of an unobtrusive measure is the use of paths worn by students in determining where to locate paved sidewalks on a college campus. It is possible, though, that students may have an aversion to paved walks and will always create paths regardless of where sidewalks are put in. The choice of unobtrusive measures, then, demands creativity and imagination.

DESIGN OF EVALUATION STUDIES

Research approaches are being constantly refined in order to produce evaluation results with the most satisfactory characteristics (Conner and associates, 1984: 417-546). By now, a wide variety of designs for evaluation is available. The selection of a specific research design for evaluation depends on when the evaluation is to be conducted, the dollars available, and the degree of accuracy desired (Hatry, Winnie, and Fisk, 1981: 53). The characteristics of four approaches are shown in Table 7-1. The *no-design* and the *hypothetical-report* approaches are extreme types. Without any planned design, many of the purposes of evaluation will not be achieved. Managers probably resort to the no-design approach only when they have no better alternatives and the evaluation must be done. The hypothetical-report approach, on the other hand, may turn out not to be useful and may also lack reliability and validity. Thus, for practical purposes, the *questionnaire* and *hypothesis-testing* approaches are the two most attractive methods.

In the questionnaire approach, success or failure depends on the design and use of the survey instrument. Survey research must also deal with serious questions of reliability. If citizens are asked about the adequacy of a service, those who do not know or do not care about the service may overload the responses with random (that is, unreliable) data; a citizen may say yes today and no tomorrow to the same survey question. This problem can be somewhat reduced by permitting a "don't know" response. In any event, citizen surveys are only one source of managerial program information. The manager must employ a critical perspective in interpreting and using the findings of surveys (Stipak, 1980: 521-525).

The hypothesis-testing approach is probably the most favored technique, since it specifies the data to be collected in relation to the evaluative propositions. Among the various ways of testing hypotheses, the *controlled experimental design* is preferred (Hatry, Winnie, and Fisk, 1981: 40-46; Fitz-Gibbon and Morris, 1978: 61-92). In this design, the experimental group receives the program service, and the control group does not receive the service but is otherwise treated exactly the same.

Table 7-1 Characteristics of Four Approaches to Evaluation

Approach	Characteristics
No-design	Primary dependence is on interviews of agency personnel by evaluators. There is little planning or consultation with management. The study can be undertaken quickly, but there is a consequent loss in the efficiency of data collection. Follow-up field visits may be necessary, and much time is spent sifting through the data.
Questionnaire	Start-up time is relatively short, and data are collected in a routine format, which may facilitate analysis. Reliability and validity of the data may be questioned if randomization of respondent selection is not assured.
Hypothesis-testing	Careful planning is required. Restrictiveness of statistical analysis, especially in use of the null hypothesis, may affect range, applicability, and usefulness of the evaluation findings.
Hypothetical report	Evaluator "predrafts" the report to the point of needing only specific data to validate or reject a tentative conclusion. This degree of preparation verges on advocacy and may raise questions about the scientific basis of the report.

Source: Adapted from U.S. Department of Housing and Urban Development, *A Guide for Local Evaluation* (Washington, D.C.: HUD, 1976), Reading 6, "Report Design," 2-5.

The effects of the program are tested by comparing the results in the experimental group with the control group.

Although the controlled experimental design is most likely to be conclusive, it is very difficult to implement. First, there are ethical constraints, since withholding program benefits may be damaging to some individuals. Furthermore, it may not be feasible to create the experimental conditions, and the benefits of a collective good such as a water-management project are not easy to measure (Burke and Heaney, 1975: 59-91). Nevertheless, differences between the costs and the benefits of institutional and community care of the mentally ill have been persuasively demonstrated with an experimental design (Weisbrod, 1981).

If tightly controlled experimental conditions are not possible, other methods may afford more or less close approximations. These other methods are generally referred to as quasi-experimental designs (Campbell and Stanley, 1963: 34-64). They are not as rigorous as controlled experimentation, since they make use of similar, often naturally existing, groups rather than groups formed by random selection from among a pool of subjects.

If groups cannot be found for comparison at all, various hypothesis-testing methods are available (Hatry, Winnie, and Fisk, 1981: 25-55). One of these is to study the same group before and after it has received the program service. Another is to compare expected performance with actual, observed performance. Time-series analysis is a third way; in this technique, a group's starting point serves as a definition of initial performance level, and later observations are measured against this base and correlated with the group's experiences (Fitz-Gibbon and Morris, 1978: 93-112).

Whatever the design for testing, a hypothesis may be stated in one of two general ways: as a null hypothesis or as an assertive hypothesis. The *null hypothesis* postulates that any patterns found in the research are due to chance; if the differences between groups are too large to be attributed to chance, the null hypothesis is rejected. The test of the null hypothesis is subject to two opposite kinds of error: rejection of the hypothesis when it is true (that is, the differences *are* due to chance), called a Type I error; and acceptance of the hypothesis when actually it is false, called a Type II error. Statistical criteria for the likelihood of chance differences help to avoid both these types of error (Welch and Comer, 1983: 166-178).

The crucial question is how large a difference is required for the null hypothesis to be rejected. A statistical test of the level of significance can be applied to answer the question. A significance level of .01 means that there is only one chance in a hundred that a difference of a given size would occur by chance; a significance level of .05 means that that difference could occur by chance five times in a hundred. The greater the tolerance for chance differences, the higher is the acceptable level of significance. A program manager may want a less stringent significance test to help build program support. The application of statistical analysis to the evaluation of programs can be very flexible.

An *assertive hypothesis* states a tentative conclusion, which the evaluator either verifies or falsifies under other assumptions and without use of the null hypothesis. The assertive approach offers a kind of shortcut when data are difficult to obtain or where statistical rigor may not be indicated. It assists in reaching usable conclusions when statistical rigor is not a major concern.

Choice of a research design is primarily the responsibility of the evaluator, who must, however, keep in mind that the findings should be usable by the manager for whom the evaluation is being made. A productive evaluation is one that is carried out in close consultation between evaluator and manager and with mutual respect for the division of labor: the evaluator is given enough flexibility to conduct the evaluation without managerial interference; the evaluator has enough trust to allow the manager full use of the findings (Weiss and Bucuvalas, 1977). Such an evaluation is said to be *utilization-focused* (Patton, 1978: 284-289).

THE FUNCTION OF EVALUATION

"Policy evaluation has entered a second generation and has begun to take new directions" (Busson and Coulter, 1983: 271). The United States General Accounting Office (1987) reports that the evaluation of federal programs used large-scale, multi-year studies less and less during the 1980s. Instead, small-scale, quick-turnaround studies are more commonly used. These "quick" studies are often done by internal personnel rather than by outside specialists. They focus on implementation and program management problems and do not typically evaluate program impact.

In part these new directions have arisen out of demands on governmental agencies for improved performance, and in part out of increased fiscal stress and the day-to-day managerial problems that seem to push program evaluation aside (Daily, 1983). Local government personnel sometimes still resist evaluation efforts, and local government managers face problems of inadequate incentives and resources for evaluation. Underlying all is a lack of trust by local officials. The contemporary public manager must acknowledge the necessity for evaluation of programs.

Technical measurements alone are not sufficient because they tend to leave out important social ingredients. They may generate useful managerial information but fall short of providing information that is useful for policy making (Gardner and Florestano, 1983: 315). Wholey, Newcomer, and associates (1989) reemphasize the importance of the case study. In place of exclusive reliance on the technical aspects of evaluation, they underscore the need of helping program managers to understand the importance of evaluation, of developing a strategy for using evaluation results, and of following up on recommended changes. Realistically, there probably should be a balance between the rapid, inexpensive, management-controlled approach to evaluation and the more rigorous, large-scale, outside-controlled study. However, organized, grand-design evaluation study still contributes significantly, especially to the evaluation of major national policy issues (Nathan, 1988).

Evaluation questions are more than technical questions about a program; evaluation also raises questions about a wide range of social

Table 7-2 Beliefs and Realities in Program Evaluation

Belief	Reality
Experimental design takes precedence over quasi-experimental and nonexperimental designs	Usable findings come from a variety of sources
Evaluation studies have better results if managers are involved at all stages	Managers may delay studies or alter their quality and content
Evaluation should give rise to specific and discrete program decisions	Evaluation may influence decisions even when no direct or explicit connection can be traced

Source: Adapted from R. F. Clark, "The Proverbs of Evaluation: Perspectives from CSA's Experience," *Public Administration Review* 39 (November/December 1979): 562-566.

problems and inquires about the usefulness of existing policies and solutions. Many professions and specialties are engaged in this broader study of society (Lindblom and Cohen, 1979). Social problem solving invokes the image of an "experimenting society," which goes beyond the technical requirements for success in a particular program and explores solutions to large-scale social problems, even at the risk of failure in a specific effort (Campbell, 1969).

The provision of governmental services offers an ideal setting within which to evaluate the impact of bureaucracy on society. Evaluations of such governmental services as job training, worker's and unemployment compensation, welfare services, hospital and medical programs, and retirement systems have been undertaken. These studies have raised questions about how various population groups use government services, how they rate the services they receive, and how their encounters with the bureaucracy affect their attitudes toward government (Katz et al., 1975).

The conduct of program evaluation may still be dominated by the obsolete and limited beliefs that Simon (1946) called "proverbs." Some beliefs about evaluation and the corresponding realities are displayed in Table 7-2.

Bureaucratic resistance to evaluation sometimes emerges if a manager fears that "bread and butter [are] at risk when the program evaluator arrives on the scene" (Greer and Greer, 1982). Another potential problem is organizational fragmentation, which was found to have been an impediment to the development of an evaluation plan in the Department of Labor (Hargrove, 1980). Major units in the department were simply unable to agree on what to study. If managers are inflexible, uncooperative, or suspicious, the quality of the evaluation is apt to be damaged. If service data and fiscal information are incomplete or of poor design, a usable evaluation study may be impossible. Utilization of evaluation findings is too narrowly conceived if they are merely used like a hammer (Weiss, 1982: 130).

Evaluation is one tool in the public manager's kit. Unlike the business manager, the public manager does not have a marketplace that provides organizational evaluations more or less automatically. The public manager must instead deliberately institute an evaluation in order to get cues on which to base future actions. Evaluation is the public manager's substitute for the private manager's balance sheet in a competitive world of needs and services.

REFERENCES

Barnard, Chester. 1938. *The Functions of the Executive.* Cambridge, Mass.: Harvard University Press.

Bennis, Warren. 1981. "Organizational Developments and the Fate of Bureaucracy." In *Perspectives on Public Bureaucracy.* 3d ed., ed. F. A. Kramer, 5-25. Cambridge, Mass.: Winthrop.

Bernstein, S. J., and Patrick O'Hara. 1979. *Public Administration: Organizations, People, and Public Policy.* New York: Harper and Row.

Burke, Roy, III, and J. P. Heaney. 1975. *Collective Decision Making in Water Resource Planning.* Lexington, Mass.: Lexington Books.

Busson, Terry, and P. B. Coulter, ed. 1983. "Policy Evaluation for Local Government: A Symposium." *Policy Studies Journal* 12 (December): 271-388.

Campbell, D. T. 1969. "Reforms As Experiments." *American Psychologist* 24 (April): 409-429.

_____, and J. C. Stanley. 1963. *Experimental and Quasi-Experimental Designs for Research.* Boston: Houghton Mifflin.

Caro, F. G., ed. 1977. *Readings in Evaluation Research.* 2d ed. New York: Russell Sage.

Clark, R. F. 1979. "The Proverbs of Evaluation: Perspectives from CSA's Experience." *Public Administration Review* 39 (November/December): 562-566.

Conner, R. F., and associates, ed. 1984. *Evaluation Studies Review Annual,* vol. 9. Beverly Hills, Calif.: Sage.

Daily, J. H. 1983. "Overcoming Obstacles to Program Evaluation in Local Government." *Policy Studies Journal* 12 (December): 287-294.

Fesler, J. W. 1980. *Public Administration: Theory and Practice.* Englewood Cliffs, N.J.: Prentice-Hall.

Fitz-Gibbon, C. T., and L. L. Morris. 1978. *How to Design a Program Evaluation.* Beverly Hills, Calif.: Sage.

Gardner, Bill, and P. S. Florestano. 1983. "The Necessity of Utilizing Social Management Techniques in Program Evaluation." *Policy Studies Journal* 12 (December): 315-325.

Gibson, F. K., and J. E. Prather. 1984. *Management of Program Evaluation.* Athens, Ga.: Carl Vinson Institute of Government, University of Georgia.

Glass, G. V., ed. 1976. *Evaluation Studies Review Annual,* vol. 1. Beverly Hills, Calif.: Sage.

Greer, T. V., and J. G. Greer. 1982. "Problems in Evaluating Costs and Benefits of Social Programs." *Public Administration Review* 42 (March/April): 151-156.

Hargrove, Erwin C. 1980. "The Bureaucratic Politics of Evaluation: A Case Study of the Department of Labor." *Public Administration Review* 40 (March/April): 150-159.

Hatry, H. P., R. E. Winnie, and D. M. Fisk. 1981. *Practical Program Evaluation for State and Local Government Officials.* 2d ed. Washington, D.C.: Urban Institute.

Havens, H. S. 1981. "Program Evaluation and Program Management." *Public Administration Review* 41 (July/August): 480-485.

Katz, Daniel, B. A. Gatek, Robert L. Kahn, and Eugenia Barton. 1975. *Bureaucratic Encounters: A Pilot Study in the Evaluation of Government Services.* Ann Arbor: Institute for Social Research, University of Michigan.

Katz, Daniel, and Robert L. Kahn. 1978. *The Social Psychology of Organizations.* New York: Wiley.

Lewis, Eugene. 1981. "Public Bureaucracy in Everyday Life." In *Perspectives on Public Bureaucracy.* 3d ed., ed. F. A. Kramer. Cambridge, Mass.: Winthrop.

Lindblom, Charles E., and D. K. Cohen. 1979. *Usable Knowledge: Social Science and Social Problem Solving.* New Haven: Yale University Press.

McGrath, J. E., and David Brinberg. 1984. "External Validity and the Research Process: A Comment on the Calder/Lynch Dialogue." In *Evaluation Studies Review Annual,* vol. 9, ed. R. F. Conner and associates, 438-447. Beverly Hills, Calif.: Sage.

Mohr, L. B. 1988. *Impact Analysis for Program Evaluation.* Pacific Grove, Calif.: Brooks-Cole.

Nathan, Richard. 1988. *Social Science in Government: Uses and Misuses.* New York: Basic Books.

Palumbo, D. J., and David Nachmias. 1984. "The Preconditions for Successful Evaluation: Is There an Ideal Paradigm?" In *Evaluation Studies Review Annual,* vol. 9, ed. R. F. Conner and associates, 102-114. Beverly Hills, Calif.: Sage.

Patton, M. Q. 1978. *Utilization-Focused Evaluation.* Beverly Hills, Calif.: Sage.

Poister, T. H., J. C. McDavid, and A. H. Hoagland. 1979. *Applied Program Evaluation in Local Government.* Lexington, Mass.: Lexington Books.

Rutman, Leonard. 1980. *Planning Useful Evaluations: Evaluability Assessment.* Beverly Hills, Calif.: Sage.

Simon, Herbert A. 1946. "The Proverbs of Administration." *Public Administration Review* 6 (Winter): 53-67.

Starling, Grover. 1986. *Managing the Public Sector.* 3d. ed. Homewood, Ill.: Dorsey.

Stillman, Richard J., II. 1984. *Public Administration: Cases and Concepts.* Boston: Houghton Mifflin.

Stipak, Brian. 1980. "Local Governments' Use of Citizen Surveys." *Public Administration Review* 40 (September/October): 521-525.

Struening, E. L., and Marcia Guttentag, ed. 1975. *Handbook of Research Evaluation,* vols. 1 and 2. Beverly Hills, Calif.: Sage.

Stufflebeam, D. L., and W. J. Webster. 1981. "An Analysis of Alternative Approaches to Evaluation." In *Evaluation Studies Review Annual*, vol. 6, ed. H. E. Freeman and M. A. Solomon, 70-85. Beverly Hills, Calif.: Sage.

Sylvia, Ronald D., K. J. Meier, and E. M. Gunn. 1985. *Program Planning and Evaluation for the Public Manager*. Monterey, Calif.: Brooks-Cole.

U.S. Department of Housing and Urban Development. 1976. *A Guide for Local Evaluation*. Reading 6, "Report Design." Washington, D.C.: HUD.

U.S. General Accounting Office. 1987. *Federal Evaluation: Fewer Units, Reduced Resources, Different Studies from 1980*. PEMD-87-9 (January). Washington, D.C.: Government Printing Office.

Van Maanen, John. 1973. *The Progress of Program Evaluation*. Washington, D.C.: National Training and Development Service Press.

Webb, Eugene, D. T. Campbell, R. D. Schwartz, and Lee Sechrest. 1965. *Unobtrusive Measures: Nonreactive Research in the Social Sciences*. Chicago: Rand McNally.

Weisbrod, B. A. 1981. "Benefit-Cost Analysis of a Controlled Experiment: Treating the Mentally Ill." *Journal of Human Resources* 16 (Fall): 523-548.

Weiss, Carol H. 1972. *Evaluation Research: Methods of Assessing Program Effectiveness*. Englewood Cliffs, N.J.: Prentice-Hall.

_____. 1973. "Where Politics and Evaluation Meet." *Evaluation* 1: 37-45.

_____. 1982. "Measuring the Use of Evaluation." In *Evaluation Studies Review Annual*, vol. 7, ed. E. R. House and associates, 129-145. Beverly Hills, Calif.: Sage.

Weiss, Carol H., and M. J. Bucuvalas. 1977. "The Challenge of Social Research to Decision Making." In *Using Social Research in Public Policy Making*, ed. Carol H. Weiss, 213-233. Lexington, Mass.: Lexington Books.

Welch, Susan, and J. C. Comer. 1983. *Quantitative Methods for Public Administration*. Homewood, Ill.: Dorsey.

White, M. J., Michael Radnor, and D. A. Tansik, ed. 1975. *Management and Policy Science in American Government*. Lexington, Mass.: Lexington Books.

Wholey, Joseph S. 1979. *Evaluation: Promise and Performance*. Washington, D.C.: Urban Institute.

_____. 1983. *Evaluation and Effective Public Management*. Boston: Little, Brown.

Wholey, Joseph S., Mark A. Abramson, and C. Bellavita. 1986. *Performance and Credibility: Developing Excellence in Public and Nonprofit Organizations*. Lexington, Mass.: Lexington Books.

Wholey, Joseph S., K. E. Newcomer, and associates. 1989. *Improving Government Performance: Evaluation Strategies for Strengthening Public Agencies and Programs*. San Francisco, Calif.: Jossey-Bass.

8

POSDCORB Revisited:
What Have We Learned?

The processes by which public organizations are managed today are constantly evolving. The elements of Gulick's POSDCORB evolve along with them. POSDCORB identifies timeless management problems but recognizes that organizational operations cannot be the same from one time to the next, from one situation to the next (Gulick, 1984).

Instead, Gulick believes that POSDCORB must be reinterpreted and that the essentials of public management must be made relevant to new public problems by each successive generation of public managers. The concluding discussion in this book is based on revisions of the components of POSDCORB that have already been discussed (see Chapter 1) and on Gulick's recent restatement of the tasks of public administration.

In the Fiftieth Anniversary issue of *Public Administration Review*, 98-year-old Luther Gulick (1990) linked contemporary management challenges to the history and future of American public administration. Although the administrative activities of American government are as old as the nation's history, Gulick notes that public administration did not appear as a distinct field in America until the early 1900s, when public administration emerged "as a reaction to the spoils and corruption of American city and county governments" (1990: 600).

Despite its relatively recent beginning, American public administration did not spring forth from a vacuum. The fundamentals of American government had been developed more than a century before the reaction to big city spoils and political machines. The framers of the new United States government had rejected hereditary elitism and praised democracy; they had reduced many of the barriers to freedom (trade restraints, unrepresentative taxation, restrictions on personal activity) and they had placed a tremendous burden on a written, flexible national constitution.

Subsequent political cycles and administrative development have interacted within the general framework of democracy, freedom, and enterprise (Gulick, 1990: 599-600). Each new wave of political and bureaucratic action has encouraged a "new" public administration in order to highlight the immediate and significant concerns of the period.

With varying but consistent emphasis throughout the twentieth century, public administration has reflected two core values. The first is maintaining that specialization is a way to develop competent workers. The second is believing that making management a profession is a way to provide adequate leadership. These underlying values are expressed in the POSDCORB of the 1930s and in a reinterpretation of POSDCORB for the 1990s.

Gulick recently stated that "the field of public administration is set by the environment, not by logic; if government does it, it is 'public administration'" (1990: 602). In addition, public administration is "a collection of operational technologies designed to overcome inefficiencies, to reduce corruption, and to help humankind on its way to survival and advancement in a changing and competitive world" (1990: 601). As a field of study and knowledge, public administration has materialized through scientific research as well as through case studies.

However, there is a tension between rigorous scientific study and the less structured case approach. The operational, or public management, features of public administration are often excluded from research by scientists. This exclusion is necessary to reduce the scope of public affairs to proportions manageable by the logic and rules of science. Many political scientists and policy analysts stress the limits of the study of public management. They focus more on recurring conceptual problems, such as resource allocation mechanisms or equity. Case study advocates sense that much of the wholeness of public administration may be lost by not investigating managerial operations. But, if applied studies are the only approach, the field will miss the scientific insights from logical inquiry.

Bailey maintains that a bond between scientific method and the case study approach to public administration best reflects "practitioner-oriented" research (1992: 47). Unavoidably, public administration connects craft and science, politics and management, research scientist and practitioner. Citizens, elected officials, political executives, and civil servants have a mutual interest in scientific generalizations as well as integrity of the specific managerial decisions. Case study research reflects an interest in solving human and social problems by a level of scientific rigor appropriate for the problem.

The central tasks of public administration in the twenty-first century will reflect changing conditions in America and in the world.

Gulick does not reject POSDCORB, but he has lived long enough to see the need to restate the original requirements and tasks for managing the public organization. His restatement (1990: 603) incorporates the traditional POSDCORB management principles and relates them to contemporary conditions and tasks in America and around the globe as follows:

1. *Planning:* "More and better planning at every decision level, making full use of the new memory, computation, and communication tools";
2. *Allocation:* "Contributing to improved allocation of resources between public and private sectors, between competing demands for public services, and between the present and the future";
3. *Market:* "Providing the framework for openness and freedom of every market—commercial and intellectual—touched by private and public centers of power";
4. *Productivity:* "Facilitating choice among alternative productive techniques and organizations to produce and deliver public services and to assure means of promoting the general welfare through these techniques";
5. *Enthusiasm:* "Developing personnel policies which capture the creativity and enthusiasm of both staff and customers, to lay the basis for increases in humanity and productivity";
6. *Coordination:* "Strengthening the process of self coordination, together with supervision and evaluation."

PLANNING

Although planning information is imperfect, planning is a very important managerial activity.

A major concern of managers is to define, forecast, and control future developments or at least place them within bounds. But there simply is no way to get around the facts that forecasts are uncertain, planning studies are quickly outdated, and controls extended into the future may prove to be unrealistic. Planning will always be based on imperfect and incomplete information.

Among the conditions that warrant constant attention are changes in economic factors (such as inflation and interest rates), changes in demographics (such as migration), changes in technology, and changes in political relationships. Today's information society is a result of technological changes and economic adaptations to them, but how could planners in the 1960s—only little more than three decades ago—anticipate the circumstances of the 1990s? However, the impossibility of making completely accurate projections does not lead to a rejection of planning. Planning lays a base for accommodating to changes, and without that base, changes would have an even more drastic impact.

The effectiveness of planning is limited by the inherent limits on human knowledge (Simon, 1976; March and Simon, 1958: 137-171), the problems of language (the word "needs," for example, means different things to different political actors), and the explosive growth of knowledge (Ostrom, 1973). Managerial decisions are always subject to error, since no one can know all of the consequences of decisions and actions. The effectiveness of planning is also limited by the resistance to change inherent in established routines, programs, and systems in an organization. Strategic planning techniques confront these limitations by using key actors in a process that identifies the truly important priorities requiring action. Often, however, even extensive strategic planning activities do not fundamentally change existing operations (Bryson and Roering, 1988).

Yet planning is still indispensable, because it allows managers to make decisions based on the best available knowledge. Some of this knowledge comes from a greater appreciation of the organization's external environment, discovered during the planning process. Other knowledge creates greater interaction between managers and "common revenue, budgeting, and expenditure control tasks" (Sacco and Ostrowski, 1991: 173).

ALLOCATION

Public managers need to be allocated adequate but controlled resources for staffing and budgeting.

Today most people agree that public administration is a part of the greater political process. Allocation refers to how the people with political process influence get political or economic benefits, as well as when and how they get them (Lasswell, 1936). The political and administrative system is a conduit for the "authoritative allocation of values," or, in other words, taxing, spending, and regulatory resources, through input into political decisions and through policy outcomes (Easton, 1965: 50; Almond and Powell, 1966).

The allocation of resources between government, business, and citizen organizations must be oriented toward a good life for every involved party (Waldo, 1948: 65-88). Part of the reform spirit behind the origin of public administration as a field was directed against misallocation of public resources through narrow, self-serving political interests. A specific example is the "pork barrel" phenomenon, where government decides to ignore the public interest and to allocate benefits to a narrow, influential constituency in order to achieve immediate political support.

Today, allocation issues reflect debate about the proper role of government in the market place as well as the control of corruption. Governments allocate resources when the private entrepreneurs in the marketplace are not able to do so. One example is to provide a public good. A public good is not divisible into parts for individual consumers and it is not a good that one person can use up (Olson, 1965). National defense in the form of the Air Force or flood control in the form of a dam are examples.

Allocations toward the future must weigh current political concerns against future needs. At the root of this problem is "budgeting for growth" or how to control the constant, almost automatic increases in federal spending (Schick, 1990: 15). Allocations through the current budget process have become disengaged from the economy and significant budget problems. Since the American political system is based on fragmented political power structures and behaviors (Long, 1962), perhaps this problem is inevitable. The current budget process is designed to control the management of agency operations, but the majority of federal spending is in transfer payments to recipients outside the government—Social Security, for example. Allen Schick maintains that "far more can be saved by a single COLA [Cost of Living Adjustment] decision than by thousands of line-item nicks in agency budgets" (1990: 106). Future budget health at all levels of government depends on the outcome of these growth decisions.

The challenges to public managers are at all levels of government— national, state, and local—and include issues such as medicaid financing, education, and corrections (Gosling, 1992: 184-203). State and local governments have been hit hard by economic, financial, and political transitions since the late 1970s. Federal aid to states stopped growing in the mid-1970s and total state and local expenditures started to decline on a per-capita basis after 1978 (Advisory Commission on Intergovernmental Relations, 1985: 193-195).

The continued cuts in federal spending for state and local governments, by about one-third during the 1980s, significantly reversed the national support pattern started during the Great Society programs of the 1960s. Coupled with the general economic recession of the early 1990s, state and local governments have experienced substantial budget pressures. These conditions have been worsened by general opposition from taxpayers to new tax rates or increased charges for services.

Perhaps the biggest difficulty state and local governments face is their lack of control over conditions in the nation at large. Cities and states are at the mercy of fluctuating interest rates and federal funding decisions. They find themselves drained of skills and economic values as citizens move to new places. The economic base for financing state and local services changes rapidly, as does the demand for services. One common reaction is to increase taxes, which usually just makes things worse. But public managers must continue to adapt; they cannot simply shut down a water or sewer system or send the police home. Another reaction might be to place more emphasis on informal, low-capital, nonprofessional methods, including even the use of informed volunteers such as social service workers or fire fighters in selected small-scale operations. Redesigning a service is another option—for example, having citizens bag garbage or cart it to the roadside to reduce the cost of municipal garbage collection. The replacement of taxes by user fees may help redistribute service burdens in a politically acceptable way. Still another possibility is to contract with private companies for the provision of some public services (Morgan, 1984: 180-184; see also Levine, 1979). An ongoing question is whether intrastate shifts of service responsibilities from local governments to the state government will provide a more effective system (Stanfield, 1991).

MARKET

> Government regulations, especially marketplace interventions, will require constant political justifications for acceptable administrative actions.

The market is traditionally free and private. A free market exists when demand and supply determine the price for a good. Consumer demand is a signal for a producer to provide voluntarily a supply at a price that satisfies the consumer and makes a profit for the producer. Price allocates resources by stimulating or slowing production. Producers respond to changing consumer demand by redirecting production away from unprofitable decisions. Under the market model, allocation occurs without the need for governmental intervention or control.

But, sometimes government does have to "touch the market" through intervention. As in the case of public goods, for example, police protection, markets may not be the best allocator since a price cannot be set. Governments intervene for other reasons, including: (1) to redistribute income when market allocations create too great an inequity between "haves" and "have-nots"; (2) to stabilize the economy, for example, to reduce the effects of inflation after extensive government spending in a war effort or to restart the economy after a time of economic stagnation; and (3) to satisfy voters if they want a national industrial policy, a trade policy, or changes in the banking system (Markovich and Pynn, 1988: 47-50).

Kenneth J. Meier has organized the various governmental interventions into markets as a series of subsystems (1985: 9-36). Meier believes that public managers have great influence in some subsystems and they may be able to arbitrate successfully the flow between public and private interests. In other situations, however, managers must negotiate with specialized interests to reach decisions.

The role of the public manager aside, the key to Gulick's emphasis on markets is openness to create responsible action. Open meetings and the free flow of information are critical components of the public manager's role in markets. This does not mean that governmental intervention in markets is undesirable, but it does mean that public managers are constantly vulnerable to suspicions of "government failure" in resource allocation. Adequate information is reassuring to a questioning public.

PRODUCTIVITY

Managers are constantly devising new performance and evaluation measures to keep the organization focused on its missions.

Public-sector managers constantly struggle with the lack of a clear bottom line that tells them how well their organization is performing. It is difficult for them even to define what performance to measure. The deployment of personnel and public funds are the basic resources of the manager. While the manager may measure these inputs objectively through agency records, it is not easy to tell how the public evaluates the results. For example, how do objective measures such as the number of police officers per 10,000 residents or the per capita expenditure on police relate to residents' feelings about public safety? One study did relate objective indicators of police response to residents' perceptions of the speed with which police responded to calls in their neighborhood. It found that residents who made calls to the police tended to have more positive perceptions of rapid response than did those who had had no need to call the police. Even if the police response was delayed, residents' satisfaction was not reduced as long as subsequent police actions were perceived as satisfactory. It was unsatisfactory experience with the police after their arrival that was associated with a perception of slow response (Parks, 1984). Public criticism often suggests that many people actually have no idea of the types and levels of service they need or receive. But even if objective measures are unrelated to public perceptions, they are important performance records for the manager. Furthermore, managers can adjust the use of their resources to increase the activities that people do observe, with a consequent favorable effect on public opinion. Changing the timing of police rounds, for example, may not change the cost of the service, but the residents of a neighborhood may be more satisfied if they see police officers more often.

However, managers must bear in mind that the perceptions of a small number of citizens may not reflect jurisdiction-wide performance. It is imperative for public managers to take a comprehensive view of service delivery, even though there may be dissatisfaction within a specific neighborhood or among a particular group of citizens (Fitzgerald and Durant, 1980).

There is no one best way to organize for productivity. We have seen one model advocated that put scattered units under a centralized executive with a unified chain of command, but we have also seen the criticisms of it: that it is too stiff, too bureaucratic. The issues identified by Gulick more than 50 years ago are still with us. How will the work of the organization be divided among positions, groups, departments, and divisions? How will these multiple activities then be coordinated? What internal control procedures, information systems, appraisal and reward systems, and status distinctions are needed?

Public management is a more rapidly changing field than the stereotypes of bureaucracy might lead us to believe. If nothing else, forces for change come from outside the organization: cutbacks in federal spending, more active policy roles of state governments, more demands for services, and heightened public interest in the productivity of spending policies. As a result, existing hierarchies are questioned, and new ones do not develop quickly. Hierarchies bring about stability, but they are expensive. Managers become responsible for solving more problems, often with no increase in resources. Managers in turn delegate greater temporary authority to supervisors to get things done. Less formal procedures, more interpersonal communications, and more participative management often result. This orientation may overshadow the reliance on formal rules and narrow spans of supervisory discretion, and the dominance of technical concerns, that characterize more stable organizations.

Evaluation is the regular collection of data concerning the efficiency, effectiveness, and economy of government operations, leading to improved policy implementation and program management. Efficiency is the measurable output of services related to the cost of the resources that went into it; effectiveness is the perceived quality of the service (Hatry, 1978: 28). Measurements of efficiency, however, may create a false sense of savings and fail to reflect the full range of evaluative considerations (Meier, 1979: 120).

Program evaluation is ultimately a political activity. The demands of the political environment may, and some would say properly, override the technical research concerns. In determining the questions to be asked and the methods of data collection, the evaluator is pulled and tugged in difficult directions by the conflicting political interests.

Once the manager has the evaluation findings in hand, the outcomes may be further altered by bureaucratic considerations, power struggles, or other political intricacies of the workplace. Program managers may defend their programs vigorously in the face of adverse findings. The politics of policy implementation and evaluation often overshadow the technical aspects. The basic principles for public managers to follow are the clarity of the evaluation focus and the research design and respectful, trusting communications between managers and evaluators.

ENTHUSIASM

The public manager's ability to motivate employees is subject to many limitations.

Civil-service regulations are often pointed to as a major barrier to successful managerial direction of a governmental organization. As early as 1948, the civil-service reform movement was characterized as a "triumph of techniques over purpose" (Sayre, 1979). The demands of standardized procedures and requirements left no room for managerial discretion. The reform certainly had some desirable results in enhancing job security, but the other side of the coin is that it made it difficult for managers to reward good performance and to mete out discipline to those in need of it (Foster, 1979).

Today's barriers lie principally in the rapid rate of change and in the need to adapt the organization to it. One approach or set of approaches to dealing with these barriers is called organizational development (Bennis, 1969). The contemporary public manager must deal with employees whose needs are different from those of public employees of previous generations and who can more easily move into private-sector employment. This new mobility of public workers should be a stimulus for more effective managerial direction.

Effective management direction is "a process for motivating and inspiring people, especially subordinate managers" (Thompson, 1991: 57). Enthusiastic personnel may be more willing to implement the established policies and purposes of an organization. If staff members recognize that the organization is flexible and open, they may be more willing to participate creatively in renewing and redefining the organization's approaches to achieving its legally defined missions.

The effective future public administrator faces a formidable array of challenges. Clearly, the conditions of work will not be smooth and stable. The manager will face change and uncertainty. Self-directed education is a key component of managerial renewal, enthusiasm, and creativity. Personnel policies—the "staffing" function—will have to develop public employees who:

1. "can deal with change, uncertainty, turbulence, ambiguity";
2. "are sensitive to and capable of working with diverse values";
3. "will continue learning and developing professionally and intellectually throughout their careers";
4. "are not passively obedient but are committed to appropriate values in ways which would make a public administrative Watergate or Iran-Contra affair unlikely";
5. "can work with colleagues, superiors, clients, and constituents in constructive and open ways while sustaining a strong sense of character, ethics, and civic and professional commitment";
6. "are flexible, open minded, and capable of finding new information on their own, absorbing new information and insights, and correcting their paths when what they learn indicates the need for correction"; and
7. "are largely self-directed, creative, and have a proper sense of autonomy as well as responsibility" (Balfour and Marini, 1991: 483).

The public manager who maintains these qualities will no doubt develop the creativity and self-motivation necessary for effective personal performance and for organizational leadership.

COORDINATION

Coordinating and reporting demand more emphasis on communications.

Before an organization is able to function, the people in it must know what it is that they are to do. Vagueness of policy is one of the many obstacles to the effective operation of public organizations. It may stem from laws that have unclear goals or objectives, from ambiguous court decisions, or from unexpected events that were not considered when the policy was formulated. The complexities of policy making, the competition among goals and approaches, the need for consensus, and the often unanticipated routes taken by political actors contribute to chaos in communications (Edwards, 1980: 17-51).

Communications are costly to produce. Formal and informal messages must be composed, transmitted, stored, retrieved, and applied. But since communications are at the hub of an organization (Katz and Kahn, 1978: 428), the essential basis of its unified action, communications failures are even more costly. "Gobbledygook" and "red tape" are terms for communications failures (Starling, 1986: 252-256, 258).

Sometimes a lack of communication can be consciously or unconsciously desired by the people in the organization. If superiors do not know what is going on at lower levels, they do not have to act; it may be easier to ignore lower-level behavior than to correct it. In addition, if there is too much communication, superiors may be unable to attend to all of it. It must be filtered out somewhere along the way, and these filters may give a distorted picture of the situation (Kaufman, 1973: 49-67).

CONCLUSION

Government today seems to overwhelm, invade, dehumanize. Citizens question the size of government, its appropriateness, its worth. Many feel that public policies and the actions of public officials are not in their best interests, individually or collectively. The circumstances demand recognition of the political side of public management.

It has been a major theme of this book that bureaucratic decisions have political origins and consequences and that administration cannot be divorced from politics. Both external and internal politics affect the practical actions a public manager can take in responding to changing organizational and social conditions.

Gulick's POSDCORB has been used as a convenient device to describe what managers do. We have tried to infuse it with the rich variety of content proper to it, and we have altered it where necessary. But the concerns and problems of POSDCORB are as relevant today as they have ever been. What has changed is the way it is interpreted and applied in public management.

Good managers will recreate a sense of trust between government and the governed. Public managers who lose touch with people become corrupt or politically bankrupt. By keeping in touch, managers help government respond to the needs and wants of citizens and thereby help to maintain the legitimacy of government.

It is also important to remember that government does not work like a machine, that managers are more than cogs in the wheels of government and public employees do not run off batteries. In his latest published work, Luther Gulick presents once more the perspective that he developed at least as early as 1915, when he helped draft documents for the New York State Constitutional Convention:

> The metaphor of the machine puts us on the wrong track. Government is made up of human beings, it operates through human beings, and serves and regulates human beings. (Gulick, 1984: 381)

In human activity, there are no comprehensive formulas and no ways to achieve perfection. Managers need flexibility to approach organizational questions, to learn, to assimilate, to act in pursuit of community values. Managers represent people assembled for action. It is the manager's task to act decisively while remaining in harmony with the ideals of the social order.

REFERENCES

Advisory Commission on Intergovernmental Relations. 1985. *The Question of State Government Capability.* Report A-98. Washington, D.C.: ACIR.

Almond, Gabriel, and G. B. Powell. 1966. *Comparative Politics: A Developmental Approach.* Boston: Little, Brown.

Bailey, M. T. 1992. "Do Physicists Use Case Studies? Thoughts on Public Administration Research." *Public Administration Review* 52 (January/February): 47-54.

Balfour, D. L., and Frank Marini. 1991. "Child and Adult, X and Y: Reflections on the Process of Public Administration Education." *Public Administration Review* 51 (November/December): 478-485.

Bennis, Warren. 1969. *Organizational Development: Its Nature, Origins, and Prospects.* Reading, Mass.: Addison-Wesley.

Bryson, J. M., and W. D. Roering. 1988. "Initiation of Strategic Planning by Governments." *Public Administration Review* 48 (November/December): 995-1004.

Easton, David. 1965. *A Framework for Political Analysis.* Englewood Cliffs, N.J.: Prentice-Hall.

Edwards, George C., III. 1980. *Implementing Public Policy.* Washington, D.C.: CQ Press.

Fitzgerald, M. R., and R. F. Durant. 1980. "Citizen Evaluations and Urban Management: Service Delivery in an Era of Protest." *Public Administration Review* 40 (November/December): 585-594.

Foster, G. D. 1979. "The 1978 Civil Service Reform Act: Post-Mortem or Rebirth?" *Public Administration Review* 39 (January/February): 78-86.

Gosling, J. J. 1992. *Budgetary Politics in American Government.* New York: Longman.

Gulick, Luther H. 1984. "The Metaphors of Public Administration." *Public Administration Quarterly* 8 (Fall): 369-381.

_____. 1990. "Reflections on Public Administration, Past and Future." *Public Administration Review* 50 (November/December): 599-603.

Hatry, H. P. 1978. "The Status of Productivity Measurement in the Public Sector." *Public Administration Review* 38 (January/February): 28-33.

Katz, Daniel, and Robert L. Kahn. 1978. *The Social Psychology of Organizations.* New York: Wiley.

Kaufman, Herbert. 1973. *Administrative Feedback: Monitoring Subordinates' Behavior.* Washington, D.C.: Brookings Institution.

Lasswell, Harold. 1936. *Who Gets What, When, How.* New York: McGraw-Hill.

Levine, Charles H. 1979. "More on Cutback Management: Hard Questions for Hard Times." *Public Administration Review* 39 (March/April): 179-193.

Long, Norton. 1962. *The Polity*. Chicago: Rand McNally.

March, James G., and Herbert A. Simon. 1958. *Organizations*. New York: Wiley.

Markovich, D. E., and R. E. Pynn. 1988. *American Political Economy: Using Economics with Politics*. Pacific Grove, California: Brooks-Cole.

Meier, Kenneth J. 1979. *Politics and the Bureaucracy: Policymaking in the Fourth Branch of Government*. North Scituate, Mass.: Duxbury.

_____. 1985. *Regulation: Politics, Bureaucracy, and Economics*. New York: St. Martin's.

Morgan, David R. 1984. *Managing Urban America*. 2d ed. Monterey, Calif.: Brooks-Cole.

Olson, Mancur. 1965. *The Logic of Collective Action*. Cambridge, Mass.: Harvard University.

Ostrom, Vincent. 1973. "Some Paradoxes for Planners: Human Knowledge and Its Limitations." In *The Politics of Planning*, ed. A. Lawrence Chickering, 243-254. San Francisco: Institute for Contemporary Studies.

Parks, Roger B. 1984. "Linking Objective and Subjective Measures of Performance." *Public Administration Review* 44 (March/April): 118-127.

Sacco, J. F., and J. W. Ostrowski. 1991. *Microcomputers and Government Management*. Pacific Grove, Calif.: Brooks-Cole.

Sayre, Wallace S. 1979. "The Triumph of Techniques over Purpose." In *Classics of Public Personnel Policy*, ed. F. J. Thompson, 30-35. Oak Park, Ill.: Moore.

Schick, Allen. 1990. *The Capacity to Budget*. Washington, D.C.: Urban Institute.

Simon, Herbert A. 1976. *Administrative Behavior*. 3d ed. New York: Macmillan.

Stanfield, R. L. 1991. "Forced Federalism." *National Journal* 23 (December 14): 3020-3023.

Starling, Grover. 1986. *Managing the Public Sector*. 3d ed. Homewood, Ill.: Dorsey.

Thompson, Fred. 1991. "Management Control and the Pentagon: The Organizational Strategy-Structure Mismatch." *Public Administration Review* 51 (January/February): 52-66.

Waldo, Dwight. 1948. *The Administrative State*. New York: Ronald Press.

Index